JUDY ZEIDLER'S
INTERNATIONAL
DELI
COOKBOOK

ALSO BY JUDY ZEIDLER

The Gourmet Jewish Cook

Master Chefs Cook Kosher

The 30-Minute Kosher Cook

Co-Author

Michel Richard's Home Cooking with a French Accent

JUDY ZEIDLER'S INTERNATIONAL DELI COOKBOOK

Great Recipes

from the Broadway Deli

by Judy Zeidler

BROADWAY DELI
SANTA MONICA, CA

Library of Congress Cataloging-in-Publication Data:

Zeidler, Judy.
[International deli cookbook]
Judy Zeidler's international deli cookbook: great recipes
from the Broadway Deli/by Judy Zeidler
         p.   cm.
Includes index.
ISBN 0-8118-0297-3 (pb)
1. Cookery, International. 2. Broadway Deli (Santa Monica,
Calif.) I. Broadway Deli (Santa Monica, Calif.) II. Title:
International deli cookbook.
TX725.A1Z43   1994
641.5—dc20   94-574
                                                        CIP

Printed in the United States of America.

Cover and book design
by Aufuldish & Warinner
Illustrations by Eric Donelan

Revised Edition
First Printing

Distributed by the Broadway Deli
1457 Third Street Promenade
Santa Monica, CA 90401

I dedicate this book to my husband, Marvin, whose

restless feet waited until I finished this book before taking

off on our annual three-month trip to Italy.

And my thanks for his expertise as a chef and

his incredible palate

ACKNOWLEDGMENTS

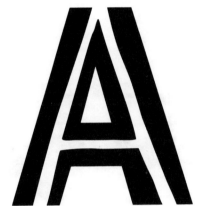 special thanks to Sara J. Mitchell for her friendship and for her red pencil and sharp eyes. ❦ To Frederick Hill for his encouragement. To Bill LeBlond of Chronicle Books for liking my idea and going with it. ❦ To Janice Wald Henderson and Jackie Killeen for their excellent editing. Another very special thanks to Joan Bram, a fabulous friend and one-woman support group. Joan arrived day after day with samples of recipes she had tested. ❦ To other loyal friends that tested the recipes for me: Francine Bartfield, Sue Cheldin, Sue and Jim Cross, Tracy Flatow, Sylvia Fox, Sue and Mort Frishberg, Yvonne Nivens, Shirley Renick, and Florine Sikking. ❦ A special acknowledgment to my children and grandchildren. Sue, Leo, Ariella, and Melina; Marc and Judy; Kathy, Steve, and Aaron; Paul, Amber, Normandie, Giamaica Day, Zane and Quest; Zeke and Jay. I love them and they love my cooking. ❦ To my friend and partner Bruce Marder the most talented chef I know.

CONTENTS

INTRODUCTION

MY

first deli memories were formed when I was six years old. Every Sunday, my parents would take me to lunch at a New York Jewish-style delicatessen. We always ordered pastrami or corned beef sandwiches served with French's mustard, kosher dill pickles out of a barrel, coleslaw or potato salad, and Delaware Punch in its distinctively shaped bottle.

❧ I may no longer be six years old, but I've never stopped eating at delis. I've discovered that they produce some of life's most satisfying meals. Today, many of my deli memories are shaped at the Broadway Deli in Santa Monica, California. My husband, Marvin, is a partner in this deli, as well as several other popular restaurants in the Los Angeles area.

❧ The Broadway Deli is also the inspiration for this cookbook. Whenever I visit it, I watch long lines of people waiting patiently for seats and I am constantly reminded just how much deli food is loved.

❧ Webster's definition of a deli only begins to touch upon all that a deli can be: "…from Latin, *delicatus*, delicate = A shop that sells cooked or prepared foods ready for serving."

❧ Actually, a delicatessen is designed to satisfy all sorts of whims, whether patrons are in the mood for a quick bagel or an elaborate, three-course chicken dinner. No matter what time of day you visit a deli—and they're usually open from breakfast to bedtime—there's always a large, yet distinctive, variety of dishes from which to choose. You can dine at a deli and be coddled by maternal waitresses, if you're lucky, or you can whisk away your favorite foods to be eaten at home. No matter where you consume them, one fact's for certain: Deli foods are comfort foods.

❧ Americans are not the only ones who do delis. Many nationalities claim delis as their own. In Italy, delis, called *salumeria*, prepare an abundance of wonderful foods such as carpaccio, roasted peppers, prosciutto, and an amazing array of cheeses and pastas. In America, Italian-style delis are often patronized for their humongous hero sandwiches, jam-packed with meats, cheeses, and peppers.

❧ The well-known Scandinavian delis, or *conditorie*, are renowned for their impressive smoked fish, herring, terrines, cheese, open-faced sandwiches made with earthy whole-grain breads, salads, meatballs, and jam-filled pastries.

❧ In France, delis are dubbed *charcuteries* and are capable of reaching the peak of epicurean perfection. Drop into a *charcuterie* and you'll be amazed at the variety of foods-to-go, including smooth pâtés, tiny savory tarts, and sophisticated salads of marinated mushrooms, artichokes, and other perfectly ripened vegetables.

❧ Mediterranean delis are ethnic treasure troves, supplying souvlakia, stuffed grape leaves, a plethora of olives and oils, feta cheese, falafel, and pita bread. Hummus, tabbouleh, kibbeh, and marinated artichokes enlivened with Middle Eastern spices are just some of the other exotic offerings.

❧ To Germans, the *delikatessen* is the place to go for hearty sausages, tangy sauerkraut, and fresh beer. Their warm potato salad, dark dense breads, and flaky strudels are more than ample reason why German delis are widely embraced by many cultures.

❧ Here at home, it's the old-time Jewish-style delis that conjure up so many fond memories. Most have evolved from the classic delis that populated New York City's Lower East Side in the early 1900s. Some of these old-fashioned delis still exist. Portly, no-nonsense waiters continue to serve thick slices of juicy, hand-carved brisket and corned beef. Patrons still pour pitchers of pure chicken fat over chopped liver and mashed potatoes; one bite and you're convinced you've died and gone to deli heaven. And those antique metal spritzers never cease to dispense bubbly seltzer—the drink of choice for delis.

❧ Today, a new style of deli is making its appearance, profoundly altering the deli definition. In cities across the country, these contemporary delis are influenced by the many ethnicities that have been absorbed into our American heritage. They offer sophisticated fare, yet still spotlight nostalgic Americana classics. In deference to current dietary concerns, many dishes are prepared in a lighter, more healthful fashion. The Broadway Deli fits comfortably into the modern-day category.

❧ To write this book, I've researched deli food in every corner of the world, as well as at home. The research was pure pleasure. I've sampled every kind of deli imaginable, from old-fashioned to contemporary, from American to Middle Eastern, in tiny corner takeout stores and upscale emporiums.

❧ I've incorporated the very best from my travels and tastings—including the most popular recipes from the Broadway Deli. Other recipes are the result of pleading with famous deli chefs, who eventually agreed to share their secrets with me. This cookbook is filled with classic and contemporary recipes for soups, salads, deli meat and seafood specialties, sandwich creations, and a complete deli bakery section highlighting richly textured breads and desserts.

❧ Each of the two hundred plus recipes in this collection is fun to prepare and, more importantly, fun to eat. Many take only thirty minutes to make and can be served at buffets, picnics, or parties for almost any occasion.

❧ Although the original Broadway Deli is a Los Angeles restaurant, there is a Broadway in just about every American town or city. And chances are, on every Broadway there's a deli. I hope you're inspired to re-create your own Broadway deli in your home.

❧ I dedicate this book to adventurous food lovers who have always wanted to duplicate delectable deli flavors in their kitchens. Fragrant chicken soup with fluffy matzo balls, robust Greek salad, the ultimate golden French fries with homemade ketchup, airy Italian frittatas, crunchy kosher-style dill pickles. These recipes and more await you.

The DELI SOUP AND STOCK KITCHEN

CHAPTER 1

Deli soups are notably homey and usually hearty. Often the end result of long, slow simmering, these soups are designed to comfort and nourish. Served steaming hot in simple bowls, along with thick slices of fresh-baked pumpernickel or rye bread, deli soups stick to your ribs, as our grandmothers used to say. ❦ No deli cookbook would be complete without the star attraction, that famous cure-all—chicken soup. In this chapter, I offer what I believe to be the best recipe for this classic soup. You will also find cream soups, plus robust split pea, cabbage, minestrone, corn soups, and for good measure a few refreshing cold soups. ❦ Soups, both hot and chilled, become more intriguing when they're garnished, with attention paid to visual appeal and textural contrast. Diced mozzarella or grated Parmesan cheese; cooked beans such as fava, cannellini, cranberry, or garbanzo; toasted croutons; pesto or sour cream; chopped fresh herbs; and even basil ice cubes (for cold soups) can transform an ordinary soup into an extraordinary one. And, of course, all soups are enhanced by homemade stocks; you'll find a section on these at the end of this chapter. ❦ A big pot of deli soup makes an easy-to-serve main course for a casual family supper. The only additions needed are a freshly tossed salad, fiber-rich bread, and a simple dessert.

RECIPES
CHAPTER 1

THE ULTIMATE CHICKEN SOUP WITH THE FLUFFIEST MATZO BALLS {Serves 12}

My chicken soup really tastes like chicken. The secret is using lots of poultry and fresh vegetables and simmering the soup until it's as rich as gravy. This soup can be frozen in ice cube trays and added to sauces or other soups, or used to moisten leftover reheated chicken. I've perfected this matzo ball recipe over the years, until I was satisfied that it produces the lightest matzo balls you've ever tasted. If you don't wish to take the time to make them, boil some noodles, macaroni, or ravioli and add to the soup instead.

One 5-pound chicken
    or two 3-pound chickens, trussed
1 pound chicken necks and gizzards
3 medium onions, diced
1 medium leek, sliced into 1-inch pieces
3 to 4 quarts water
16 small carrots, cut into 1-inch pieces
5 stalks celery with tops,
    cut into 1-inch pieces
3 medium parsnips, sliced
8 sprigs fresh parsley
Salt, to taste
Freshly ground black pepper, to taste
The Fluffiest Matzo Balls (recipe follows)

❦ In a large heavy Dutch oven or pot, place trussed chicken, necks and gizzards, onions, leek, and enough water to cover. Over high heat, bring to a boil. Using a large spoon, skim off the scum that rises to the top. Add carrots, celery, parsnips, and parsley. Cover, leaving the lid ajar, reduce heat to low, and simmer for 1 hour. Season with salt and pepper to taste. Uncover and simmer 30 minutes longer. Add water if needed.

❦ With a slotted spoon, remove chicken from the soup. Let soup cool to room temperature, then chill. Skim off fat that hardens on the surface and discard. Meanwhile prepare the matzo balls.

❦ Bring soup to a slow boil and gently drop in matzo balls. Cover, reduce heat to low, and simmer for about 10 minutes (do not uncover during this cooking time). Ladle into heated soup bowls.

THE FLUFFIEST MATZO BALLS {Makes 12 balls}

3 eggs, separated
About ½ cup water or chicken stock
1 to 1½ cups matzo meal
⅛ teaspoon salt
Pinch freshly ground black pepper

❦ Place egg yolks in a measuring cup and add enough water or chicken stock to fill 1 cup. Beat with a fork until well blended. Set aside.

❦ In a large bowl, using an electric mixer, beat egg whites until they form stiff peaks; do not overbeat. In a small bowl, combine matzo meal with salt and pepper. With a rubber spatula, gently fold the yolk mixture alternately with the matzo mixture into beaten egg whites. Use only enough matzo to make a light, soft dough. Season with additional salt and pepper to taste. Cover and let firm up for 5 minutes.

❦ With wet hands gently shape mixture into 1½-inch balls. Add to and cook in soup according to directions in recipe.

VARIATION *For low-cholesterol matzo balls, replace egg yolks with ¼ cup cooked, puréed carrots.*

FRENCH ONION SOUP {Serves 8}

The key to making classic onion soup is to slowly sauté the onions in butter, allowing them to develop a rich, sweet taste. To cook this properly you will also need large ovenproof soup bowls. Serve this straight from the oven with the cheese still bubbling on top. It's a complete meal when presented with a green salad, garlic toast, and dessert.

¼ pound unsalted butter or margarine

3 large onions, thinly sliced (about 4 cups)

1 teaspoon sugar

6 cups vegetable or chicken stock (pages 26–27)

½ cup brandy

Salt, to taste

Freshly ground black pepper, to taste

8 slices French bread, toasted

1 cup shredded Swiss or Gruyère cheese

❦ In a large heavy pot, melt butter over low heat and add onions and sugar. Sauté gently, stirring occasionally, until onions are golden brown, about 20 minutes.

❦ Gradually add stock and continue stirring. Bring soup to a boil, reduce heat to low, cover, and simmer gently for 1 hour. The last 20 minutes, stir in brandy and season with salt and pepper to taste.

❦ Preheat the broiler. Place 8 heated, ovenproof soup bowls on a very heavy baking sheet and ladle the soup into the bowls. Top each bowl with a slice of toasted French bread and sprinkle generously with cheese. Place under the broiler until cheese melts and begins to bubble. Serve immediately.

SHIITAKE MUSHROOM AND BARLEY SOUP {Serves 4 to 6}

The technique of sautéing all the ingredients, before adding the stock, brings out the intense mushroom flavor of this robust soup—a favorite of Broadway Deli patrons.

2 tablespoons olive oil

1 onion, diced

2 stalks celery, diced

2 carrots, diced

¾ pound fresh shiitake mushrooms, thinly sliced

2 cloves garlic, minced

6 cups Basic Chicken Stock (page 27)

2 tablespoons soy sauce

3 tablespoons pearl barley

2 tablespoons minced fresh thyme

1 tablespoon dry sherry

Salt, to taste

Freshly ground black pepper, to taste

❦ In a large heavy pot, heat olive oil over medium-high heat and sauté onion, celery, and carrots, stirring occasionally, until tender, about 10 minutes. Add mushrooms and garlic and cook uncovered, stirring occasionally, until lightly browned, about 5 minutes.

❦ Add chicken stock, soy sauce, barley, thyme, and sherry. Reduce heat to low, cover partially, and simmer gently for 45 minutes. Season with salt and pepper to taste. To serve, ladle into heated soup bowls.

VEGETARIAN MINESTRONE

{Serves 10 to 12}

This hearty Italian soup is wonderfully versatile. Choose fresh vegetables according to the season and don't be overly concerned with exact measurements. Substitute part chicken or beef stock for the vegetable stock, if you wish. Be sure to allow time for soaking beans overnight.

¼ cup olive oil

2 medium onions, chopped

2 cloves garlic, minced

1 cup chopped carrots

1½ cups chopped celery

¼ cup minced fresh parsley

2 cups peeled and diced potatoes

2 cups unpeeled diced zucchini

2 cups chopped Swiss chard

1 cup dried cannellini beans or Great
    Northern beans, soaked overnight

1 can (28 ounces) peeled
    tomatoes with liquid

6 to 8 cups vegetable stock (page 26)

1 teaspoon dried basil, crumbled

½ teaspoon dried thyme, crumbled

1 bay leaf, crumbled

Salt, to taste

Freshly ground black pepper, to taste

4 to 8 ounces dried macaroni or penne pasta

½ head cabbage, cored and shredded

1 can (12-ounces) garbanzo beans, drained

Freshly grated Parmesan cheese

In a large heavy pot, heat olive oil over medium heat. Add onions, garlic, carrots, celery, parsley, potatoes, zucchini, chard, beans, and tomatoes. Sauté 5 minutes, stirring occasionally. Add stock, basil, thyme, and bay leaf. Season with salt and pepper to taste. Cover, reduce heat to low, and simmer until beans are soft, about 2 hours.

Add pasta, cabbage, and garbanzo beans. Cook, partially covered, for 30 minutes, stirring frequently. Serve in heated soup bowls and sprinkle with grated Parmesan cheese.

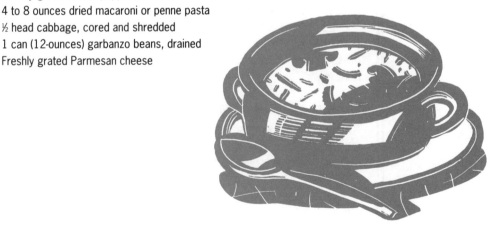

DELI SPLIT PEA SOUP

{Serves 8}

No packaged mix or canned soup can come close to the rich, intense flavor of this Dutch-style, green split pea soup. Its taste is remarkably lively, even if you omit the salami or ham. This nourishing soup requires only a salad and a suitably rich dessert to make a complete meal. Be prepared for the inevitable demand for seconds. And remember to allow time for soaking peas overnight.

1½ cups dried green split peas
2 tablespoons olive oil
2 medium onions, finely diced
3 cloves garlic, minced
1 large carrot, peeled and finely diced
1 medium parsnip, peeled and finely diced
2 stalks celery, finely diced
1 small rutabaga, peeled and finely diced
¾ cup diced salami or ham, optional
10 cups chicken or vegetable stock
Salt, to taste
Freshly ground black pepper, to taste
Toasted Oil-Free Croutons (page 31), for garnish

❦ Soak dried split peas in water to cover overnight.

❦ In a large heavy pot, heat olive oil over medium-high heat and sauté onions, garlic, carrot, parsnip, celery, rutabaga, and salami (if using) until soft, about 10 minutes. Add stock and drained split peas and mix well. Season with salt and pepper to taste. Bring to a boil, reduce heat, and simmer, partially covered, for 1 hour, stirring frequently. Ladle into heated soup bowls and garnish with toasted croutons.

SEASONING WITH SALT AND PEPPER

 The secret ingredient to a recipe is the addition of salt or pepper. What does "salt and pepper to taste" really mean?

❦ *Adding enough salt and pepper to satisfy your own personal taste, plus the taste of the people you are cooking for. Hot dishes need less salt to taste—cold need more.*

❦ *Salt gives sparkle to a dish. It brings out the flavor and often adds life to a dull dish.*

❦ *Do not add all of the salt called for in a recipe at the beginning. Adjust the amount when finished.*

❦ *If added too soon, salt creates unwanted moisture in tomatoes, meats, etc. And when the volume is reduced through cooking, the dish becomes too salty. Add salt to meat just before roasting or sautéing.*

❦ *A few grains of kosher or sea salt sprinkled on top of a finished dish add a flavorful crunch. So does freshly ground black pepper, but use it sparingly.*

GREEN GARDEN SOUP

{Serves 4 to 6}

Take a cue from the deli and make a soup out of salad greens. It's an ingenious way to use up extra greens and you'll love the soup's glorious emerald-green color.

3 tablespoons olive oil or butter
½ cup chopped green onions
1½ cups chopped celery
3 cups coarsely chopped lettuce
2 cups chopped watercress
2 cups chopped spinach leaves
½ cup chopped fresh parsley
2 tablespoons minced fresh basil
6 cups vegetable or chicken stock (pages 26–27)
Salt, to taste
Freshly ground black pepper, to taste
Freshly grated Parmesan cheese or Toasted
    Oil-Free Croutons (page 31), for garnish

❦ In a large pot, heat olive oil over medium heat and sauté green onions and celery until tender, about 5 minutes. Add lettuce, watercress, spinach, and parsley; sauté until softened but still firm, about 3 minutes. Add basil and stock, and season with salt and pepper to taste. Bring to a boil, reduce heat, and simmer until vegetables and broth thicken, 20 to 25 minutes. Ladle into 6 heated soup bowls and garnish with grated Parmesan cheese or toasted croutons.

SWEET AND SOUR BORSCHT

{Serves 6}

This hearty beet soup scores high in the versatility department. It can be served hot or cold, with or without meat, potatoes, or cabbage. I often give borscht an Italian flair by adding balsamic vinegar instead of the usual lemon juice to heighten its sweet-and-sour flavor.

2 pounds beets (about 6 medium), tops
    removed, peeled, and shredded
2 tablespoons unsalted butter or margarine
2 cloves garlic, minced
2 cups finely chopped onions
¼ cup firmly packed dark brown sugar
¼ cup balsamic vinegar
3 cups vegetable or chicken stock (pages 26–27)
Salt, to taste
Freshly ground black pepper, to taste
Sour cream, for garnish
¼ cup minced fresh mint leaves, for garnish

❦ Place beets in a large nonreactive pot and cover with water. Bring to a boil, reduce heat, and simmer until tender, about 30 minutes. Drain, reserving 2 cups of liquid. Return beets and reserved liquid to pot and set aside.

❦ In a small skillet, heat butter over medium heat and sauté garlic and onions until softened, about 5 minutes. Add brown sugar and cook, stirring constantly, about 3 minutes. Add to cooked beets along with vinegar and stock. Bring to a boil, reduce heat, and simmer, stirring occasionally, about 20 minutes. Season with salt and pepper to taste.

❦ To serve, ladle the hot soup into heated bowls. Top each with a dollop of sour cream and sprinkle with minced mint leaves.

CHILLED BORSCHT *Chill and serve cold; remove layer of oil that forms on top before serving.*

SOUTHWESTERN CORN CHOWDER {Serves 6}

Check out this creamy corn chowder with a spicy flair. Crisp tortilla squares, zesty chilies, and jack cheese contribute to that special Santa Fe flavor. If using fresh corn, after cutting off the kernels with a sharp knife, scrape the cobs for remaining corn "milk" and add to soup. Serve this hearty soup piping-hot with additional crispy tortillas and cheese.

3 ½ cups fresh (about 10 ears) or
    frozen corn kernels
1 cup vegetable stock (preferably homemade,
    page 26)
½ teaspoon dried oregano, crumbled
½ teaspoon minced garlic
4 tablespoons unsalted butter
2 cups milk
Salt, to taste
⅓ cup diced canned or fresh roasted
    Anaheim chilies (see Note) or
    Roasted Red Bell Peppers (page 81)
18 fried tortilla chips
1 cup cubed jack cheese

❦ Place corn kernels and stock in a food processor or blender. Blend briefly to break up kernels, do not overblend.

❦ In a large pot, combine corn mixture, oregano, garlic, and butter. Bring to a boil, reduce heat, and simmer 5 minutes, stirring well. Add milk and season with salt to taste. Bring to a boil and add 2 tablespoons of the chilies.

❦ Just before serving, stir in cheese and ladle into 6 heated soup bowls. Top each bowl with 2 or 3 tortilla squares and remaining chilies.

NOTE *If using fresh chilies, roast according to directions for Roasted Red Bell Peppers (page 81).*

POTATO AND LEEK SOUP {Serves 6 to 8}

The first time I prepared a huge pot of this delicious soup, my husband and I discovered that its homey taste was habit-forming. We proceeded to enjoy it three nights in a row, looking forward to its peppery flavor each time.

2 large potatoes (about 1½ pounds)
⅓ cup olive oil
4 medium leeks (white part and some green
    parts), thinly sliced (about 3 cups)
3 cloves garlic, minced
1 stalk celery, thinly sliced
5 cups vegetable or chicken stock (pages 26–27)
Salt, to taste
Freshly ground black pepper, to taste
Freshly grated Parmesan cheese, for garnish

❦ Peel potatoes, slice in thirds lengthwise, then slice crosswise very thin. Place in cold water to remove the starch; drain before using.

❦ In a large heavy pot, heat olive oil over medium heat and sauté leeks, garlic, and celery until soft, about 5 minutes. Add potatoes to the leek mixture, cover partially, and saute until soft, about 10 minutes, mixing with a wooden spoon to avoid sticking. Add stock, bring to a boil, reduce heat, cover, and simmer 40 minutes.

❦ Season with salt and pepper to taste. Ladle into heated shallow soup bowls. Sprinkle each serving generously with grated Parmesan cheese.

COLD TOMATO SOUP WITH BASIL AND MOZZARELLA

{Serves 6}

This soup tastes best in late summer, when tomatoes are ripe and sweet. A tomato press used for puréeing tomatoes is most efficient. You can also purée peeled tomatoes in a blender or food processor and then press them with the back of a spoon through a strainer.

6 large tomatoes, peeled
1 teaspoon sugar or more, to taste
¼ cup thinly sliced fresh basil leaves
1 teaspoon salt or more, to taste
Freshly ground black pepper, to taste
6 ounces soft mozzarella cheese,
    cut into 1-inch cubes
Olive oil, for drizzling

Purée tomatoes and strain into a glass bowl. Add sugar to taste and basil. Season with salt and pepper to taste; mix thoroughly. Spoon an equal amount of mozzarella into the center of 6 shallow bowls and ladle tomato mixture over each. Drizzle olive oil over tops.

VARIATIONS *Garnish with cooked or canned fava, cannellini, or garbanzo beans instead of mozzarella.*

GAZPACHO

{Serves 8}

On a sultry summer day, few soups taste as refreshing as this chilled blend of tomatoes, cucumbers, and bell peppers. Since it's primarily made in a blender, it takes only minutes to prepare. Poured into a wide-mouth thermos, gazpacho is the ultimate first course for picnics or outdoor concerts. Add Basil and Lemon Peel Ice Cubes just before serving.

Basil and Lemon Peel Ice Cubes
    (recipe follows)
5 ripe tomatoes, peeled,
    seeded, and quartered
1 medium cucumber, peeled,
    seeded, and diced
1 green bell pepper, seeded and diced
1 red bell pepper, seeded and diced
1 medium onion, diced
1 tablespoon minced fresh parsley

(continued)

Prepare ice cubes and freeze.
In a food processor or blender, combine tomatoes, cucumber, bell peppers, onion, parsley, and garlic. Blend until almost smooth. Transfer to a large glass bowl and stir in tomato juice, olive oil, vinegar, and paprika. Season with salt and pepper to taste. Chill.

A FAST AND EASY WAY TO PEEL TOMATOES

Using a sharp knife, cut a shallow X in the skin at the bottom of each tomato.

Drop the tomatoes, 2 or 3 at a time into boiling water; count to ten and then lift them out with a slotted spoon and plunge them into a bowl filled with ice and water. Then tomatoes will peel easily.

1 clove garlic, minced
1¼ cups tomato juice
3 tablespoons olive oil
2 tablespoons balsamic vinegar
¼ teaspoon paprika
Salt, to taste
Freshly ground black pepper, to taste
For garnish: ½ cup *each* finely diced tomato,
    green bell pepper, cucumber, and red
    onion

GAZPACHO, *continued*

❦ Serve in chilled bowls. Add a Basil or Lemon Peel Ice Cube to each serving and garnish with chopped tomatoes, green peppers, cucumbers, and red onions.

BASIL OR LEMON PEEL ICE CUBES

Water for ice cubes
Small fresh basil leaves or ½-inch-wide slices
    lemon peel

❦ Fill an ice cube tray with water and place a basil leaf or lemon peel in each section. Freeze.

ORANGE FRUIT SOUP

{*Serves 4*}

Your local deli may not serve this soup, but I often serve it for deli brunches at my home. The flavor of freshly squeezed orange juice topped with sliced strawberries and bananas is always a pleasant surprise to friends who taste this fruit soup for the first time. In the spring, be sure to use blood oranges, which yield a strikingly beautiful raspberry-colored juice.

12 Valencia oranges or blood oranges
16 strawberries, hulled and sliced
4 small bananas, thinly sliced
Fresh mint leaves, for garnish

❦ Thirty minutes before serving, squeeze oranges, strain juice (about 4 cups), cover, and chill. At serving time, pour orange juice into 4 shallow soup bowls. Arrange strawberries, bananas, and mint leaves decoratively on top. Serve immediately.

VARIATIONS *For a dramatic presentation, arrange fruits on the bottom of bowls. Place bowls on table and when guests are seated, pour chilled orange juice over fruit. Or substitute such seasonal fruits as raspberries or thinly sliced melons, figs, peaches, or pears for the strawberries.*

BASIC STOCKS

Stocks can be the cook's best friend! If you like to make soups, vegetables, pasta, sauces, and stews, you should keep a supply of flavorful stocks in your freezer. Using water as a liquid makes everything taste watery. But a rich chicken, beef, vegetable, or fish-based stock enhances every sauce you add it to. ❦ Take the time to make a big batch of stock. You may double or even triple the quantities in these recipes. Freeze stock in ice cube trays to be used in small quantities, maybe to perk up some gravy, or use larger containers for larger batches to be added to soups. Stocks are a standby with professional chefs, who always keep a stockpot going. ❦ If you're pressed for time, you can use concentrated stock, available in cubes or powdered form. If you're diet-conscious, select the low-sodium varieties. For vegetarian or Kosher cooking; there's even a chicken-less stock that tastes like the real thing!

BASIC VEGETABLE STOCK {Makes 8 cups}

An intensely flavorful vegetable stock, which can be stored in the freezer, serves as a handy shortcut when making good vegetable soups. It can also be used in stews or as a sauce base. Onions, celery, carrots, and leeks are indispensable to making good stock, but feel free to add a few of your favorites as long as their flavors aren't overpowering.

3 stalks celery, sliced

3 medium carrots, sliced

2 medium leeks (white and green parts), sliced

1 medium onion, stuck with 2 whole cloves

2 medium tomatoes, diced

1 medium zucchini, sliced

Greens only of 4 beets

1 small head garlic, unpeeled and sliced in half
     crosswise

6 sprigs fresh parsley

2 bay leaves, crumbled

½ teaspoon dried thyme, crumbled

5 whole black peppercorns

8 cups water

2 teaspoons salt

❦ In a large heavy pot, combine all ingredients and bring to a boil over high heat. Reduce heat to low, partially cover, and simmer slowly for at least 2 hours.

❦ Pour broth through a strainer lined with cheesecloth and cool. Then cover tightly and place in the refrigerator for up to 2 or 3 days or freeze in small containers for up to 1 month.

BASIC FISH STOCK {Makes about 4 cups}

To prepare this stock, it's easier and less expensive to buy assorted fish for chowder at the fish market. Be sure to ask for some extra fish bones, too. Fish stock does wonders for fish soups, stews, and sauces.

2 pounds fresh fish for chowder

2 medium onions, diced

1 clove garlic, halved

2 medium carrots, sliced

2 stalks celery, sliced

¼ cup herb bouquet (bay leaf, fennel seed,
     fresh parsley sprigs, dried thyme, and
     black peppercorns tied in cheesecloth)

1 cup dry white wine

Salt, to taste

White pepper, to taste

❦ In a large heavy pot, combine fish, onions, garlic, carrots, celery, herb bouquet, and wine. Add water to cover, bring to a boil over high heat. Season with salt and pepper to taste. Reduce heat to low and simmer, partially covered, 45 minutes.

❦ Pour broth through a strainer lined with cheesecloth into a heatproof bowl and cool. Cover with plastic wrap and refrigerate for up to 2 or 3 days or store in small containers (ice cube trays) and freeze for up to 1 month.

BASIC CHICKEN STOCK   {*Makes about 6 cups*}

Concentrated chicken seasoning mixtures are available and are perfectly acceptable. Preparing chicken stock from scratch, however, guarantees a rich, not-so-salty product. Make a big batch; freeze in small containers or ice cube trays and use to enhance soups and sauces.

4 pounds chicken necks and giblets
3 quarts cold water
1 large onion, stuck with 3 cloves
1 whole head garlic, unpeeled
    and sliced in half
2 large leeks (white and green parts),
    halved lengthwise
3 large carrots, peeled and sliced
3 stalks celery, sliced
6 sprigs fresh parsley
1 bay leaf, crumbled
1 tablespoon whole black peppercorns
Salt, to taste

❦ In a large pot, combine chicken parts and the cold water. Bring to a boil and skim off the foam. Add onion, garlic, leeks, carrots, and celery. Place parsley, bay leaf, and peppercorns in a cheesecloth bag tied with twine and add to the pot. Bring to a boil, reduce heat and simmer 2 hours, partially covered. Season with salt to taste. Simmer another 2 hours, partially covered, adding boiling water if needed to keep chicken and vegetables covered.

❦ Strain stock through a fine sieve into a large bowl, lightly pressing on chicken and vegetables. Cool. Chill and remove fat that hardens on top. Pour into small containers or ice cube trays and refrigerate or freeze.

BASIC BEEF STOCK   {*Makes about 12 cups*}

A few quarts of savory, rich beef stock in the freezer are worth their weight in gold. Homemade beef stock tastes much better than the store-bought variety and contains much less sodium. Freeze the stock in small containers—even in ice cube trays—and you'll be able to make a variety of soups, sauces, and stews on a moment's notice. Have butcher cut up bones or use them whole—no problem.

5 pounds chopped beef bones
¼ cup safflower or vegetable oil
½ cup tomato paste
2 medium onions, corsely diced
2 carrots, thickly sliced
5 stalks celery, thickly sliced
1 head garlic, sliced in half crosswise
15 whole black peppercorns
3 bay leaves, crumpled
1 bunch fresh thyme

❦ Preheat the oven to 400°F.
❦ Place bones and oil in a large roasting pan and bake, stirring occasionally, until bones are browned, about 20 minutes. Add tomato paste, spreading evenly to coat bones. Bake 20 minutes more. Using a slotted spoon, transfer bones to a large, heavy stock pot. Add to fat in roasting pan onion, carrots, celery, garlic, peppercorns, bay leaves, and thyme. Roast until golden brown, about 30 minutes.
❦ Cover bones with warm water, about 1½ gallons. Bring to a boil, reduce heat and simmer, skimming off fat as it builds up, about 1 hour. Add vegetables and spices to bones. Cover and simmer 12 hours, adding more water as needed.
❦ Pour stock through a strainer lined with cheesecloth into a heatproof bowl and cool. Skim fat from top. Cover with plastic wrap and refrigerate for up to 2 or 3 days or store in small containers and freeze for up to 1 month.

DELI SALADS

CHAPTER 2

Deli salads are often much more than the dainty mixture of field greens served in upscale restaurants. In fact, deli salads are usually substantial enough to be considered main courses. When displayed in those glass cases, they tempt everyone to buy more varieties than intended. Depending upon the deli, these salads can run the gamut from traditional to out-of-the-ordinary. ❦ In this chapter, I've included many of the beloved classics—such as coleslaw and both hot and cold potato salads—as well as more creative selections like Asian Pasta Primavera and Sweet Potato and Turkey Salad. You'll also discover a wealth of ethnic salads, delightful as main courses, side dishes, or starters. The key to a great salad is its freshness. Vegetables should be crisp, and unless a salad is marinated, don't add the dressing until serving time. Toss from the bottom up, so every ingredient glistens with homemade dressing. ❦ At the end of this section, you will find a dressing for each salad, but I encourage you to experiment with matching salads and dressings any way you choose.

RECIPES

CHAPTER 2

THE BEST CAESAR SALAD {Serves 6}

C aesar salad—a classic mixture including crisp romaine, pungent anchovies, and crunchy croutons—is an all-time Southern California favorite. This version is the creation of chef/restaurateur Bruce Marder, owner of the renowned West Beach Cafe in Venice, California, and also a partner at the Broadway Deli, where a thousand Caesar salads are served weekly. Now you have his exclusive recipe, and it's simpler than you ever imagined a great Caesar salad could be.

3 heads romaine lettuce, hearts and tender
　　leaves only
¾ cup Mustard Vinaigrette (page 49)
1 cup Toasted Oil-Free Croutons
　　(recipe follows)
2 teaspoons finely minced garlic
1 tablespoon mashed anchovies
　　(about 8 anchovy fillets)
1 tablespoon minced anchovies
　　(about 8 anchovy fillets)
3 tablespoons freshly grated Parmesan cheese

❦ Separate lettuce leaves and discard coarse outer leaves. Wash, drain well, pat dry with paper towels, and tear into pieces. Chill.

❦ Prepare Mustard Vinaigrette and Toasted Oil-Free Croutons and set aside.

❦ Just before serving, mix vinaigrette with minced garlic and mashed anchovies.

❦ In a large glass or stainless-steel bowl, toss lettuce with minced anchovies and enough vinaigrette to coat. Add Parmesan cheese and toss. Spoon onto 6 chilled salad plates and top with croutons.

TOASTED OIL-FREE CROUTONS {Makes about 4 cups}

1 loaf good-quality white or
　　egg bread, unsliced

❦ Preheat the oven to 250° F.

❦ Remove crusts from bread and cut loaf into ¼-inch slices. Stack slices and cut into ¼ x 1½-inch strips. Place in a single layer on a baking sheet and bake until lightly golden and crisp, about 20 minutes. (Leftover croutons can be stored in plastic bags in refrigerator or freezer and toasted just before serving.)

CLASSIC CREAMY COLESLAW {Serves 8}

W hen I was growing up in Los Angeles, Clifton's Cafeteria, a downtown landmark, served the creamiest coleslaw. I never realized that the delicious dressing was prepared with only three ingredients—mayonnaise, sugar, and lemon juice—until I coaxed the recipe from their chef some twenty years later. Prepare no more than two hours before serving.

1 cup Mayonnaise Sauce (page 52)
1 large head green cabbage (about 2 pounds),
　　cored and shredded
2 large carrots, shredded

❦ Prepare mayonnaise sauce.

❦ In a large bowl, combine cabbage and carrots. Toss with mayonnaise sauce, cover with plastic wrap, and chill.

CELERY ROOT SALAD {Serves 4}

While little known in the United States, celery root, or celeriac, is exceptionally popular in France. Cut into thin, noodlelike shreds, it's usually tossed with dressing and served as a slaw or crudité. In this recipe, the subtle flavor of celeriac is enhanced by a tangy mustard mayonnaise. Allow at least two hours for chilling.

Mustard Mayonnaise (page 51)
1 celeriac root (about 1½ pounds)
1 teaspoon salt
1 tablespoon white wine vinegar
Boiling water, for blanching

❦ Prepare Mustard Mayonnaise.

❦ Peel celeriac, wash in cold water, and cut into julienne strips. Place in a large bowl, cover with cold water, salt, and vinegar. Allow to stand 15 minutes, then drain.

❦ Transfer celeriac to a colander and pour boiling water over it; drain and refresh under cold running water. Pat dry with paper towels and transfer to a large bowl.

❦ Add Mustard Mayonnaise to celeriac. Toss gently, cover, and refrigerate for at least 2 hours.

CHAYOTE SALAD WITH MAYONNAISE SAUCE {Serves 4}

A root vegetable related to squash and native to Mexico, chayote tastes best served raw in salads rather than cooked. The easiest way to julienne chayote, as well as other vegetables, is with a slicer/grater, which is sold in most cookware stores. However, a sharp knife will work well, too.

¼ cup Mayonnaise Sauce (page 52)
2 chayote squash (about ¾ pound each)
2 small heads radicchio or red leaf lettuce, shredded
2 tablespoons olive oil
Salt, to taste

❦ Prepare Mayonnaise Sauce, cover with plastic wrap, and chill.

❦ Using a vegetable peeler, peel chayote, then cut or grate into thin julienne, discarding the small pit in the center. Place in a large bowl and toss with Mayonnaise Sauce.

❦ In a medium bowl, toss shredded radicchio with olive oil and season with salt to taste. Mound on salad plates, forming a well in the center of each mound. Pile an equal amount of the chayote salad in each well. Serve immediately.

DALLMEYER'S TOMATO, PEPPER, AND MOZZARELLA SALAD {Serves 10 to 12}

Munich is known to gastronomy fans as a "food city," and it is famous for food stalls, restaurants, and fancy markets. This salad is a specialty of Dallmeyer, one of the city's most colorful and exciting eateries. The basic salad, prepared all over Europe, alternates layers of sliced tomatoes and mozzarella cheese, topped with fresh basil and olive oil. But Dallmeyer includes tricolor peppers, zucchini, and cucumber for visual appeal and crunch.

1 red bell pepper, seeded and cut
    into ½-inch dice
1 yellow bell pepper, seeded and cut
    into ½-inch dice
1 green bell pepper, seeded and cut
    into ½-inch dice
1 zucchini, unpeeled and cut into ½-inch dice
2 cucumbers, peeled, seeded, and cut
    into ½-inch dice
8 ounces fresh mozzarella cheese, cut
    into ½-inch dice (2 cups)
About ¼ cup olive oil
1 pound cherry tomatoes, cut in half
¼ cup minced fresh basil leaves
Salt, to taste
Freshly ground black pepper, to taste

In a large bowl, combine peppers, zucchini, cucumbers, and cheese. Toss with just enough olive oil to moisten. Add tomatoes and basil, and gently toss. Season with salt and pepper to taste. Spoon into salad bowls.

PREPARING SALAD GREENS

Store unwashed salad greens in plastic bags in the refrigerator and wash carefully in cold water, just before using.

❧ If greens must be washed before storing, dry them well, preferably in a salad spinner. Layer greens between paper towels; wrap and store in plastic bags in the refrigerator.

❧ Never toss greens with dressing until just before serving unless you want a wilted salad.

CAULIFLOWER-ANCHOVY SALAD {Serves 4}

Cauliflower's taste and color is subdued, so the zippy flavor of this salad's anchovy dressing gives the understated vegetable a dynamic flavor boost.

1 cup Parsley-Anchovy Dressing (page 50)
1 head cauliflower, rinsed and
    separated into florets

❦ Prepare Parsley-Anchovy Dressing, cover with plastic wrap, and chill.

❦ In a large saucepan, using a vegetable rack, steam cauliflower until tender when pierced with a fork, about 10 minutes. Transfer to a large bowl, cover with plastic wrap, and chill for at least 30 minutes.

❦ Spoon just enough dressing over cauliflower to moisten and toss. Serve immediately.

GREEK SALAD {Serves 6}

The chef who shared this recipe with me swears it's the original and only Greek salad served in authentic Greek delis. Use the freshest vegetables, real Greek olives, and top-quality feta cheese to create this melange of idyllic Mediterranean flavors.

½ cup Basic French Dressing (page 48)
6 tomatoes, cut into wedges
1 large cucumber (preferably hothouse),
    peeled, halved lengthwise, seeded,
    and sliced on bias
1 large red onion, julienned
1½ medium-size red bell peppers,
    seeded and cut into 1-inch strips
1½ medium-size green bell peppers,
    seeded and cut into 1-inch strips
¾ cup pitted Greek or kalamata olives
1½ teaspoons minced garlic
½ pound feta cheese, cut into ½-inch cubes
Salt, to taste
Freshly ground black pepper, to taste

❦ Prepare Basic French Dressing.

❦ In a large bowl, toss tomatoes, cucumber, onion, bell peppers, olives, garlic, and feta cheese. Add just enough of the French dressing to moisten and toss. Season with salt and pepper to taste.

SPINACH AND JÍCAMA SALAD

{Serves 4 to 6}

This cultural blend of Californian and Middle Eastern flavors is as delicious as it is exotic. Jícama is a crisp tart root vegetable of Mexican origin, now widely available at supermarkets. You can substitute hard pears or tart apples.

Tahini-Honey Dressing (page 53)
1 cup peeled and diced jícama
1 large cucumber, peeled and diced
3 green onions, thinly sliced
3 celery stalks, diced
1 bunch spinach, stemmed and
    torn into bite-size pieces
¼ cup toasted sesame seeds

❦ Prepare Tahini-Honey Dressing.

❦ In a large bowl, toss jícama, cucumber, onions, and celery. Spoon Tahini-Honey Dressing into jícama mixture and toss. Cover with plastic wrap and chill.

❦ Just before serving, toss jícama mixture with spinach. Spoon onto salad plates and garnish with sesame seeds.

CONFETTI LENTIL SALAD

{Serves 6}

If you've only eaten lentils in soups and stews, you should try them in salads. These legumes are the star ingredient in a colorful vegetable salad crowned with creamy goat cheese.

¾ cup Basic French Dressing (page 48)
4 cups water
1 teaspoon salt
2 cups red or brown lentils
¼ cup seeded and finely chopped
    green bell peppers
¼ cup seeded and finely chopped
    red bell peppers
1 stalk celery, finely chopped
3 green onions, finely chopped
¼ cup sliced California olives
4 ounces goat cheese, cut into pieces

❦ Prepare Basic French Dressing, cover with plastic wrap, and chill.

❦ In a large pot, bring the water and salt to a rolling boil. Add lentils and simmer 5 minutes. Remove from the heat and allow lentils to soften, about 5 minutes. Drain them well and transfer to a large bowl.

❦ Pour French dressing over lentils and toss thoroughly. Stir in bell peppers, celery, green onions, and olives. To allow the flavors to develop, let stand at room temperature for 30 minutes before serving. Add goat cheese, toss, and serve.

ITALIAN BREAD SALAD

{*Serves 6 to 8*}

*K*nown as panzanella, *this is a traditional Italian peasant salad. There are many variations: some are mixtures of marinated vegetables placed on crusty bread, others are layers of bread and vegetables. This one is special: it reminds me of the Middle Eastern tabbouleh salad, substituting bread for cracked wheat and adding a colorful array of green and red diced vegetables.*

6 slices day-old country-style bread,
    without crust
1 small red onion, sliced or diced
    (about 1 cup)
2 cloves garlic, minced
1 yellow bell pepper, seeded and
    cut into ½-inch dice
2 medium-size ripe, firm tomatoes,
    diced (2 cups)
1 cucumber, peeled and diced
1 cup fresh basil leaves, torn into
    small pieces
1 tablespoon capers, rinsed and dried
2 anchovy fillets, drained and minced
½ cup olive oil
2 tablespoons red wine vinegar
Salt, to taste
Freshly ground black pepper, to taste

❦ In a bowl, soak bread in water to cover for a few minutes. Squeeze dry and drain well. Crumble into a large bowl.

❦ Add onion, garlic, bell pepper, tomatoes, and cucumber; toss with bread. Add basil, capers, and anchovy fillets and mix well. Add enough olive oil to moisten. Then add vinegar, salt, and pepper to taste; toss.

TABBOULEH

{*Serves 8*}

*E*very Middle Eastern deli includes *this Lebanese cracked wheat salad in its display case. Parsley, olive oil, lemon juice, and mint contribute a distinctive taste to this healthful salad, and the addition of bell peppers gives it an extra crunch. Serve with traditional pita bread.*

1 cup fine bulgur (cracked wheat)
½ cup minced green onions
1 cup minced fresh parsley
½ cup minced fresh mint
1 cup peeled and diced cucumber
1 small green bell pepper,
    seeded and diced
2 cups peeled and coarsely
    chopped tomatoes
⅓ cup fresh lemon juice
Salt, to taste
Freshly ground black pepper, to taste
⅓ cup olive oil
Romaine lettuce leaves
Tomato slices, for garnish

❦ In a small bowl, soak bulgur in cold water to cover until tender, about 20 minutes. Drain and squeeze as dry as possible in cheesecloth or a clean towel, or by pressing against a sieve with a spoon.

❦ Place drained bulgur in a bowl. Add green onions, parsley, mint, cucumber, bell pepper, and tomatoes. Stir in lemon juice. Season with salt and pepper to taste. Let stand about 30 minutes, to allow flavors to blend. Stir in olive oil. Cover with plastic wrap and marinate in the refrigerator for at least 2 hours.

❦ To serve, line a serving bowl with romaine lettuce leaves and mound salad in the center. Garnish with tomato slices.

RICE AND GARDEN VEGETABLE SALAD

{Serves 10}

A crunchy, colorful salad, which is appealing for a barbecue, a picnic, or a buffet. When cold vinaigrette is added to the hot rice all the flavors meet in a tangy, delicious blend. Perfect served with cold meat or poultry.

¾ cup Mustard Vinaigrette (page 49)

4 cups hot cooked rice

½ cup finely chopped green onions

½ cup seeded and finely chopped green bell peppers

½ cup peeled and finely chopped tomatoes

½ cup chopped fennel bulb

½ cup minced fresh parsley

½ cup fresh or frozen green peas

Salt, to taste

Freshly ground black pepper, to taste

Tomato wedges, for garnish

❦ Prepare Mustard Vinaigrette.

❦ In a large salad bowl, toss hot rice with ½ cup of the vinaigrette and chill.

❦ In a medium bowl, combine green onions, bell peppers, tomatoes, fennel, and parsley and toss. Add this mixture and the green peas to the rice and toss again. Add the remaining vinaigrette if needed. Season with salt and pepper to taste. Garnish with tomato wedges.

FRENCH POTATO SALAD

{Serves 8}

T he inspiration for this potato salad comes from French chefs, who often add the dressing (usually vinaigrette) when the potatoes are still warm. They believe it's the best way for the potatoes to absorb all of the dressing's tangy taste. Rich in texture and flavor, this salad especially complements simply prepared chilled poultry or poached fish.

½ to ¾ cup Basic French Dressing (page 48)

3 pounds new potatoes, unpeeled, cooked, and cut into small cubes

⅓ cup dry white wine

⅓ cup vegetable or chicken stock (pages 26–27)

⅓ cup minced fresh parsley

⅓ cup sliced green onions

4 ounces Roquefort cheese or other blue cheese

¼ pound sliced bacon, cooked crisp (optional)

❦ Prepare Basic French Dressing.

❦ In a large bowl, combine hot potatoes, white wine, chicken stock, parsley, and green onions. Toss mixture gently; cool.

❦ Crumble Roquefort over mixture, add enough French dressing to moisten, and toss gently. Cover with plastic wrap and chill at least 4 hours.

❦ Crumble bacon, if using, over salad and serve at room temperature.

BEST-EVER POTATO SALAD {Serves 8}

Potato salad can always come to the rescue at party time, as it can be made ahead and served with so many dishes, from sandwiches to entrées. I add lots of crunchy, colorful vegetables to a classic recipe to perk up the potato flavor.

12 small red-skinned potatoes
   (2½ to 3 pounds)
1 tablespoon kosher salt
1½ cups diced celery
1 red bell pepper, seeded and diced
1 green bell pepper, seeded and diced
1 yellow bell pepper, seeded and diced
4 hard-cooked eggs, coarsely chopped
1 cup Deli Mayonnaise (page 51)
4 green onions, finely sliced (½ cup)
½ cup minced fresh parsley
Salt, to taste
Freshly ground black pepper, to taste
Red and yellow bell pepper slices, for garnish
½ cup minced chives, for garnish

❧ Scrub potatoes well with a vegetable brush, but do not peel. In a large heavy pot, cover potatoes with cold water and add salt. Bring to a boil over high heat, cover, reduce heat, and simmer until tender when tested with the tip of a knife, 15 to 20 minutes (remove smaller potatoes first to prevent overcooking). Cool and dice.

❧ In a large bowl, combine potatoes, celery, diced bell peppers, and hard-cooked eggs. Add just enough mayonnaise to moisten ingredients and toss gently. Add green onions and parsley; season with salt and pepper to taste and toss again. Garnish with red and yellow bell pepper slices and chives.

MODERN MACARONI SALAD {Serves 8}

Make your own macaroni salad and you'll discover it's crunchier than any deli's when it's tossed with fresh vegetables just before it's served. I add fennel to my recipe for an intriguing flavor twist. If you like, substitute small macaroni shells for the elbow variety.

1 cup Mayonnaise Vinaigrette (page 52)
8 ounces elbow macaroni, boiled until tender
   and drained
1 cup finely diced fennel or celery
½ cup seeded and finely diced red or green bell
   pepper
⅓ cup sliced green onions
3 tablespoons minced fresh parsley
Salt, to taste
Freshly ground black pepper, to taste

❧ Prepare Mayonnaise Vinaigrette.

❧ In a large bowl, combine macaroni with ½ cup of the vinaigrette. Cover with plastic wrap and chill for 1 hour.

❧ To the macaroni, add fennel, bell pepper, green onions, 2 tablespoons of the parsley, and the remaining ½ cup vinaigrette. Stir gently but thoroughly to blend well. Season with salt and pepper to taste.

❧ Sprinkle with remaining parsley and serve immediately. You can also cover and refrigerate, but the salad will lose some of its crunch.

ASIAN PASTA PRIMAVERA {Serves 8}

Pasta and grilled chicken infused with aromatic Asian spices create an explosion of flavors in this beguiling salad.

1 cup Piquant Chinese Dressing (page 49)

2 pounds linguini, cooked al dente

1 pound boned chicken breasts, grilled, skinned, and shredded

½ pound snow peas, julienned

1 pound bean sprouts

½ red onion, thinly sliced

1 cup shredded red cabbage

1 cup toasted chopped cashews (page 182)

¼ cup black sesame seeds

❦ Prepare Piquant Chinese Dressing.

❦ In a large bowl, toss together linguini, chicken, snow peas, bean sprouts, onion, and cabbage until complete mixed. Add cashews and sesame seeds and toss. Add just enough dressing to moisten and toss to coat.

JUDY'S STANDBY HERRING SALAD {Serves 6 to 8}

This is my favorite salad to make when I'm pressed for time, as it starts with a jar of herring in sour cream, easily found in most supermarkets. Try preparing it my way, then incorporate your own ideas, using herbs, spices, and vegetables such as cucumbers, pickles, beets, or boiled new potatoes. It's easy to double or triple the recipe: just buy more herring! Note that this salad should be chilled before serving.

1 jar (16 ounces) pickled herring fillets in sour cream

½ cup sour cream

1 small red onion, thinly sliced

1 tart apple, such as pippin or Granny Smith, peeled, cored, and chopped

6 to 8 large Boston or Bibb lettuce leaves

Paprika, for garnish

2 tablespoons minced fresh dill, for garnish

❦ Cut herring fillets into bite-size strips and place with their sour cream in a large glass bowl. Gently fold in additional sour cream. Fold in onion and apple. Cover with plastic wrap and chill before serving.

❦ To serve, arrange lettuce leaves on chilled salad plates; spoon herring mixture on top and sprinkle with paprika and dill. Serve with thin slices of Deli Onion-Rye Bread (page 152).

SCANDINAVIAN HERRING-
POTATO SALAD

{ *Serves 8* }

A delectable variation on a Danish favorite, this salad marries the flavors of herring, potatoes, apples, and beets, which create a lovely rosy hue.

⅓ cup Mustard Mayonnaise (page 51)

2 large beets

4 large potatoes

2 cups pickled herring, drained and cubed

2 medium red apples, unpeeled,
    cored, and thinly sliced

½ cup thinly sliced onions

❦ Prepare Mustard Mayonnaise.

❦ In separate saucepans, boil beets and potatoes in water until tender. Drain, peel, and cut into ½-inch cubes.

❦ In a large bowl, combine beets, potatoes, herring, apples, and onions. Toss with just enough Mustard Mayonnaise to moisten. Chill.

TUSCAN BEAN AND TUNA SALAD

{ *Serves 6 to 8* }

D uring a recent three-month vacation in Chianti, much of my time was spent creating new recipes from Tuscany's fabulous array of farm-fresh produce in local markets. I grew addicted to this combination of arugula, tuna, and cannellini beans for leisurely lunches in the garden overlooking the grape vines. Note that the beans must be soaked overnight.

1 cup dried cannellini beans or
    Great Northern beans

About ½ cup olive oil

Salt, to taste

Freshly ground black pepper, to taste

2 cups thinly sliced arugula or
    radicchio leaves

1 can (6⅛ ounces) tuna in oil,
    drained and flaked

1 small red onion, thinly sliced

❦ Soak beans overnight in water to cover.

❦ Drain beans and place in a pot with enough cold water to cover by 2 inches. Bring to a boil and simmer until tender, about 1 hour, adding additional water to cover beans, as needed. Drain well and cool. Toss with 2 to 3 tablespoons of the olive oil. Season with salt and pepper to taste.

❦ In a small bowl, toss arugula with 3 to 4 tablespoons of the olive oil; season with salt and pepper to taste. Arrange arugula in the center of each salad plate and spoon the prepared beans on top. Top with flaked tuna and sliced onion. Sprinkle each serving with another teaspoon of olive oil and more black pepper.

FRESH TUNA SALAD NICOISE

{ Serves 4 to 6 }

A ndrew Sikking, a talented young chef formerly at Beverly Hills Maple Drive restaurant, shared his technique for searing fresh tuna over an open flame. Andrew's method provides wonderful results, but if you don't have a gas stove, sear the tuna in a nonstick skillet.

Vinaigrette Niçoise (page 51)

½ pound fresh tuna fillet

Freshly ground black pepper, to taste

1 tablespoon anchovy paste

2 tablespoons olive oil, if using skillet

¾ cup small cooked white beans,
  drained and cooled

1 medium-size ripe tomato, cut into cubes

1 small red bell pepper, seeded and diced

1 small yellow bell pepper, seeded and diced

12 Italian oil-cured olives, pitted and thinly sliced

3 green onions, thinly sliced

6 fresh basil leaves, julienned

Salt, to taste

3 cups mixed baby lettuce leaves

4 to 6 sprigs fresh parsley, for garnish

❦ Prepare Niçoise Vinaigrette, cover, and chill.

❦ Gas Stove Method: Cut tuna lengthwise into 1-inch-thick spears and skewer 1 slice on a long 2-pronged fork. Brush the entire surface of the skewered tuna with vinaigrette and sprinkle with pepper. Turn the gas burner up to high and hold the tuna over the fire until charred, 15 to 20 seconds on each side. Outside is cooked but center should be very rare. Brush with more vinaigrette, remove from skewer, and place on a platter. Repeat with the remaining spears. Cut into ¼-inch slices. Add anchovy paste to the remaining vinaigrette, cover with plastic wrap, and chill.

❦ Skillet Method: In a small, heavy, nonstick skillet, heat olive oil over high heat. Sprinkle tuna spears with pepper and sear until cooked through, about 1 minute on each side or to desired doneness; do not overcook. Cut into slices, brush with vinaigrette, and place on a platter. Add anchovy paste to the remaining vinaigrette, cover with plastic wrap, and chill.

❦ To Prepare Salad: In a large bowl, combine beans, tomato, red and yellow peppers, olives, green onions, basil, and tuna. Toss with half of the remaining chilled vinaigrette. Season with salt and pepper to taste.

❦ To serve, toss baby greens with remaining vinaigrette just to coat and arrange on chilled salad plates. Spoon bean mixture on top of the salad. Garnish each plate with parsley.

CHINESE CHICKEN SALAD

{ *Serves 12 as an appetizer; 6 to 8 as a main course* }

Y ou could always find Chinese chicken salad in Chinese restaurants, but it also has become the most popular menu item at many neighborhood delis. This delicious recipe contains all the authentic ingredients: chicken, shredded lettuce, bean sprouts, ginger, wontons, and almonds. It was created by Hugh Carpenter, a noted chef who developed the original recipe for Chopstix, a popular Southern California Chinese deli/cafe. Look for less common ingredients in the ethnic section of supermarkets or in Asian grocery stores.

Piquant Chinese Dressing (page 49)
2 cooked whole chicken breasts, skinned,
    boned, and shredded
4 cups shredded romaine lettuce
    (about 2 heads)
1 cup fresh bean sprouts
1 red bell pepper, seeded and shredded
½ cup slivered almonds
10 wonton skins
3 cups peanut oil, for shallow frying
2 ounces rice sticks
¾ cup preserved ginger in syrup, thinly sliced

❦ Prepare Piquant Chinese Dressing.

❦ In a large bowl, combine chicken, lettuce, bean sprouts, and bell peppers. Cover with plastic wrap and refrigerate until ready to serve salad.

❦ Preheat the oven to 325° F.

❦ Place almonds on a baking sheet lined with aluminum foil and bake until light golden in color, about 15 minutes.

❦ Cut wonton skins into ¼-inch-wide strips. In a 10-inch skillet heat ½-inch oil over medium-high heat until a strip of wonton bounces across surface when added. Cook wontons, one-third at a time, until golden. Drain on paper towels.

❦ Add additional oil to skillet if needed. Test oil temperature for rice sticks: The end of a rice stick placed in the oil should puff up immediately. When hot, add a small amount of rice sticks at a time and push apart with chopsticks. As soon as they expand (about 5 seconds), turn rice sticks over with chopsticks or tongs and push back into hot oil. Cook 5 seconds more and remove with tongs. Drain on paper towels. Store on dry paper towels at room temperature up to 4 hours.

❦ Just before serving, add toasted almonds and preserved ginger to the chicken and vegetable mixture. Shake dressing, add enough to bowl to moisten salad, and toss immediately. Gently fold in wontons and rice sticks, taking care not to crush them. Serve at once.

SWEET POTATO AND TURKEY SALAD

{Serves 8 to 10}

The Broadway Deli's chef prepared this original recipe on my television show, "Judy's Kitchen." The combination of sweet potatoes, turkey, and mustard vinaigrette is so appealing, don't expect leftovers. You'll also like his time-saving technique for cooking sweet potatoes: Simply peel, slice, toss in oil, and bake.

¾ cup Mustard Vinaigrette (page 49)
2 pounds sweet potatoes or yams
   (about 4 medium)
¼ to ½ cup olive oil
Salt, to taste
Freshly ground black pepper, to taste
4½ cups cooked, diced (½ inch) turkey breast
½ cup thinly sliced green onions

❦ Preheat the oven to 350° F.

❦ Prepare Mustard Vinaigrette, cover with plastic wrap, and chill.

❦ Peel sweet potatoes and cut into 1-inch slices, then cut each slice into quarters. Place in a large bowl, add just enough olive oil to coat, season with salt and pepper, and toss. Arrange sweet potatoes in a single layer on a nonstick or foil-lined baking sheet. Bake until tender, about 20 minutes, turning occasionally to bake evenly.

❦ Transfer sweet potatoes to a large bowl and toss with turkey and green onions. Pour enough Mustard Vinaigrette over the salad to coat. Season with additional salt and pepper to taste.

CHICKEN-ENDIVE SALAD

{Serves 6}

Crisp endive leaves, tossed with tender chicken, slender asparagus, and toasted almonds, are transformed into an elegant salad for a wedding reception, bridal shower, or cocktail buffet.

3½ heads endive
½ pound pencil-thin asparagus,
   ends trimmed
1 whole chicken breast (about ½ pound),
   poached and cut into 1- to 2-inch dice
2 ounces sun-dried tomatoes
½ cup toasted whole almonds (page 182)
1½ tablespoons chopped fresh tarragon or 1
   teaspoon dried tarragon, crumbled
2 tablespoons fresh lemon juice
¼ cup olive oil
Salt, to taste
Freshly ground black pepper, to taste

❦ Pull off and discard wilted outside leaves of endives. Discard hard core. Cut leaves into 2-inch pieces.

❦ In a large pot or steamer, steam asparagus so it is cooked but still crisp, about 15 minutes. Run under cold water to stop the cooking. Cut into 2-inch pieces.

❦ In a large bowl, gently toss endive, asparagus, chicken, and tomatoes. Add almonds and tarragon and toss. Toss again with the lemon juice and olive oil. Season with salt and pepper to taste.

COBB SALAD {Serves 4}

This Cobb salad varies only slightly from the original recipe served at the Brown Derby Restaurant, which was once the most famous Hollywood dining establishment. Now a staple on most deli menus, the classic salad was named for Bob Cobb, the Brown Derby's owner.

½ cup Basic French Dressing (page 48)
6 hearts of romaine lettuce, shredded
1 cup cooked, diced chicken or turkey breast
2 tomatoes, diced
2 tablespoons crumbled crisp bacon
1 avocado, diced
¼ cup crumbled blue cheese

❦ Prepare Basic French Dressing.
❦ In a large salad bowl, place lettuce, chicken, tomato, bacon, and avocado and toss well with French dressing. Arrange on salad plates and top with blue cheese.

TURKEY AND WILD RICE SALAD {Serves 8}

Deli chefs favor rice salads because they stay fresh and colorful for hours in a display case. Wild rice, toasted pecans, and an aromatic raspberry vinaigrette add notes of elegance to my version. If you like, substitute chicken for the turkey.

¾ cup Raspberry Vinaigrette (page 50)
2 cups cooked wild rice
1½ cups diced, roasted turkey breast
    (skin removed) (page 126)
1 cup toasted pecan halves (page 182)
¼ cup *each* seeded and diced red, yellow, and
    green bell peppers
¼ cup diced red onion
¼ cup thinly sliced green onions
½ teaspoon minced garlic

❦ Prepare Raspberry Vinaigrette.
❦ In a large bowl, combine remaining ingredients. Toss with ½ cup of the vinaigrette; add remaining vinaigrette if needed to moisten.

SANTA FE CHICKEN AND BLACK BEAN SALAD

{*Serves 6 to 8*}

This spicy, robust salad contains corn, chilies, black beans—all the ingredients that have made southwestern cooking a culinary sensation. For an authentic salad, which packs even more punch, add more chilies.

3 whole chicken breasts (about 1½ pounds),
   poached or grilled, skin removed
1 cup fresh or frozen corn kernels
2 tablespoons julienned sun-dried tomatoes
2 tablespoons thinly sliced green onions
2 tablespoons julienned red onions
½ tablespoon minced garlic
1¼ serrano chilies, seeded and minced
1 cup cooked black beans
3 tablespoons fresh lime juice
¼ cup olive oil
½ cup chopped cilantro
Salt, to taste
Freshly ground black pepper, to taste

❦ Cut chicken breasts into strips. In a large bowl, combine chicken, corn, tomatoes, green onions, red onions, garlic, chilies, and black beans. Add lime juice and olive oil; toss to coat. Add cilantro and toss. Season with salt and pepper to taste.

ANTIPASTO SALAD

{*Serves 6 to 8*}

Italian delis are famous for their antipasti and you can be too! This recipe uses all the authentic ingredients for a perfect mix. Serve as a salad or first course.

1 cup Italian Herb Vinaigrette (page 48)
¾ pound Provolone cheese
½ pound Tuscano-style salami
½ pound mortadella sausage
¼ pound prosciutto
½ cup *each* seeded and julienned red, yellow,
   and green bell peppers
½ cup kalamata olives

❦ Prepare Italian Herb Vinaigrette.
❦ Cut provolone, salami, mortadella, and prosciutto into 2-inch-long julienne strips. In a large bowl, toss them with bell peppers and olives. Add vinaigrette and toss to coat.

CALIFORNIA CHEF'S SALAD {*Serves 6 to 8*}

No two chefs' salads are alike, but this one probably comes closest to the typical California rendition. Get creative and add some of your favorite vegetables, meats, or cheeses to this protein-packed entrée. Thousand Island Dressing is the traditional accompaniment, but for a compelling taste twist, try this salad with Parsley-Anchovy Dressing (page 50).

½ cup Thousand Island Dressing (page 53)
8 cups torn assorted salad greens, chilled
3 medium tomatoes, each cut into 8 wedges
¼ cup sliced green onions
2 medium cucumbers, peeled and thinly sliced
4 slices salami or cooked ham, julienned
½ cup cooked, cubed turkey or chicken
4 slices Swiss cheese, julienned

❧ Prepare Thousand Island Dressing.

❧ In a large, chilled salad bowl, toss greens, tomatoes, green onions, and cucumbers and top with salami, turkey, and cheese. At serving time, toss with just enough Thousand Island dressing to moisten or serve on the side.

SALAD DRESSINGS  alad dressings, as their name implies, dress up a salad. They add color, flavor, and interest, besides blending the ingredients. Salad dressings add a delicious accent to vegetables and lend zip to bland lettuce, such as iceberg, Bibb, or red leaf. Try tossing cold, leftover, steamed or cooked vegetables (such as broccoli, brussel sprouts, cauliflower, asparagus, and carrots) with a dressing of your choice for a second-day treat. Many of the dressings in this chapter would be perfect with cold fish or chicken and are especially good on sandwiches. The choice is yours; there is more than one for every day of the week. After preparing a salad with its matching dressing, feel free to select an alternate dressing the next time.

BASIC FRENCH DRESSING

{Makes about 1 cup}

Homemade vinaigrette is far more flavorful than even the highest-quality bottled dressing. Although this recipe contains quite a few ingredients, it's made in a flash.

¾ cup safflower oil
⅓ cup white vinegar or fresh lemon juice
½ teaspoon salt
¼ teaspoon freshly ground black pepper
2 teaspoons Dijon mustard
2 teaspoons sugar
½ teaspoon paprika
½ teaspoon dried basil, crumbled
½ teaspoon dried tarragon, crumbled
2 cloves garlic, minced

In a 1-pint jar, combine all ingredients. Cover tightly and shake well. This will keep up to 1 week in the refrigerator. Makes about 1 cup.

ITALIAN HERB VINAIGRETTE

{Makes about ½ cup}

If you're using dried herbs in this dressing, be sure to crumble them first to release their flavor and aroma. To avoid deterioration, dried herbs should always be stored in an airtight container in a cool, dark place.

¼ cup olive oil
2 tablespoons red wine vinegar
1 teaspoon minced garlic
1 tablespoon finely chopped fresh oregano
    or ½ tablespoon dried oregano, crumbled
2 teaspoons finely chopped fresh rosemary
    or 1 teaspoon dried rosemary, crumbled
1 teaspoon coarse-grained mustard
Salt, to taste
Freshly ground black pepper, to taste

In a large bowl, combine olive oil, vinegar, garlic, oregano, rosemary, and mustard. Using a wire whisk, blend well. Season with salt and pepper to taste. Cover with plastic wrap and chill. This will keep for several days in the refrigerator. Makes about ½ cup.
VARIATION *Replace red wine vinegar with 1 tablespoon balsamic vinegar and replace oregano and rosemary with 1 tablespoon finely chopped fresh basil.*

MUSTARD VINAIGRETTE

{*Makes about 2 cups*}

With the addition of egg and mustard, this vinaigrette is richer and more assertive in flavor than most. However, salmonella, which can be transferred through raw eggs, is a concern. You might want to purchase the pasteurized, reduced-cholesterol eggs sold at many supermarkets, as they claim to be free of salmonella.

1 egg yolk
1 tablespoon Dijon mustard
3 tablespoons red wine vinegar
1 cup safflower oil
½ cup olive oil
Salt, to taste
Freshly ground black pepper, to taste
Sugar, to taste

❦ In a blender or food processor, with the metal blade in place, blend egg yolk, mustard, and vinegar. Continue processing while pouring both safflower and olive oil in a thin stream through the feeder tube, by tablespoons at first, then in a steady stream until well blended. Season to taste with salt, pepper, and sugar. Cover with plastic wrap and chill. This will keep for several days in the refrigerator.

PIQUANT CHINESE DRESSING

{*Makes about 1 cup*}

This flavorful dressing is perfect with Chinese Chicken Salad (page 42) or Asian Pasta Primavera (page 39). Use the preserved ginger in cookie dough, ice cream, or sauces.

½ cup red wine vinegar
2 tablespoons light soy sauce
2 tablespoons sesame oil
¼ cup syrup from jar of preserved
    ginger in syrup
1 tablespoon hoisin sauce
1 teaspoon Chinese chili sauce, optional
1 teaspoon salt
⅓ cup minced green onions

❦ In a medium bowl, combine all ingredients and blend well. Cover with plastic wrap and chill. This will keep for about a week in the refrigerator.

RASPBERRY VINAIGRETTE {*Makes about ¾ cup*}

The combination of raspberry and sherry vinegars lends a fruity flavor to the Turkey and Wild Rice Salad. Have fun by pairing this vinaigrette with other salads in this cookbook.

¼ cup raspberry vinegar
2 tablespoons sherry vinegar
½ cup olive oil
Salt, to taste
Freshly ground black pepper, to taste

❦ In a small bowl, blend together all ingredients. Cover with plastic wrap and chill. This will keep for several days in the refrigerator.

PARSLEY-ANCHOVY DRESSING {*Makes about 1½ cups*}

If you like anchovies, you'll love this pesto-like dressing. It quickly enhances a simple salad, but it's also a delight when tossed with steamed vegetables such as broccoli, cauliflower, asparagus, or spinach. I also use it as a dip for crudités, as an accompaniment to pickled tongue, and in any recipe calling for pesto. Be sure the parsley is very well dried after washing so the dressing will not be watery.

¼ small onion, diced
1 can (2 ounces) anchovy fillets, drained
¾ cup olive oil
2 tablespoons balsamic vinegar
2 cups tightly packed parsley sprigs, stems removed (about 1 bunch)
Freshly ground black pepper, to taste

❦ In a blender or food processor fitted with the metal blade, blend onion, anchovies, olive oil, and vinegar. Add parsley, a little at a time, and purée until the dressing is a bright green color. Season with pepper to taste. Transfer to a glass bowl, cover with plastic wrap, and chill. If dressing thickens after chilling, add additional olive oil and mix well. This will keep for several days in the refrigerator.

VINAIGRETTE NICOISE

{*Makes about 1 cups*}

Created for the Tuna Niçoise Salad, this vinaigrette, with its three vinegars, would enhance crisp baby lettuce leaves as well.

¾ cup olive oil
1 tablespoon balsamic vinegar
1 tablespoon white wine vinegar
1 tablespoon fresh lemon juice
1 teaspoon chopped fresh thyme
Salt, to taste
Freshly ground black pepper, to taste

In a medium bowl, mix together all ingredients. This will hold for several days, well covered, in the refrigerator.

MUSTARD MAYONNAISE

{*Makes about ¾ cup*}

In this recipe, dry mustard and extra lemon juice brighten a basic mayonnaise.

½ cup Deli Mayonnaise
2 tablespoons dry mustard
2 tablespoons fresh lemon juice
Salt, to taste
Freshly ground black pepper, to taste

In a small bowl, blend together all ingredients. Cover with plastic wrap and chill. This will keep for several days in the refrigerator.

DELI MAYONNAISE

{*Makes about 1 cup*}

Few condiments taste as wonderful as homemade mayonnaise. The depth of flavor is remarkable, and the texture is much creamier than the bottled variety. See Mustard Vinaigrette recipe regarding raw eggs (page 49).

2 egg yolks
Juice of ½ lemon
¼ teaspoon salt
⅛ teaspoon freshly ground black pepper
¾ cup safflower oil or olive oil

In a blender or food processor with the metal blade in place, blend egg yolks, lemon juice, salt, and pepper. Continue processing while pouring oil in a thin stream through the feeder tube, by tablespoons at first, then continuing in a steady stream until the mayonnaise thickens. Transfer to a bowl, cover with plastic wrap and chill. This will hold for a few days in the refrigerator.

MAYONNAISE VINAIGRETTE

{Makes about 1 cup}

Homemade mayonnaise is a wonderful base for salad dressings when it's thinned with additional lemon juice and Dijon mustard and enhanced with fresh chives and shallots. This vinaigrette will perk up the flavor of even the most simple salad.

½ cup Deli Mayonnaise (page 51)
2 tablespoons fresh lemon juice
2 tablespoons Dijon mustard
1 shallot, minced
¼ cup minced fresh chives
Salt, to taste
Freshly ground black pepper, to taste

In a small bowl, blend together all ingredients. Cover with plastic wrap and chill. This will keep for several days in the refrigerator.

MAYONNAISE SAUCE

{Makes about 1½ cups}

This basic sauce can be used for coleslaw or other salads. Mix in a teaspoon of Dijon mustard, dry mustard, and fresh chopped dill, and this classic sauce becomes an excellent accompaniment to cold seafood and poultry, as well as to cold steamed or grilled vegetables.

1 cup Deli Mayonnaise (page 51)
2 tablespoons sugar
2 tablespoons fresh lemon juice
Salt, to taste
Freshly ground black pepper, to taste

In a bowl, blend together all ingredients. Cover with plastic wrap and chill. This will keep for several days in the refrigerator.

RUSSIAN DRESSING

{Makes about 1 cup}

With its vivid color and slightly crunchy texture, this traditional dressing doubles as a superlative sandwich spread and chilled seafood sauce.

½ cup Deli Mayonnaise (page 51)
½ cup chili sauce
1 tablespoon minced celery
1 tablespoon seeded and minced
    red bell pepper
1 tablespoon seeded and minced
    green bell pepper
Salt, to taste
Freshly ground black pepper, to taste

In a small bowl, blend together all ingredients. Cover with plastic wrap and chill. This will keep for several days in the refrigerator.

THOUSAND ISLAND DRESSING

{*Makes about 2 cups*}

When I was growing up, it became my job to prepare this dressing for dinner every night. I used to love to fold in chopped hard-cooked eggs and sweet pickle relish. My tastes have changed since childhood, but I still believe Thousand Island is one of the best additions to salads and sandwiches—with or without the hard-cooked eggs and relish.

1½ cups Deli Mayonnaise (page 51)
1 tablespoon fresh lemon juice
1 tablespoon ketchup (preferably homemade, page 73)
1 teaspoon Worcestershire sauce
½ cup chili sauce
1 tablespoon minced fresh parsley
½ teaspoon salt
¼ teaspoon black pepper
Pinch cayenne

❧ In a small bowl, blend together all ingredients. Adjust seasoning to taste. Cover with plastic wrap and chill. This will keep for several days in the refrigerator.

TAHINI-HONEY DRESSING

{*Makes about ¾ cup*}

This out-of-the-ordinary, sweet-tart dressing harmonizes well with most fruit or vegetable salads.

¼ cup Deli Mayonnaise (page 51)
¼ cup tahini (crushed sesame seeds)
2 tablespoons honey
Juice of 1 lemon

❧ In a blender or in a small bowl using a whisk, blend together all ingredients. (Mixture will be very thick.) Cover with plastic wrap and chill. This will keep for several days in the refrigerator.

SUPER DELI SANDWICHES

CHAPTER 3

In most American delis, it's the sandwich that pays the rent. Today's deli sandwiches go far beyond such traditional staples as a BLT or brisket. Apparently whatever can be packed between two slices of bread, tucked into a roll, or stuffed into a pita pocket sells. I have even come across an Italian recipe, which is included, using bologna as a substitute for bread. ⚑ It seems every deli chef has his own ideas about the art of sandwich making. One suggests piling on wafer-thin, instead of thick, slices of meat or poultry. He claims that the many cut edges release all the flavor and provide greater textural satisfaction. ⚑ Another chef insists that lettuce shouldn't come anywhere near a deli sandwich, as it soaks up all the condiments. And, he even claims that an authentic deli sandwich is *never* made with buttered bread. ⚑ When serving sandwiches, I like to present bowls of garnishes like lettuce, cucumbers, and sliced tomatoes and let guests make their own selections. Since no sandwich is better than its bread, this book includes recipes for some fabulous deli breads. And all these sandwiches will taste even better if you use homemade Deli Mayonnaise (page 51).

RECIPES

PAN BAGNA NICOISE

{Makes 1 sandwich}

Pan bagna *translates as "bathed bread." This upgraded tuna sandwich is sold on the streets of Nice much as pizza is sold in Rome. The bread is sprinkled with olive oil and vinegar and filled with tuna, anchovies, vegetables, and herbs. The sandwich is then topped for a few minutes with a heavy plate to compress it and to ensure that the bread soaks up the good flavors of the filling.*

1 clove garlic

1 large kaiser roll or French roll

1 tablespoon olive oil

1 teaspoon red wine vinegar

Salt, to taste

Freshly ground black pepper, to taste

4 thin slices firm tomato

4 thin slices red onion

2 tablespoons drained canned tuna (packed in oil or water)

2 anchovy fillets

4 pitted black olives, sliced

2 fresh basil leaves

1 large lettuce leaf

❦ Cut garlic clove in half and rub crust of roll with cut ends. Slice roll in half crosswise and scoop out some of the inside of the bottom half to make room for the filling.

❦ Sprinkle roll slices with olive oil and vinegar and season with salt and pepper to taste. On bottom half, arrange tomato and onion slices, tuna, anchovy fillets, olives, basil leaves, and lettuce. Cover with the remaining half of roll and weigh down with a heavy plate for 2 minutes to compress the filling. Serve immediately.

VEGETARIAN SUBMARINE SANDWICH FOR A CROWD

{Makes 12 sandwiches}

This four-foot sandwich was created especially for the gala opening of the Broadway Deli. The chef couldn't make the sandwiches fast enough to meet the demand. Order a four-foot loaf of French bread from your local bakery.

1 loaf French bread (4 feet long)

¼ cup red wine vinegar

½ cup olive oil

2 cups shredded iceberg lettuce

3 cups thinly sliced cucumbers

2 cups alfalfa sprouts

6 Roasted Red Bell Peppers (page 81)

3 medium avocados, peeled and thinly sliced

6 medium tomatoes, thinly sliced

4 ounces jack cheese, thinly sliced

❦ Slice loaf of bread in half lengthwise. Sprinkle each half with vinegar and olive oil. Arrange lettuce on half of the loaf; arrange cucumber slices on top of lettuce, then sprouts, peppers, avocado, tomatoes, and cheese. Cover with top half of loaf. At 4-inch intervals, fasten with frilled toothpicks and then slice each section.

PITA ROLL-UPS
{*Makes 8 to 10 sandwiches*}

Pita roll-ups make great picnic food because each sandwich is individually wrapped and ready to go. The layering of the vegetables adds appealing color. Present the pita roll-ups, side by side, on a large platter. Ten-inch pita rounds are sold in many cities as "Extra Large Arabic Bread." If you can't find them, use smaller rounds.

Four 10-inch rounds or five 8-inch rounds pita bread
6 cups chopped romaine lettuce
8 thin slices tomato
12 thin slices red onion
4 thin slices jack cheese
1 Roasted Red Bell Pepper (page 81), cut into strips
1 avocado, peeled and thinly sliced
1 cup alfalfa sprouts

❦ Split each pita round through its pocket into 2 round halves. Place 1 round half on a 12x18-inch sheet of parchment or waxed paper. Arrange ¼ of the lettuce across the center of the pita half. Top with 2 tomato slices and 3 onion slices. Continue to layer with 1 slice cheese, roasted pepper strips, avocado slices, and ¼ cup of the sprouts. Roll up tightly, jelly-roll fashion. Place rolled-up pita on edge of remaining pita half, seam-side down. Roll up tightly, jelly-roll fashion, enclosing completely.

❦ Place the sandwich, seam-side down, diagonally on a square of parchment paper. Then fold corner of parchment paper closest to you over sandwich. Fold 2 sides of parchment over and continue to roll up tightly, envelope fashion. Using a very sharp knife, cut the pita roll in half, crosswise through the parchment, exposing the colorful filling.

❦ Repeat process with remaining pita rounds and filling ingredients.

VARIATION *Substitute thin turkey or chicken slices for cheese, roasted pepper, and alfalfa sprouts.*

TOMATO, MOZZARELLA, AND BASIL SANDWICH
{*Makes 2 sandwiches*}

Not only is the Italian flag red, white, and green, but so is this delicious Italian sandwich. Marinate the tomatoes in a little balsamic vinegar, if you like, to bring out their garden-fresh flavor.

¼ cup Mustard Vinaigrette (page 49)
10 slices Roma tomatoes
10 slices soft mozzarella cheese
10 small fresh basil leaves
2 long French baguettes (6 to 7 inches)
Salt, to taste
Freshly ground black pepper, to taste

❦ Prepare Mustard Vinaigrette, cover with plastic wrap, and chill.

❦ On a large plate, arrange tomato slices in a single layer. Top each tomato slice with a slice of cheese and a basil leaf.

❦ Slice baguettes in half lengthwise (without cutting all the way through). Drizzle vinaigrette on each of the cut sides.

❦ Arrange 5 of the tomato stacks overlapping slightly, lengthwise, along the center of each baguette. Season with salt and pepper to taste.

VEGETABLE SANDWICH LOAF

{Makes 1 large round loaf: serves 8}

Here's an unusual and delicious sandwich; the filling is baked right into the bread. Famed culinary instructor and author Lorenza De' Medici prepares this loaf for her cooking school at Badia a Coltibuono, in Tuscany, and graciously allowed me to include it in this book. Just add a salad for a balanced lunch or brunch. Note that this yeast dough will require several hours for rising and baking.

1 package active dry yeast

1 tablespoon sugar

¾ cup lukewarm water

2 tablespoons olive oil, plus more for baking sheet

1 teaspoon salt

2 cups plus unbleached all-purpose flour, plus ½ cup flour for board

Vegetable Filling (recipe follows)

❦ Dissolve yeast with a pinch of the sugar in ½ cup of the lukewarm water and set aside until foamy, about 2 minutes.

❦ In a large bowl, using a heavy-duty mixer, blend 1 tablespoon of the olive oil, the remaining sugar, salt, and the remaining ¼ cup lukewarm water. Blend in yeast mixture. Add 2 cups of the flour gradually until the dough comes together. Turn out onto a floured board and knead until dough is smooth and elastic, about 3 minutes. Form into a ball, brush top of dough with the remaining tablespoon olive oil, cover with a towel, and let rise in a warm place 30 minutes. Punch down, shape into a ball, and let rise an additional hour.

❦ Prepare Vegetable Filling and set aside.

❦ Line a baking sheet with aluminum foil and brush with oil. Punch the dough down to flatten and roll out on a floured board into a 12x16-inch rectangle. Cover with Vegetable Filling and roll rectangle lengthwise, jelly-roll fashion, to enclose filling. Form roll into a ring; pinch ends to seal and place on prepared baking sheet. For second rising, cover with a towel and let rise in a warm place until doubled, about 30 minutes.

❦ Meanwhile preheat the oven to 375°F. When loaf has risen bake until golden brown, about 20 minutes. Cool on a wire rack.

VEGETABLE FILLING

{Makes about 2 cups}

1 tablespoon olive oil

1 cup diced onions

1 cup seeded and diced red bell peppers

1 cup diced zucchini

Salt, to taste

Freshly ground black pepper, to taste

In a nonstick skillet, heat olive oil over medium heat and sauté onion, bell pepper, and zucchini until tender, about 5 minutes. Season with salt and pepper to taste. Transfer to a bowl and cool.

VARIATION *Substitute diced salami and provolone cheese for the peppers and zucchini.*

BAGEL, CREAM CHEESE, AND LOX SANDWICH

{*Makes 4 sandwiches*}

This star of the deli sandwich repertoire humbly worked its way from New York's Lower East Side to Park Avenue and across the United States. Small wonder it's popular coast to coast; a lox sandwich may be simple, but the taste combination is indescribably delicious. Don't preassemble the sandwiches for a buffet crowd. Simply provide large bowls and platters of the ingredients and let guests have fun making their own sandwiches.

4 bagels (preferably homemade, page 160)
1 cup Whipped Cream Cheese (recipe follows)
8 slices lox (smoked salmon)
4 thin slices onion
4 slices Swiss cheese
8 slices tomato, for garnish
4 Boston or butter lettuce leaves, for garnish

❦ Slice bagels in half and toast lightly. Spread all bagel halves with cream cheese; then top 4 of the halves with layers of lox, sliced onions, and Swiss cheese. Top with the remaining cheese-spread bagel halves. Garnish with sliced tomatoes and lettuce leaves.

WHIPPED CREAM CHEESE

{*Makes about 1 cup*}

4 ounces cream cheese, at room temperature
1 tablespoon cold water

❦ In a medium bowl, using an electric mixer, blend cream cheese until fluffy. Gradually add enough water until mixture is the consistency of heavy whipped cream.

SARDINE SANDWICH

{*Makes 2 sandwiches*}

My good friend Lora Gerson is a cook who likes no-frills food. One of her favorites is a simple sardine sandwich on homemade onion-rye bread, served with a glass of chilled beer.

2 tablespoons unsalted butter,
    at room temperature
4 slices onion-rye bread
    (preferably homemade, page 152)
1 can (3.75 ounces) sardines in oil, drained
6 thin slices red onion
2 thin slices tomato
Salt, to taste
2 crisp iceberg lettuce leaves
Lemon wedges, for garnish

❦ Butter bread slices generously. Arrange drained sardines on 2 of the slices. Top 2 of the slices with onion, tomato, salt, and lettuce leaves. Cover with the remaining bread slices. Garnish with lemon wedges.
VARIATION *Mash sardines, blend with lemon juice and some of the oil from the can. Serve on buttered bread with thin slices of onion.*

CHICKEN SALAD AND SPROUTS SANDWICH

{Makes 4 sandwiches}

Forget about those old-fashioned chicken-salad sandwiches which were primarily mayonnaise, celery, and bread. The nineties call for a healthier deli version that puts the emphasis on the chicken, instead of fatty dressing. Kalamata olives, red onion, and alfalfa sprouts add color, flavor, and crunch.

3 cups skinned and diced roasted chicken

1 cup finely diced celery

8 kalamata olives, pitted and diced

2½ tablespoons finely diced tomatoes

2 tablespoons finely diced red onion

½ cup mayonnaise

2 teaspoons balsamic vinegar

Salt, to taste

Freshly ground black pepper, to taste

8 slices French Country Bread (page 154)
    or egg bread

1 cup alfalfa sprouts

4 Boston or Bibb lettuce leaves

❦ In a large bowl, combine chicken, celery, olives, tomato, and red onion. Toss with ⅓ cup of the mayonnaise and vinegar. Season with salt and pepper to taste.

❦ Spread 4 of the bread slices with the remaining mayonnaise. Spread chicken salad on 4 slices of bread. Arrange sprouts on top and then lettuce. Cover with the remaining 4 slices of bread. Cut in half and serve.

THANKSGIVING TURKEY SANDWICH

{Makes 4 sandwiches}

All the best flavors of a fabulous Thanksgiving dinner wind up in this delectable sandwich. Don't forget the leftover stuffing; it really adds extra pizzazz.

4 kaiser rolls or whole-wheat braided rolls
    (preferably homemade, pages 163 and 162)

¼ cup mayonnaise

2 tablespoons Dijon mustard

4 large slices roasted turkey breast

¼ cup Cranberry-Onion Relish (page 77)

¼ cup leftover turkey stuffing, optional

4 large red leaf lettuce leaves

❦ Slice rolls in half and spread bottom halves with mayonnaise and top halves with mustard. Place 1 slice of turkey on each bottom half; spread with relish, then stuffing, if using. Top with a lettuce leaf and the remaining half of the roll. Cut each in half and serve immediately.

TURKEY AND ARUGULA SANDWICH

{*Makes 2 sandwiches*}

Arugula, a salad green with a peppery bite, grows wild in our vegetable garden. I like to use it in sandwiches instead of the more benign-flavored lettuces. Arugula is particularly good paired with roasted turkey. Cranberry-Onion Relish (page 76) and Best Ever Potato Salad (page 38) are perfect plate companions.

2 tablespoons Italian Herb Vinaigrette (page 48)
4 slices whole-wheat bread or
    French Country Bread (page 154), toasted
8 slices cooked turkey breast (about 6 ounces)
2 thin slices soft Parmesan cheese, optional
1 small tomato, thinly sliced
1 small red onion, thinly sliced
1 cup coarsely chopped arugula
Salt, to taste
Freshly ground black pepper, to taste

❦ Prepare Italian Herb Vinaigrette, cover with plastic wrap, and chill.

❦ On 2 of the toasted bread slices arrange sliced turkey, cheese, tomato, and onion; top with arugula. Sprinkle with vinaigrette and season with salt and pepper to taste. Cover with the 2 remaining slices of bread. Cut in half and secure with toothpicks.

GRILLED EGGPLANT, TOMATO, AND CHICKEN SANDWICH

{*Makes 4 sandwiches*}

Juicy chicken breast slices are topped with grilled eggplant and tomato and sandwiched between slices of country bread brushed with tangy olive purée. The end result is a sophisticated sandwich, ideal for casual entertaining.

16 thin slices unpeeled eggplant
16 thin slices tomato
4 tablespoons olive oil
¼ cup olive paste (preferably homemade,
    page 74)
8 slices French Country Bread (page 154)
    or crusty white bread or
    cracked-wheat bread
2 boneless chicken breasts (6 ounces each),
    poached or grilled, skinned,
    and sliced on an angle

❦ On a work area, overlap 4 slices each of the eggplant and tomato in 2 rows overlapping. Repeat with remaining eggplant and tomato slices.

❦ In a large nonstick skillet, heat 2 tablespoons of the olive oil and, using a spatula, add eggplant and tomato combination and brown on both sides, adding the remaining 2 tablespoons of the olive oil as needed. Transfer to baking sheets and keep warm. Repeat with remaining eggplant and tomato slices.

❦ Spread olive paste on all 8 bread slices and arrange sliced chicken breasts on 4 of the slices. Using a metal spatula, carefully transfer eggplant and tomato combinations on top of sliced chicken breasts. Cover with the remaining 4 prepared slices of bread. Cut each sandwich in half and secure each half with a toothpick.

TRIPLE-DECKER CLUB SANDWICH *{Makes 4 sandwiches}*

As newlyweds, my husband and I enjoyed creating club sandwich combinations. At its heyday back in the 1950s, the club sandwich is now making a comeback. Improvise on this classic recipe with your own variations—it's a perfect way to use up leftovers. Serve with *Creamy Coleslaw (page 31)* or *Celery Root Salad (page 32)* and *Quick Dill Pickles (page 78)*.

12 slices white bread, cracked-wheat bread, or French Country Bread (page 154), toasted
½ cup mayonnaise
¼ cup prepared mustard
12 slices bacon, cooked crisp
2 large tomatoes, thinly sliced
12 small iceberg lettuce leaves
8 slices cooked turkey breast (about 8 ounces)
1 ripe avocado, peeled and sliced
Salt, to taste
Freshly ground black pepper, to taste

❦ Spread toasted bread with mayonnaise and mustard. Place an equal amount of bacon, tomato, and lettuce on 4 of the slices.

❦ Place 4 more toast slices on top. Place on each slice an equal amount of turkey and avocado. Season with salt and pepper to taste and cover with the remaining 4 slices of toast. Cut each sandwich into 4 triangles and arrange on a plate.

OPEN-FACE GARLICKY CUBE-STEAK SANDWICH *{Makes 4 sandwiches}*

When funds are low and the family craves steak, inexpensive cube steaks can come to the rescue. Cube steaks are run through a machine that tenderizes them. In this recipe their rich meaty taste is enhanced with fresh garlic. They're topped with sautéed onions and peppers and served on a toasted kaiser roll. Accompanied with dill pickles, coleslaw, potato salad, or French fries, this sandwich makes a satisfying lunch or casual dinner.

About 6 tablespoons olive oil
2 medium-size red bell peppers, seeded and thinly sliced
2 onions, thinly sliced
2 teaspoons minced garlic
4 cube steaks (about 3 ounces each)
Salt, to taste
Freshly ground black pepper, to taste
2 kaiser rolls (preferably homemade, page 163), split
8 fresh basil leaves

❦ Preheat broiler or prepare charcoal grill.

❦ In a nonstick skillet, heat 2 tablespoons of the olive oil over medium-high heat and sauté peppers and onions, stirring frequently, until soft, about 3 minutes. Set aside.

❦ In a cup or small bowl, combine 2 tablespoons of the oil with garlic and brush over steaks. Season with salt and pepper to taste. Broil or grill until cooked to desired degree of doneness.

❦ Brush cut sides of rolls with additional olive oil. Broil or grill until toasted and top each with a steak. Arrange peppers and onions over steaks and top each with 2 basil leaves.

BOLOGNA SANDWICH STACKS {Makes 12 mini-sandwiches}

Chef Davide Brovelli created these panini (small Italian sandwiches) as an appetizer for Del Sole, his family-owned restaurant on Lago Maggiore in northern Italy. When we were served this dish, I immediately thought it would be ideal for a deli buffet or picnic. Small rounds of bologna replace the usual bread slices and are filled with Davide's delicious version of potato salad, made with new potatoes, green beans, diced red peppers, and peas.

Potato Salad Filling (recipe follows)
24 rounds of bologna,
    2 inches in diameter (see Note)
Julienned zucchini and diced tomatoes,
    for garnish

❦ Prepare Potato Salad Filling, cover with plastic wrap, and chill.

❦ Place 1 round of bologna in the bottom of a 2-inch round cookie cutter and spoon in about 1 tablespoon potato salad until it reaches a height of 1 inch. Cover with a second bologna round. Press down gently and carefully remove cookie cutter. Repeat the process with the remaining rounds of bologna and potato salad. Garnish with "flowers" made of zucchini stems and diced tomato petals.

NOTE Some specialty meat stores sell 2-inch stick bologna. If you can't find it, cut 2-inch rounds out of larger slices with a cookie cutter. Mince the leftover bologna and add to a salad (including this Potato Salad Filling), a sandwich, or an omelet.

POTATO SALAD FILLING {Makes 3 cups}

4 small new potatoes (about 1 pound),
    boiled and cut into ¼-inch dice
½ cup diced green beans, steamed
½ cup seeded and diced red bell pepper
½ cup fresh or frozen peas, cooked
½ cup mayonnaise

❦ In a large bowl, combine potatoes, green beans, bell pepper, and peas. Blend in mayonnaise, 1 tablespoon at a time. Gently mix until vegetables are moistened.

GRILLED SALAMI SANDWICH {Makes 2 sandwiches}

When my children were growing up, they could always count on finding kosher salami in the refrigerator. I like to broil thin slices for sandwiches: the salami gets crisp, the edges curl, and it tastes a lot like bacon, only better. Serve with coleslaw and pickle spears.

12 thin slices kosher salami, casing removed
Dijon mustard, for bread
4 slices rye bread

❦ Line broiler pan with aluminum foil and preheat broiler.

❦ Broil salami close to heat until crisp. Transfer to paper towels to drain. Spread mustard on each slice of bread, arrange broiled salami on 2 of the slices, and top with remaining slices. Cut in half and serve immediately.

NEW YORK PASTRAMI AND CHOPPED LIVER SANDWICH

{ *Makes 1 sandwich* }

If you're seeking the ultimate deli sandwich experience, try this indulgent combination of lean pastrami and smooth, homemade chopped liver. It's the sandwich of deli lovers' dreams—compliments of Wolf's Deli in New York. Serve with mustard, coleslaw, and pickle spears.

2 slices onion-rye bread
(preferably homemade, page 152)
3 ounces Deli Chopped Chicken Livers
(page 118)
7 ounces pastrami or corned beef, thinly sliced

❦ Spread 1 slice of bread with chopped liver and top with slices of pastrami. Cover with second slice of bread; cut in half and fasten with frilled tooth picks.

THE ALL-AMERICAN BLT

{ *Makes 2 sandwiches* }

In case you've forgotten how to make this all-American sandwich, here's the classic recipe. The chef at the Broadway Deli taught me a great way to precook bacon; see note following recipe.

4 slices white sandwich bread, toasted
Mayonnaise, for bread
1 large ripe tomato, thinly sliced
8 to 10 slices bacon, cooked until crisp
4 large leaves Boston or Bibb lettuce, coarsely
shredded

❦ Spread 2 slices of toast generously with mayonnaise. Cover with tomato slices and top with bacon strips and lettuce. Cover with the other 2 slices of toast. Cut in half or quarters. Secure each sandwich with a toothpick.

PRECOOKED BACON *Preheat oven to 350°F. Arrange strips of bacon on a parchment-lined baking sheet and bake for 15 to 20 minutes. Drain on paper towels and brown in a skillet just before serving.*

CLASSIC REUBEN SANDWICH {*Makes 6 sandwiches*}

A true classic, this sandwich is named after Reuben's, a landmark New York delicatessen where actors and theatergoers gather. I've experimented with many variations; my recipe testers liked this one best. Consult the On The Side chapter for some ideas for accompaniments.

½ cup Russian Dressing (page 52)
12 slices pumpernickel or onion-rye bread
     (preferably homemade, page 152), toasted
Safflower oil, for griddle or skillet
12 slices Swiss cheese
12 slices lean corned beef
1 cup sauerkraut (preferably homemade,
     page 00), drained
Dijon mustard, for bread

❦ Prepare Russian Dressing.

❦ Place 6 slices of the bread on a heated, lightly oiled griddle or skillet and layer each with 2 slices of the cheese, 2 slices corned beef, and a heaping spoonful of sauerkraut. Spoon dressing on top of sauerkraut. Using a spatula, carefully transfer cheese-topped bread to a cutting board and cut in half.

❦ Spread a thin layer of mustard on the remaining 6 slices of toasted bread; cut in half and place on top of sauerkraut. Flatten sandwiches with a heavy weight or plate and serve immediately.

VARIATION *A delectable sandwich served piping hot.*

SUBMARINE SANDWICH {*Makes 1 large sandwich; serves 4 to 6*}

I talian delis are legendary for making terrific submarine sandwiches. I often drive by the Bay City Deli in Santa Monica at lunchtime and notice long lines of people waiting to buy those sandwiches that include everything but the kitchen sink. But why stand in line when you can make at home one that's equally good? For a casual party, layer a long loaf with fillings and let guests cut off as much as they like.

¼ cup Italian Herb Vinaigrette (page 48)
1 long crusty loaf (about 16 inches) French or
     Italian bread
¼ cup mayonnaise
2 small ripe tomatoes, thinly sliced
4 ounces prosciutto, thinly sliced
6 ounces Italian salami, thinly sliced
3 ounces Cheddar cheese, thinly sliced
6 ounces boiled ham, thinly sliced
4 ounces provolone cheese, thinly sliced
12 slices Quick Dill Pickles (page 78)
1 cup shredded iceberg lettuce
12 small sweet pickled peppers, sliced

❦ Prepare Italian Herb Vinaigrette.

❦ Slice loaf of bread in half lengthwise and spread both cut sides with mayonnaise. Layer bottom half of loaf with tomato slices, prosciutto, salami, Cheddar, ham, provolone, and pickles. Top with lettuce and pickled peppers. Spoon vinaigrette over the filling and cover with top half.

MEAT LOAF SANDWICH

{ *Makes 4 sandwiches* }

Hot or cold, as a main course or a sandwich, homemade meat loaf remains an American classic. This sandwich is easy to pack for picnics, kept chilled in your ice chest along with beer and soft drinks.

2 tablespoons Dijon mustard
8 slices onion-rye or Squaw Bread (pages 151-152), lightly toasted
4 thick slices Roasted Meat Loaf (page 135)
2 Roasted Red Bell Peppers (page 81)
4 crisp iceberg lettuce leaves, optional

❦ Spread mustard on all the toasted bread slices. Arrange a slice of meatloaf on 4 of the slices; top with roasted peppers and lettuce leaves, if using. Cover with remaining 4 slices of bread. Cut in half and fasten with toothpicks.

DELI CHEESEBURGER

{ *Serves 4* }

Cheeseburgers, like malts and drive-in movies, make me feel like a teenager again. This version has some grown-up additions that make the difference. Serve with French-Fried Onion Rings (page 81).

4 Hamburger Patties (recipe follows)
¼ cup olive oil
4 hamburger buns (preferably homemade, page 159)
¼ cup mayonnaise
¼ cup Dijon mustard
1 red onion, thinly sliced
4 slices Cheddar or jack cheese
Thinly sliced tomatoes and lettuce leaves, for garnish

❦ Prepare hamburger patties. Heat oil in a heavy, cast-iron skillet and brown patties on both sides, pressing down with metal spatula to cook evenly.

❦ Slice each hamburger bun in half and toast. Spread each half with equal parts of mayonnaise and mustard. Cover lower half with cooked burger patty. Top each patty with a slice of onion and a thin slice of cheese. Place on broiler pan lined with aluminum foil and broil until cheese melts. Top burger with other half of bun and arrange on serving plates with sliced tomatoes and lettuce leaves.

HAMBURGER PATTIES

{ *Makes 4 patties* }

1 pound ground beef or turkey
2 cloves garlic, minced
½ teaspoon salt
¼ teaspoon freshly ground black pepper
1 teaspoon dried oregano, crumbled

❦ In a bowl, thoroughly combine all ingredients, kneading to mix well. Shape into four 4-inch round patties.

BARBECUED BEEF SANDWICH   *{Makes 4 sandwiches}*

Serve this barbecue sandwich with oven baked beans and sauer-kraut (page 80). Be sure to provide plenty of paper napkins.

4 kaiser rolls or hamburger buns (preferably
    homemade, pages 163 and 159)
1 cup Deli Barbecue Sauce (page 139), heated
12 thin slices Broadway Deli Brisket (page 140)

❦ Slice rolls in half and toast. Spoon about 2 tablespoons of heated barbecue sauce over each bottom half. Pile on sliced brisket and top with 2 more tablespoons of the sauce. Cover with top half of the roll. Serve additional barbecue sauce on the side.

SWEDISH MEATBALL SANDWICH

{Makes 8 open-faced sandwiches}

This recipe was inspired by Swedish meatballs made by my friend Kerstin Marsh and a frikadeller sandwich that originated in Scandinavia.

1 recipe Kerstin's Swedish Meatballs (page 136)
4 tablespoons unsalted butter or margarine,
    at room temperature
8 slices onion-rye bread
    (preferably homemade, page 152)
3 medium cucumbers, peeled and thinly sliced
2 pickled beets (preferably homemade,
    page 79), thinly sliced
3 hard-cooked eggs, chopped

❦ Prepare Swedish meatballs.
❦ Spread butter or margarine on all the bread slices. Divide cucumber slices over bread. Place 4 meatballs on each slice. Top with several slices of pickled beets. Sprinkle tops of sandwiches with chopped egg.

GRILLED CHEESE AND
HAM SANDWICH

{ *Makes 4 sandwiches* }

I n Italy, coffee bars, similar to mini-delis, are found on almost every street corner. One of their specialties is the irresistible panini. Assembled in advance, these sandwiches are wrapped in paper napkins and then grilled to order. Italians make them with mozzarella or provolone cheese, but you can substitute Swiss or jack. Serve with the Best French Fries (page 83).

¼ pound unsalted butter, at room temperature
8 slices white sandwich bread or sourdough bread
8 slices cheese (Swiss, mozzarella, jack, or provolone)
8 slices boiled or baked ham

❦ Spread butter on all the bread slices. Arrange a slice of cheese and ham on each of 4 slices of the buttered bread. Cover with the other buttered slice. Heat a heavy cast-iron skillet; place one sandwich on it and weight it down with a heavy frying pan or brick. Brown on both sides until the cheese and ham are very hot; cut in half. Repeat with the remaining sandwiches.

ON THE SIDE:
RELISHES, SAUCES, LITTLE EXTRAS

CHAPTER 4

Half the fun of eating in delis is sampling all the extras served on the side. For example, before an order is placed in a Jewish-style deli, a basket of assorted sliced breads, rolls, or bagels is placed on the table to tempt. Sauerkraut, dill pickles, and garlicky green tomatoes are often standard offerings, too. ❦ In an Italian deli, you're served pickled peppers and other pickled vegetables, olive paste, and fresh anchovies. The French present a crock of pâté for spreading on baguettes. ❦ "On the side" not only translates to what you get before a meal, but also to what accompanies an order. Most deli plates are generous. At the Broadway Deli, a hot sandwich is presented with mashed potatoes or French fries and perhaps their famous creamed spinach, while meat entrées are served with such sides as baked beans, fried or mashed potatoes, or potato pancakes and applesauce. (At the Broadway Deli, no one goes hungry!) ❦ I like to garnish sandwiches and other deli foods with unusual relishes. Sauerkraut and Cranberry-Onion Relish are two of my favorites. When entertaining, consider planning a menu that includes a number of different side dishes to duplicate the fun of deli-style dining.

RECIPES

CHAPTER 4

ALAIN'S HOMEMADE KETCHUP

{Makes about 3 cups}

Most delis no longer make their own ketchup, but a deli cookbook without an authentic ketchup recipe to use as a condiment for French fries or sandwiches is inconceivable. Alain Giraud, a chef at Citrus restaurant in Los Angeles, developed this recipe to serve with homemade turkey sausages for "The Taste of L.A.," a local food festival.

¾ cup red wine vinegar
3 tablespoons sugar
4 cups tomato sauce
1 tablespoon tomato paste
1 tablespoon beet juice (from canned beets)
2 tablespoons onion powder
½ teaspoon salt
3 drops Tabasco sauce
Pinch cayenne pepper

❦ In a small, heavy nonreactive saucepan, combine ½ cup of the vinegar and 2 tablespoons of the sugar and simmer over low heat, stirring until sugar dissolves and the mixture is caramelized. Add tomato sauce and tomato paste, beet juice, onion powder, and the remaining ¼ cup vinegar and bring to a boil over high heat. Add the remaining tablespoon sugar, salt, Tabasco, and cayenne. Reduce heat and simmer 20 minutes.

❦ Season with additional salt and sugar to taste. Cool, transfer to a glass bowl, cover with plastic wrap, and chill. This will keep for several weeks in the refrigerator.

DELI HOT MUSTARD

{Makes about 1 cup}

Hot mustard is a deli must—and it's easy to make your own! Basically this condiment is made from mustard seeds and spices, mixed with vinegar, plus water or wine. Salami, knockwurst, or a bologna sandwich would not be complete without mustard—sweet, mild, or hot. This recipe covers a variety of those tastes.

⅓ cup mustard seeds
¼ cup dry mustard
½ cup cold water or white wine
1 cup apple cider vinegar
1 small onion, chopped
2 cloves garlic, finely minced
3 tablespoons firmly packed dark brown sugar
½ teaspoon ground cinnamon
¼ teaspoon ground allspice
¼ teaspoon dried tarragon, crumbled
⅛ teaspoon ground turmeric
1 teaspoon salt
¼ cup honey, or more to taste

❦ In a small bowl, soak mustard seeds and dry mustard in the cold water for 2½ to 3 hours.

❦ In a 2-quart nonreactive saucepan, combine vinegar, onion, garlic, brown sugar, cinnamon, allspice, tarragon, turmeric, and salt. Bring to a boil, reduce heat to medium, and simmer, uncovered, until reduced by half, about 5 minutes. Strain into the mustard seed mixture and then spoon into a blender or food processor and blend until thick and mustard seeds are well blended.

❦ Pour into the top of a double boiler and cook over simmering water, stirring occasionally, until thickened, about 5 minutes. Stir in honey to taste and cool. Store in a sterilized, tightly covered jar in the refrigerator up to 3 months.

CREAMED HORSERADISH SAUCE {*Makes about 2 cups*}

This sauce provides a wonderful way to capture that robust horse-radish taste without overpowering a sandwich, cold meat, or fish.

¾ cup whipping cream
½ cup mayonnaise
½ cup prepared horseradish, drained
2 tablespoons Dijon mustard
Salt, to taste

❦ In a medium bowl using an electric mixer, beat cream until soft peaks form.

❦ In another medium bowl, combine mayonnaise, horseradish, and mustard. Using a rubber spatula, fold in the whipped cream. Season with salt to taste. Stir well, transfer to a serving bowl, and chill before serving.

JANIE'S OLIVE PASTE {*Makes 1 cup*}

On a recent visit with our good friends Janie and Melvin Masters at their home in the south of France, my husband and I were served a delicious olive paste spread on homemade focaccia. Its flavor was so complex, we were sure it was difficult to make. But Janie's recipe is easy; all the ingredients are blended together in a food processor in minutes. This olive paste is not only wonderful on focaccia, it also tastes superb spread on thick slices of grilled bread.

8 ounces Greek or cured olives, pitted
2 medium shallots
1 tablespoon drained capers
4 anchovy fillets
Pinch crushed red pepper
Freshly ground black pepper, to taste

❦ Place olives, shallots, capers, and anchovies in a blender or food processor fitted with a steel blade and blend until smooth. Add crushed red pepper and pepper to taste. Transfer to a glass bowl, cover with plastic wrap, and chill. Will keep a week in the refrigerator.

MUSTARD-DILL SAUCE

{*Makes about ½ cup*}

*S*erve this sauce with cured salmon or pickled fish and thin slices of rye bread for an ideal appetizer, first course, or light lunch.

3 tablespoons Dijon mustard
1 teaspoon dry mustard
2 tablespoons sugar
1 tablespoon white wine vinegar
⅓ cup olive oil
3 tablespoons chopped fresh dill

In a small deep bowl, combine Dijon mustard, dry mustard, sugar, and vinegar and blend well. With a wire whisk, slowly beat in the oil until the sauce reaches the consistency of mayonnaise. Stir in the chopped dill. Cover with plastic wrap and chill. This will keep for several days in the refrigerator.

CALIFORNIA AÏOLI

{*Makes about 1½ cups*}

*T*his sauce is a cross between those two classic garlic mayonnaises of southern France—aïoli and rouille. It is versatile enough to serve as a sophisticated spread for seafood sandwiches or as a delicious garlicky spread for toast. And, of course, it's the ideal accompaniment for a seafood soup or stew.

2 slices white bread, crusts removed
4 cloves garlic
2 tablespoons tomato paste
Drop Tabasco sauce
½ cup olive oil
½ cup fish stock or chicken stock (pages 26–27)

In a bowl, soak bread in cold water and squeeze dry.

In a blender or food processor, process bread, garlic, tomato paste, Tabasco, olive oil, and stock, turning the machine on and off for 5 seconds. Continue processing to make a smooth paste, about 10 seconds, adding additional stock if needed. Transfer to a small bowl, cover with plastic wrap, and chill. This will keep for several days in the refrigerator.

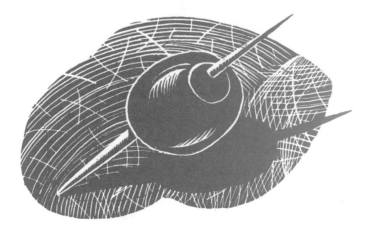

LEEK AND ONION RELISH

{*Makes about 3 cups*}

*T*his exotic relish can be made in minutes and adds an elegant touch to fish or poultry. It's also a great addition to meat or sausage sandwiches.

2 tablespoons olive oil
½ pound red onions, minced
2 bunches green onions
    (white and green parts), chopped
1 cup sliced leeks (white part only)
¼ cup sliced shallots
⅓ cup dry white wine
1 teaspoon sugar
Salt, to taste

❦ In a medium-size heavy saucepan, heat olive oil over low heat. Add red and green onions, leeks, and shallots; cook slowly, stirring occasionally, until tender, about 10 minutes. Increase heat to high. Add wine and sugar; cook, stirring occasionally, until wine has evaporated. Season with salt to taste. Transfer to a glass bowl and cool.

❦ Cover with plastic wrap and chill until ready to serve. Keeps for several days in the refrigerator.

CRANBERRY-ONION RELISH

{*Makes about 3 cups*}

A wicked amount of onions gives cranberry relish new appeal. This aromatic recipe is too good to save for Thanksgiving; consider serving it year-round with roasted chicken or meat or as a sandwich garnish. Since it takes less than one-half hour to make a big batch, increase the recipe proportionally and prepare extra to give as gifts.

½ cup dry white wine
¼ cup white wine vinegar
½ cup sugar
⅛ teaspoon ground cinnamon
⅛ teaspoon ground ginger
2 whole cloves
Grated zest of 1 orange
¼ teaspoon dried thyme, crumbled
3 medium onions, quartered and thinly sliced
    (about 4 cups)
2 cups cranberries (about 8 ounces),
    picked through
1 tart green apple, peeled, cored, and diced

❦ In a heavy nonreactive saucepan, stir together wine, vinegar, sugar, cinnamon, ginger, cloves, zest, and thyme. Bring to a boil, reduce heat, and simmer uncovered until slightly syrupy, about 5 minutes.

❦ Stir in onions and simmer, covered, until crisp-tender, about 12 minutes. Stir in cranberries and apple and cook, uncovered, until cranberries burst, about 6 minutes. Ladle relish into a glass bowl or jars, cool, cover securely, and chill. Will keep up to 1 week in the refrigerator.

ONION-RAISIN RELISH

{Makes about 3 cups}

This slightly sweet and aromatic relish is admirably versatile. It can be served hot or cold, as an appetizer on toast, or as an accompaniment to tongue, corned beef, pastrami, or other deli sandwiches.

1 pound pearl onions, unpeeled with
    root end cut off
3 tablespoons unsalted butter or margarine
1 tablespoon brown sugar
⅓ cup golden raisins
1 tablespoon fresh parsley, minced
Pinch dried thyme, crumbled
1 bay leaf, crumbled
1¼ cups dry white wine
Salt, to taste
Freshly ground black pepper, to taste

In a large saucepan, place onions and water to cover. Bring to a boil, reduce heat, and simmer until tender, about 5 minutes. Drain onions, slip off the outer skins, and set aside.

In a large nonstick skillet, melt butter over medium heat, add brown sugar, and mix until sugar dissolves. Add reserved onions and cook over low heat until a light golden brown, about 8 minutes. Add raisins, parsley, thyme, bay leaf, and wine. Season with salt and pepper to taste. Cover tightly and simmer gently for 1 hour.

With a slotted spoon, transfer onions and raisins to a glass bowl. Remove bay leaf from skillet and bring pan juices to a rapid boil; cook until reduced to a syrup. Pour over onions and raisins. Cool slightly, cover with plastic wrap, and chill. Will keep up to 1 week in the refrigerator.

SUZANNE'S CURED OLIVES

{*Makes 4 cups*}

If you're lucky enough to have an olive tree growing in your backyard, this recipe is a cinch. Suzanne Dunaway, a wonderful California artist and chef, has graciously shared her technique for handling a bountiful olive crop. It's easy and foolproof. Use for appetizers or in recipes like Janie's Olive Paste (page 74). Fresh uncured olives are not available commercially.

4 cups fresh green or ripe olives
About 1 cup kosher salt
Olive oil and minced garlic, for storing

❦ Place olives in a crock, sprinkle with ¼ cup of the salt, and add water to cover completely. Cover with a tea towel, allowing towel to fall into the water, which keeps the olives submerged. Place in a corner of the kitchen for 2 or 3 days. Pour off water and salt and repeat the process every 2 or 3 days. After 3 or 4 weeks the olives are ready. Rinse well before using.

❦ To store olives, rinse, drain, cover with olive oil and minced garlic, cover with plastic wrap, and chill. Will keep up to 3 weeks in refrigerator.

QUICK DILL PICKLES

{*Makes 10 to 12 pickles*}

These pickles taste just like the ones grandma used to make only they're faster and easier to prepare. To transform bumpy little cucumbers into crisp, garlicky dill pickles, place all the ingredients in a jar, cover, and shake. In four days you'll have the best dill pickles you've ever tasted.

4 quarts boiling water, for cleansing jar
3 tablespoons pickling spices
6 cloves garlic
10 to 12 firm small pickling cucumbers
    (about 1½ pounds)
¼ cup kosher salt
1 bunch fresh dill

❦ Pour boiling water into a 1-gallon canning jar and pour out. Drop pickling spices and 3 of the garlic cloves into the bottom of the jar. Arrange cucumbers in the jar to fill just up to the neck. Top with salt, remaining 3 cloves garlic, and dill. Add cold water to cover. Cover securely with the lid. Shake well and let stand for 3 to 4 days in a cool, dark place before serving.

❦ Refrigerate after 4 days to stop the pickling process. The pickles will keep for several weeks, covered, in the refrigerator.

VARIATION *Replace cucumbers with green tomatoes.*

PICKLED BABY BEETS

{*Serves 6*}

Ruby-red, sweet-and-sour beets look and taste great with a myriad of deli foods. You can double the recipe since it keeps in the refrigerator for weeks. The pickling liquid can be boiled and used again.

12 small fresh baby beets
    (about 1½ pounds)
1 teaspoon mustard seeds
1 teaspoon pickling spices
½ teaspoon whole allspice
½ teaspoon whole cloves
½ stick cinnamon or
    ½ teaspoon ground cinnamon
1 cup red wine vinegar
¾ cup sugar
½ teaspoon salt

❦ Trim beets, leaving ¼ inch of the stem. Scrub beets and place in a saucepan, covered with cold water. Bring to a boil, reduce heat, cover, and simmer until tender when pierced with a fork, about 40 minutes. Reserve 1 cup of the cooking liquid. While beets are still warm, slice off stems and peel off and discard outer skins. Transfer beets to a large glass bowl. Set aside.

❦ Place mustard seeds, pickling spices, allspice, cloves, and cinnamon stick in a cheesecloth bag and tie securely. In a medium nonreactive saucepan, combine vinegar, reserved cooking liquid, sugar, salt, and the spice bag. Bring to a boil, mixing until the sugar dissolves, reduce heat, and simmer 5 minutes. Pour this mixture over beets; cover with plastic wrap and refrigerate overnight. Slice before serving. Will keep up to 1 week in the refrigerator.

APPLE-CITRUS SAUCE

{*Makes about 4 cups*}

Applesauce is a classic deli side dish for poultry and brisket. To dress it up, add a little beet or cranberry juice, which gives it a pretty rosy color. Remember, the sweeter the apples, the less sugar is necessary. The slicer attachment of the food processor is a real time-saver for slicing and dicing apples.

6 large Golden Delicious apples, peeled,
    cored, and diced
Juice of 2 lemons
½ cup water or apple juice
⅓ cup sugar
3 tablespoons orange marmalade

❦ Place diced apples in a large glass bowl, toss with lemon juice, and set aside.

❦ In a large nonreactive saucepan, combine the water, sugar, and marmalade. Bring to a boil, stirring constantly until sugar dissolves. Reduce heat and simmer until syrupy, about 3 minutes. Add reserved apples and toss with the syrup. Simmer until apples are very soft.

❦ Transfer apples with a slotted spoon to a large glass bowl and mash. Over high heat, reduce syrup remaining in saucepan until thick and blend into the apples. Cover with plastic wrap and chill. Sauce will keep for several days in the refrigerator.

DELI SAUERKRAUT

{Makes six 12-ounce jars; serves about 12}

To many, the art of making sauerkraut remains a mystery, but in reality, it's a breeze. Sauerkraut pops up in countless deli dishes, from a Reuben sandwich to barbecued ribs.

2 large heads cabbage
(about 2¼ pounds each), cored
2 tablespoons sugar
2 tablespoons coarse kosher salt
Salt solution of ¼ cup salt to each ½ cup water

❦ In the bowl of a food processor, using the slicing blade, or with a sharp knife, shred cabbage. It should yield about 32 cups tightly packed.

❦ In a small bowl, combine sugar and salt. In a large glass bowl, toss shredded cabbage with sugar mixture and mix well. Using a potato masher, press cabbage to release juice. Cover the bowl with a tea towel and set aside for 3 hours.

❦ Sterilize in boiling water, six 12-ounce wide-mouth canning jars. Spoon cabbage into jars, pack down as hard as possible, and pour in the remaining liquid from the bowl. Cover each jar loosely, which allows the sauerkraut to ferment. Let stand at room temperature until mixture stops bubbling, 2 or 3 days.

❦ Open jar and press down again. If more liquid is needed, add enough salt solution to fill jars to the top. Sterilize the lids and screw on tightly. Store in a cool, dark place for 2 to 3 weeks. Use immediately or store in refrigerator up to 1 month.

BROADWAY DELI
CREAMED SPINACH

{Serves 4}

You won't find creamed spinach at any ordinary deli, but the Broadway Deli is far from ordinary. Customers love the creamed spinach and order it with every dish imaginable—even with sandwiches. One note of warning! One bite of this creamed spinach and you're hooked.

12 cups spinach leaves, stems removed
(about 4 bunches)
6 tablespoons unsalted butter
1 small onion, finely diced
3 cloves garlic, minced
1¼ cups milk, heated until warm
Salt, to taste
Freshly ground black pepper, to taste

❦ Wash spinach leaves and drain, repeating twice. In a large pot, place spinach with only the water clinging to the leaves after rinsing. Simmer until spinach is wilted, about 10 minutes. Drain, cool, and squeeze completely dry in cheesecloth. Chop coarsely.

❦ In a large heavy saucepan, melt butter over medium heat and sauté onion and garlic until tender, about 5 minutes. Add milk, bring to a boil, reduce heat, and simmer, whisking constantly, until thick. Add spinach and mix well. Season with salt and pepper to taste. Simmer a few minutes to heat through.

FRENCH-FRIED ONION RINGS {Serves 6}

Delis are expected to serve fried onion rings, but wouldn't you be surprised to find them at a chic California-French restaurant? At Citrus in Los Angeles, the demand is so great that the chefs can hardly keep servers supplied with crisp rings piled like minimountains on oval platters. Citrus uses pricey sweet Maui onions, but the mild Bermudas will do just as well.

3 large onions
Ice water, for soaking
2 large eggs
¾ cup fine bread crumbs
Safflower oil, for frying
Salt, to taste

❦ Slice onions into ¼-inch slices and separate into rings. Soak in a bowl of ice water for 2 hours, adding more ice if necessary. Remove and dry on paper towels.

❦ Preheat oven to 225°F for warming.

❦ In a medium bowl, beat eggs and spread out bread crumbs on a plate. Dip onion rings, a few at a time, in eggs, stir to coat well, and then place in single layer on bread crumbs. Turn pieces over to coat evenly with crumbs. Place coated onion rings in a large shallow bowl or on a large plate. Repeat process to coat all onion rings. Let stand 10 minutes before frying.

❦ In a deep fryer or heavy skillet, heat at least 2 inches of oil to 350°F. Fry a few prepared onion rings at a time until nicely browned, 45 to 60 seconds. Remove from oil with a slotted spoon and drain on paper towels. Season lightly with salt. Keep warm in the oven until ready to serve.

ROASTED RED OR YELLOW
BELL PEPPERS {Makes about 2 cups; serves 6}

Some chefs roast peppers over an open fire; others deep-fry them in oil. For me, roasting in the oven is the easy, foolproof way. Serve as an appetizer, garnished with anchovy fillets, or in salads and sandwiches. If roasting the peppers to use in another recipe, omit the garlic and oil.

6 large, firm, red or yellow bell peppers
3 cloves garlic, minced, optional
About 1 cup olive oil, optional

❦ Preheat the oven to 400°F.

❦ Turn up the edges of a large double sheet of aluminum foil to resemble a baking sheet. Place it on the lower rack of the oven to prevent spattering. Place peppers on the center rack just above the lower rack. Bake until the skin begins to puff and darkens lightly on top, about 20 minutes. Turn each pepper upside-down and continue baking 10 to 15 minutes. (The hotter the oven the quicker the peppers puff and brown; they must be watched.)

❦ Remove peppers from the oven and while they are still warm, very carefully peel off skins. Pull out stems and discard seeds, and slice as directed in a recipe. If you plan to serve the peppers as an appetizer or relish, cut them into thirds and layer them in a bowl with minced garlic and enough oil to cover. Cover with plastic wrap and chill.

POTATO KNISHES

{*Makes about 2 dozen knishes; serves 12*}

Deli Chopped Chicken Livers (page 118)
4 large russet potatoes, peeled and diced
2 eggs
¼ cup unbleached all-purpose flour
Salt, to taste
Freshly ground black pepper, to taste
Safflower or vegetable oil, for baking

This New York deli favorite from the Lower East Side is similar to an Irish potato cake, except that it's filled with chopped liver. Think about other creative knish stuffings like chopped corned beef, cheese, hard-cooked eggs, or even nuts and raisins for a sweetened version. I like this old-fashioned recipe the way it is, because it was my mother's. The crisp potato crust hides a filling overflowing with good rich flavor.

❦ Prepare Deli Chopped Chicken Livers, cover with plastic wrap, and chill.

❦ Preheat the oven to 375° F.

❦ In a large saucepan, boil potatoes in salted water to cover until tender, about 15 minutes. Drain and mash through a ricer or large-hole strainer into a large bowl. Add 1 of the eggs and flour and mix well. Season generously with salt and pepper to taste. Cover with plastic wrap and chill.

❦ Shape a heaping tablespoonful of the potato mixture into a 3-inch round. Press a tablespoon of the liver mixture in the center. Shape the potato mixture around the filling to completely enclose it.

❦ Line a baking sheet with aluminum foil and brush with oil. In a small bowl lightly beat the remaining egg. Place each knish on the prepared baking sheet, brush with egg, and bake until golden brown on both sides, about 45 minutes.

HASH BROWN POTATOES

{*Serves 4*}

¼ pound plus about 3 tablespoons
unsalted butter or margarine
4 large potatoes, peeled and
coarsely shredded
Salt, to taste
Freshly ground black pepper, to taste

Hash brown potatoes that score a perfect "ten" are crispy and crusty on the bottom as well as the top, and soft and moist in the center. My favorite hash browns are dished up at the landmark Pantry Restaurant in downtown Los Angeles; this recipe duplicates their marvelous flavor and texture.

❦ In a large cast-iron skillet or on a griddle, heat ¼ pound of the butter and add potatoes, forming them into a flat cake and pressing them down. Cook over medium heat until potatoes form a crisp crust on the bottom, about 5 to 6 minutes. Run a spatula around the edges and shake the pan occasionally. Add 2 or 3 tablespoons of the remaining butter and let it melt through the potatoes. Season with salt and pepper to taste.

❦ Place a large plate over the pan and quickly invert onto the plate, then slide the potatoes back into the pan to brown on the other side, about 4 minutes. Serve immediately.

GERRI'S COLCANNON

{*Serves 6 to 8*}

Gerri Gilliland is the Irish chef-owner of several renowned Los Angeles restaurants: Gilliland's, Lula's, and Jake and Annie's. On my television show, she prepared this popular Irish dish of mashed potatoes and cabbage. It tasted so good, I immediately incorporated it into my repertoire of favorite dishes. I like to serve it instead of plain mashed potatoes with traditional deli fare such as pot roast, corned beef, or poultry.

4 medium Idaho or white rose potatoes
    (about 2 pounds), peeled
    and cut into chunks
Salt, to taste
5 tablespoons unsalted butter or margarine
1 bunch green onions, trimmed and chopped
½ large head green napa or savoy cabbage,
    shredded
¼ cup milk or vegetable stock (page 26), heated
White pepper, to taste

❦ Place potatoes in a large pot with salted water to cover. Bring to a boil over high heat, cover, reduce heat, and simmer until tender, about 10 minutes.

❦ In a nonstick skillet, melt 3 tablespoons of the butter over medium heat and sauté green onions, stirring occasionally, until tender, about 5 minutes. Add cabbage and mix well. Cover and wilt cabbage until it turns bright green, about 5 minutes.

❦ Put potatoes through a ricer or mash them well in a large bowl. Add cabbage mixture and hot milk and mix well. Season with salt and pepper to taste and top with remaining 2 tablespoons of the butter.

THE BEST FRENCH FRIES

{*Serves 10*}

When I was growing up, I thought the French fries I bought at the beach in Ocean Park, California, were the best in the world. I suppose when you're young and hungry, everything tastes wonderful. I was determined to re-create those French fries for this book and did a lot of experimenting to discover the secrets of their success. For starters, use russet potatoes; the sugar-starch content makes the difference. To make ultracrispy fries, fry them twice. The first frying cooks them through and the second frying produces the golden color and delectable crisp texture. For fries of uniform size, cutters are available in most cookware stores.

2 pounds russet potatoes (about 7 medium)
4 cups peanut oil, for frying
Salt, to taste

❦ Peel potatoes and slice lengthwise into ¼- to ⅛-inch-wide sticks. Place them in a large bowl of cold water to remove the starch. Drain and dry well on paper towels before frying.

❦ Pour oil into a deep fryer or large heavy saucepan and heat to 350° F. Carefully drop in potatoes in small batches without crowding and fry until completely cooked but barely colored, turning occasionally, about 3 minutes. Remove potatoes with a slotted spoon and drain on paper towels.

❦ For the second frying, reheat oil to 350° F. and fry potatoes in small batches until crisp and golden brown, turning occasionally, about 3 minutes. Remove with a slotted spoon and drain on paper towels. Season lightly with salt. Serve in a bowl lined with cloth or paper napkin.

POTATO PIZZA WITH
CHOPPED OLIVES

{ Serves about 8 }

I *first created this potato pizza for a holiday brunch; the next day, every one of my guests asked for the recipe. A cross between a pizza and a potato pancake, this dish makes a distinctive appetizer or first course. It also works as a side dish for brisket or pot roast.*

2 large russet potatoes
    (about 1 pound), peeled and shredded
1 tablespoon fresh lemon juice
1 egg, lightly beaten
7 tablespoons olive oil
1 teaspoon salt
Freshly ground black pepper, to taste
2 cups Chopped Olive Spread (recipe follows)

❦ Place shredded potatoes in a large bowl and add lemon juice, egg, and 1 tablespoon of the olive oil. Season with salt and pepper to taste and mix well. Drain the accumulated liquid from the bottom.

❦ In a 6-inch nonstick skillet, heat 2 tablespoons of the olive oil over medium-high heat. Spoon half of the potato mixture into the hot oil and gently flatten with a fork, spreading evenly. Cook until golden brown on the bottom, about 10 minutes. Using a metal spatula, turn carefully and brown on the other side. Drain on paper towels. Repeat with 2 tablespoons of the olive oil and the remaining potato mixture.

❦ To serve: For each pancake, spread a generous amount of chopped olives on top, sprinkle each with a tablespoon of olive oil, and cut into 4 wedges.

CHOPPED OLIVE SPREAD

{ Makes about 2 cups }

1 cup black olives, pitted
1 cup green olives, pitted
1 tablespoon olive oil
2 tablespoons minced fresh parsley

❦ Chop olives coarsely, transfer to a bowl, and toss with olive oil and parsley.

GARLIC MASHED POTATOES
{Serves 6}

The union of garlic and potatoes is a marriage made in heaven. For the best results, use russet potatoes and mash them by hand. Avoid mashing or puréeing them in a blender or food processor, which makes them rubbery.

4 medium russet potatoes (about 2 pounds),
    peeled and cut into chunks
8 whole cloves garlic
Salt, to taste
4 tablespoons unsalted butter,
    at room temperature
½ cup half-and-half, heated until warm
Freshly ground black pepper, to taste

❦ In a heavy saucepan, place potatoes with enough cold water to cover. Add garlic and a pinch of salt. Bring to a boil, reduce heat, cover, and simmer until tender, about 15 minutes. Drain.

❦ Mash potatoes and garlic with a ricer or through a coarse strainer. Put potato mixture back into the saucepan. Simmer over low heat, mixing constantly with a wooden spoon, until potatoes are dried out. Stir in butter and half-and-half, a little at a time, while beating with a wooden spoon. Season with salt and pepper to taste.

OLD-FASHIONED
VEGETARIAN BEANPOT
{Serves 8}

For years I opened cans of vegetarian baked beans bought at delis, never knowing how easy it was to make great beans from scratch. This recipe duplicates the tantalizing aroma and mouthwatering flavor of authentic New England baked beans. They taste great with almost anything—even a corned beef sandwich! If you forget to soak the beans overnight, see following note on quick soaking.

2 cups dried navy beans (small white beans)
2 teaspoons dry mustard
6 tablespoons dark brown sugar
¼ cup dark molasses
2 tablespoons red wine vinegar
Salt, to taste
Freshly ground black pepper, to taste

❦ In a large bowl, cover beans with water and soak overnight.

❦ Preheat the oven to 350°F. Place beans and soaking liquid in a large bean pot or Dutch oven.

❦ In a small bowl, blend mustard, brown sugar, molasses, and vinegar. Pour over beans and mix well. Cover and bake 5 hours, mixing every 30 minutes and adding additional water as needed. Then bake uncovered until beans are completely tender and the liquid reduces and thickens, 30 minutes to 1 hour. Season with salt and pepper to taste.

QUICK-SOAKING BEANS *For shorter soaking time, put beans in pot, cover with 6 cups water, bring to a boil, and cook 2 minutes. Remove from the heat, cover, and let stand 1 hour before cooking.*

DELI BREAKFAST SPECIALS

CHAPTER 5

I love to drop into a deli in the morning. The aroma of fresh-baked breads and pastries and freshly brewed coffee is undeniably enticing. A deli's homey, comforting ambience is irresistible; it's like coming in from the cold, even when it's 85 degrees outside. ❦ A deli is an idyllic place to catch your breath before a hectic day begins. For starters, deli hospitality is legendary. It's easy to establish a camaraderie with the servers or the other customers. Small wonder so many delis offer newspapers to their customers to linger over with bottomless cups of coffee. ❦ I often try to duplicate the cozy deli atmosphere in my own kitchen. I usually set the table the night before so I have time for a long morning walk. My weekday breakfast never varies; it's always a grapefruit half or orange juice, a toasted bagel or sweet roll, and foamy cappuccino topped with a dusting of powdered sugar and cocoa. ❦ Saturday and Sunday breakfasts are particularly special as there's always more time to enjoy a substantial repast. Try some of my time-honored recipes and you'll discover that entertaining for Sunday brunch can be a breeze. ❦ The unusual Orange Fruit Soup in this book is my favorite starter, usually followed by scrambled eggs, bagels, lox, and cream cheese. Other times I serve waffles, pancakes, or French toast with breakfast meats or with assorted fruit preserves and applesauce. Lots of freshly brewed coffee is a must, and sometimes I splurge with a coffee cake or even a cheesecake. And for a special occasion, I serve champagne, a welcome addition to any menu.

RECIPES

BELGIAN WAFFLES

{Makes eight 8-inch waffles}

Belgian waffles were first introduced to the United States at the New York World's Fair, in 1939. Called gaufres in Belgium, they're baked on a special waffle iron, which makes extra-thick, very light, crisp waffles, and often sandwiched with crème fraîche, whipped cream, or ice cream. Many American delis prefer to serve them with bacon or sausage, instead.

Butter, for waffle iron

3 eggs, separated

1 cup sour cream

1 cup unbleached all-purpose flour

1 teaspoon baking soda

¼ teaspoon salt

3 cups buttermilk

¾ cup yellow cornmeal

4 tablespoons unsalted butter, melted

2 tablespoons vegetable oil

❦ Preheat an 8-inch waffle iron and brush with butter.

❦ In a large bowl, using an electric mixer, beat egg yolks with sour cream. Beat in flour, baking soda, and salt. Add buttermilk, 1 cup at a time, beating well after each addition. Beat in cornmeal, then add melted butter and oil and mix until thoroughly incorporated.

❦ In another large bowl, using clean beaters, beat egg whites until stiff peaks form. Stir half of the egg whites into the batter. Using a rubber spatula, fold in the remaining whites.

❦ Spoon 1 cup of the batter into the prepared waffle iron and cook until golden brown and crisp. Serve hot.

THE BEST FRENCH TOAST {Serves 2}

The quintessential French-toast experience means drenching the bread in flavored egg mixture and sautéing it in butter until it's crisp and golden outside and luxuriously soft inside. Serve with homemade preserves and a dusting of powdered sugar for breakfast. Or for an elegant dessert, accompany French toast with raspberry sauce and whipped cream.

4 thick slices (1½ to 2-inches) challah (egg bread), (preferably homemade, page 157)

3 eggs, lightly beaten

1 tablespoon powdered sugar

¾ cup milk

1 tablespoon grated orange zest

4 tablespoons unsalted butter

Powdered sugar and preserves of choice, for garnish

❦ Cut each slice of bread in half diagonally.

❦ In a large bowl, blend eggs, the 1 tablespoon sugar, milk, and orange zest. Place each slice of bread into the egg mixture and let soak on both sides until the bread absorbs the egg mixture.

❦ In a large nonstick skillet, heat butter over medium-high heat and fry bread until golden brown on both sides and egg mixture is cooked, about 5 minutes. Arrange on heated serving plates, sprinkle with powdered sugar, and top with a spoonful of preserves.

CLASSIC CHEESE BLINTZES {*Makes about 2 dozen blintzes*}

Blintzes are eastern European pancakes, cousins to crêpes, but they're always served with one of a variety of fillings and folded over like an envelope. I've included two fillings: The classic low-fat hoop cheese version may be served with bowls of sour cream and preserves or with marinara sauce. The Italian-style ricotta and spinach blintzes should be served with marinara sauce.

Hoop Cheese Filling or
  Ricotta-Spinach Filling (recipes follow)
3 eggs
1½ cups milk
1 tablespoon unsalted butter, melted
1 tablespoon sugar
1¼ cups unbleached all-purpose flour
½ teaspoon salt
Unsalted butter, for frying blintzes
Bowls of sour cream and preserves or
  Basic Marinara Sauce (page 102)

❦ Prepare the filling of your choice, cover with plastic wrap, and chill.

❦ In a large bowl, using an electric mixer, beat eggs. Add milk, melted butter, sugar, flour, and salt, and blend well. Pass through a fine strainer to remove any lumps that form.

❦ In an 8-inch skillet or crêpe pan, melt 1 tablespoon of butter over medium heat. When butter begins to bubble, pour in about 2 tablespoons of batter to cover the bottom of the pan with a thin layer. Rotate the pan quickly to spread batter as thin as possible. Cook on one side until the edges begin to brown, about 1 minute. Turn onto a tea towel and transfer to a platter. Repeat with the remaining batter and stack blintzes with waxed paper in between them. Cover with plastic wrap and refrigerate until ready to fill.

❦ Fill the browned side of each blintz with the prepared filling and fold, tucking ends in.

❦ In a nonstick skillet, heat 3 tablespoons of butter. Cook blintzes on both sides until lightly browned, 2 or 3 minutes on each side. With a metal spatula, carefully transfer blintzes to serving plates. Serve with bowls of sour cream and preserves or with marinara sauce.

HOOP CHEESE FILLING {*Makes about 3 cups*}

2 pounds hoop cheese
1 tablespoon sugar
½ teaspoon salt
2 eggs

❦ In a large bowl, mix together all ingredients until blended. Cover with plastic wrap and chill until ready to assemble the blintzes.

RICOTTA-SPINACH FILLING {*Makes about 3 cups*}

1 pound fresh ricotta cheese
½ pound spinach, steamed,
  drained, and chopped
Pinch freshly grated nutmeg
Salt, to taste
Freshly ground black pepper, to taste

❦ Place ricotta cheese in a strainer for 30 minutes to drain water. In a large bowl, mix drained ricotta with remaining ingredients. Cover with plastic wrap and chill until ready to assemble the blintzes.

WHOLE-WHEAT PANCAKES

{*Makes about eight 8-inch pancakes or two dozen 2-inch pancakes*}

Delis usually serve stacks of eight-inch-round pancakes. I often use an old Swedish skillet with shallow wells, about two inches in diameter. When the butter bubbles and the batter is poured in, these mini pancakes become crispy and buttery around the edges. Serve with maple syrup and/or preserves.

½ cup unbleached all-purpose flour
½ cup whole-wheat flour
1 tablespoon baking powder
1 tablespoon sugar
½ teaspoon salt
1 egg, lightly beaten
1 cup milk
2 tablespoons unsalted butter, melted
Unsalted butter, for frying

❦ In a large bowl, using a wire whisk or an electric mixer, blend both flours, baking powder, sugar, and salt. In a small bowl, beat egg, milk, and melted butter. Add to flour mixture and stir until moistened.

❦ Preheat a skillet or griddle to 425°F. Add butter, melt until bubbly, and brush to evenly coat surface, adding more if needed. Pour in batter (about ⅓ cup for an 8-inch pancake or 2 tablespoons for a 2-inch pancake). When bottom is browned and bubbles form on top, about 1½ minutes, turn pancakes with a metal spatula and cook until bottom is golden brown, about ½ minute. Repeat procedure until all the batter is used, keeping cooked pancakes warm in the oven.

CORNED BEEF HASH

{*Serves 4*}

This robust hash is a satisfying breakfast or brunch entrée. It's delicious topped with poached eggs or eggs-over-easy and served with thick slices of toasted homemade bread. Ketchup is a crowd-pleasing accompaniment.

2½ cups peeled and diced (½ inch) russet
　　potatoes (about 8 medium potatoes)
½ pound diced corned beef
　　(preferably homemade, page 141)
¼ cup olive oil
1 medium onion, finely diced
Salt, to taste
Freshly ground black pepper, to taste

❦ In a large saucepan, place vegetable steamer and add enough water to reach bottom of steamer. Bring water to a boil, reduce heat, and steam diced potatoes until tender, about 5 minutes. Transfer steamed potatoes to a large bowl, and combine with corned beef.

❦ In a large nonstick skillet, heat 3 tablespoons of the oil over medium-high heat and sauté onion until soft, about 7 minutes. Add corned beef mixture and remaining 1 tablespoon olive oil; season with salt and pepper to taste. Sauté, tossing lightly, until potatoes are nicely browned and crisp, about 10 minutes.

EGG-IN-THE-HOLE

{*Serves 4*}

When our children were very young, they were taught how to make this simple family specialty of eggs cooked in challah (egg bread). We thought it was our own invention until we discovered it served as an appetizer at Citrus restaurant in Los Angeles. For an authentic deli breakfast, serve with crisp bacon, hash browns, and preserves.

4 slices (about 1 inch thick) challah
(preferably homemade, page 157)
2 tablespoons unsalted butter or margarine
4 eggs
Salt, to taste
Freshly ground black pepper, to taste

❦ Using a 2-inch-round cookie cutter, cut a hole in the center of each slice of bread.

❦ In a large nonstick skillet, melt butter over medium-high heat and fry bread slices on one side until golden brown; turn bread slices over. Drop an egg in each hole, season with salt and pepper to taste, and cook until eggs are firm, about 1 minute. Using a metal spatula, transfer to individual serving plates.

SALAMI AND EGGS

{*Serves 4*}

New York delis call this a breakfast dish, which is fine, if you like garlicky salami for breakfast. This robust combination is a cold-weather morning treat along with hash brown potatoes. For a light Sunday supper, serve with a bowl of soup and kaiser rolls.

20 slices kosher salami, quartered and casing
removed
6 extra-large eggs
Salt, to taste
Freshly ground black pepper, to taste

❦ In a nonstick skillet, sauté salami until crisp, about 5 minutes.

❦ In a medium bowl, beat eggs with salt and pepper to taste and pour over the crisp salami, stirring as the mixture sets. Remove from the heat when cooked through.

LOX AND ONION OMELET {Serves 6}

Serve this glorious deli specialty with all the right trimmings—hash brown potatoes and bagels with cream cheese. When serving a crowd, take a tip from deli chefs and sauté the onions and lox in advance; slightly undercook omelets and keep warm in a very low oven.

3 tablespoons unsalted butter
1 small onion, diced
¼ pound thinly sliced lox (smoked salmon), diced
10 eggs, lightly beaten
Salt, to taste (optional)
Freshly ground black pepper, to taste
Chopped fresh parsley or dill, for garnish

In a large nonstick skillet, heat butter over medium-high heat and sauté onions until soft, about 4 minutes. Add lox and sauté until lightly browned. Pour in eggs and let them set lightly around the edges. Season with salt and pepper to taste. Then shake the skillet and stir until cooked through. Spoon onto heated serving plates and garnish with parsley or dill.

LOX AND CAVIAR OMELET {Serves 2}

This is a Zeidler specialty, for two, unabashedly conceived with decadence in mind. We serve it with toasted French Country Bread (page oo) and for a just-right festive touch—champagne.

2 tablespoons olive oil
¼ cup thinly sliced green onions
3 slices lox (smoked salmon), cut into pieces
3 eggs, lightly beaten
Salt, to taste
Freshly ground black pepper, to taste
1 jar (3 ounces) osetra, beluga,
     or salmon caviar

In a nonstick skillet, heat oil over medium-high heat and sauté onions, until soft, about 5 minutes. Add lox and sauté 1 minute. Pour eggs into the onion mixture and cook until they begin to set around the edges. Season with salt and pepper to taste. Using a spoon, gently stir the egg mixture, starting from the edge, until it is cooked through. Spoon onto heated plates and top with caviar.

BROADWAY DELI'S
ITALIAN FRITTATA

{Makes 4 frittatas}

At the Broadway Deli, I watched the omelet chef begin this frittata in a large skillet and then slide it into a smaller one. It is the deli technique for shaping this Italian frittata into a very puffy omelet.

Potato-Onion Filling (recipe follows)
2 cups Basic Marinara Sauce (page 102)
4 tablespoons olive oil
12 eggs
Salt, to taste
Freshly ground black pepper, to taste

❦ Preheat oven to 200°F.

❦ Prepare Potato-Onion Filling and Basic Marinara Sauce and keep warm.

❦ In a nonstick 7-inch skillet, heat 1 tablespoon of the oil and brown about 6 tablespoons of the filling. In a small bowl, using a fork, lightly beat 3 of the eggs. Pour into skillet, season with salt and pepper to taste, and mix well, stirring with a fork until set. Using a metal spatula, slide the frittata into a smaller 4-inch skillet, shaping it to fit evenly, and brown lightly on both sides. Transfer frittata to a serving plate and keep warm in oven. With remaining filling, olive oil, and eggs, repeat the process to make 3 more frittatas.

❦ Heat the marinara sauce until bubbling and spoon some alongside each omelet. Serve remaining marinara in a bowl.

POTATO-ONION FILLING

{Makes about 1½ cups}

2 tablespoons olive oil
1 small onion, diced
1 clove garlic, minced
1 small potato, peeled and cut into ½-inch dice
¼ cup seeded and diced green bell peppers
½ cup peeled and diced eggplant
Salt, to taste
Freshly ground black pepper, to taste

❦ In a nonstick skillet, heat olive oil over medium heat and sauté onion, garlic, potato, peppers, and eggplant until soft, about 5 minutes. Season with salt and pepper to taste.

The MAIN EVENT

CHAPTER 6

A lthough this is a deli cookbook, in this section you'll find a selection of hearty main dishes. I have also included a few appetizers that will enhance any meal—from a simple buffet to a festive family dinner for a special occasion. ❦ For your convenience, they are arranged by category: noodles, fish, poultry, and meat. In each one you'll find traditional favorites, as well as up-dated new recipes from eateries like the Broadway Deli. ❦ Some are quick and easy—ready in minutes—others simmer slowly for hours to blend flavors together and help tenderize some cuts of meat. Many need only a crisp green salad and a loaf of crunchy bread or rolls to complete the meal. ❦ In planning menus using these main dishes, it helps to follow some simple guidelines. Decide on a menu, select the main course, then choose side dishes that will complement. Keep in mind contrasting colors, textures, and flavors for added interest. And you know the rest—a hearty dessert balances a light main course and visa versa.

RECIPES

NOODLES AND PASTA

ven inexperienced cooks can manage pasta! If you know how to boil water, the rest is easy. With so many different shaped pastas available, it's simple to prepare new dishes by playing mix-and-match with a variety of sauces. ❧ Although Italy now has staked its place in the deli, there's one all-American pasta dish synonymous with delis—macaroni and cheese. In my updated version, this traditional dish is deliciously enhanced by its blend of four different cheeses. And to lend intriguing new appeal to that old-time favorite, spaghetti and meatballs, I added a variety of herbs. ❧ So many of my vegetarian students and friends love pasta, because with a little creativity, the range of dishes you can make is endless without using an ounce of meat. Vegetarian Lasagna, Ravioli with Sage, and Rigatoni Puttanesca are perfect examples. ❧ For a change of pace on a warm day, try preparing a chilled pasta salad. It's a refreshing alternative to one based on the usual salad greens. Toss with a simple vinaigrette or mayonnaise-based dressing. I've included several pasta recipes in the Deli Salads chapter—there's even one for Asian Pasta Primavera. ❧ Finally, to make this chapter ethnically complete, I added a succulent and crispy noodle fruit kugel, which conjures up nostalgic memories of the Lower East Side delis in New York. The puddinglike kugel is such a versatile dish; it can be consumed as a main course, side dish, or even dessert.

MACARONI WITH FOUR CHEESES {*Serves 6 to 8*}

This dish became a Broadway Deli classic from the day the restaurant opened. When premium quality cheese is used, the rich pungent flavors mingle in the most memorable way.

4 tablespoons unsalted butter
¼ cup unbleached all-purpose flour
3 cups cold milk
1 cup shredded sharp Cheddar cheese
1 cup diced fontina or jack cheese
1 cup shredded Swiss cheese
Salt, to taste
10 ounces elbow macaroni
Paprika, to taste
Freshly ground black pepper, to taste
Freshly grated Parmesan cheese, for garnish
Chopped fresh parsley, for garnish

❦ In a heavy saucepan, melt butter over medium heat. Add flour all at once and cook 5 minutes, mixing constantly. Add cold milk, whisking until thick and creamy. Simmer about 15 minutes, stirring constantly. Stir in Cheddar, fontina, and Swiss cheeses, reduce heat, and stir until smooth and thick. Set aside, cover, and keep warm.

❦ In a large pot of salted boiling water, cook macaroni until al dente, about 10 minutes; drain in a colander.

❦ Return cheese sauce to medium heat, add macaroni, and stir until completely blended and very hot. (Do not overcook or sauce may separate.) Season with paprika, salt, and pepper to taste. Spoon into heated serving bowls and sprinkle with Parmesan cheese and parsley.

BAKED PENNE WITH
TOMATOES AND CHEESE {*Serves 6*}

Italian pastas come in many shapes and sizes; penne resembles little quills. If you're heading to an Italian deli to purchase the imported variety of pasta, splurge on authentic Romano, fontina, and Gorgonzola cheeses for a memorable main course.

2 cups whipping cream
1 cup canned chopped tomatoes in heavy purée
½ cup grated Pecorino Romano cheese
½ cup coarsely shredded fontina cheese
¼ cup crumbled Gorgonzola cheese
6 fresh basil leaves, chopped
Salt, to taste
1 pound penne
4 tablespoons unsalted butter or olive oil
Olive oil, for baking dishes

❦ Preheat oven to 400°F.

❦ In a large mixing bowl, combine cream, tomatoes with purée, cheeses, and basil leaves. Mix well to combine.

❦ In a large pot of salted boiling water, cook penne until al dente, about 10 minutes; drain in a colander. Add to the cream mixture, tossing to coat penne completely.

❦ Divide penne into 6 individual 2-cup ovenproof baking dishes that have been brushed with oil. Dot with the butter and bake until bubbly and brown on top, 8 to 10 minutes.

VARIATION *If individual baking dishes are not available, bake in 1 large baking dish for 15 to 20 minutes. To serve as an appetizer, bake in 12 shallow 1-cup baking dishes.*

SOME TIPS ABOUT PASTA

Fresh pasta is lighter and richer than dried pasta because it is made with eggs. It cooks more quickly, but usually never al dente.

❦ *Dried pasta or packaged pasta has a longer shelf life and adapts to many recipes. It usually takes 10 to 12 minutes to cook, al dente.*

❦ *What does cooking pasta al dente mean? In Italian slang, al dente means "to the tooth" or "to the bite." Firm, but tender, not too hard, not too soft, just right. In other words, chewy. But in the end it is a matter of personal taste.*

❦ *Always add pasta to sauce in skillet and serve immediately.*

VEGETARIAN LASAGNA

{*Serves 10 to 12*}

Granted, when you're serving lasagna for two, it makes sense to buy it premade at your favorite Italian deli. But when you're entertaining a group, it makes sense to make your own. The fragrant, homemade flavors and elegant three-layer presentation of this recipe are unmatched by store-bought versions. Much can be assembled in advance, so it's easier to prepare than you might think.

5 cups Basic Marinara Sauce (recipe follows)
4 cups Ricotta Filling (recipe follows)
17 ounces dried lasagna noodles
Olive oil, for baking dish
1 pound provolone cheese, thinly sliced
1 cup fresh basil leaves
Salt, to taste
Freshly ground black pepper, to taste

❦ Prepare Basic Marinara Sauce and Ricotta Filling.

❦ In a large pot of salted boiling water, cook a few sheets of noodles at a time and simmer until just tender, about 3 minutes. Carefully remove from the water, drain, and place on a towel.

❦ Preheat the oven to 350°F.

❦ Generously oil a 13x8-inch ovenproof baking dish. Place a thin layer of marinara sauce on the bottom. Arrange a layer of noodles, spoon a layer of Ricotta Filling over noodles, arrange a single layer of sliced provolone on top of the ricotta, then another layer of noodles. Top with more sauce, a few basil leaves, and a sprinkling of salt and pepper to taste. Repeat with 2 more layers of noodles, ricotta filling, sauce, and provolone. Bake for about 1¼ hours.

BASIC MARINARA SAUCE

{*Makes about 5 cups*}

3 tablespoons olive oil
3 cloves garlic, minced
2 medium onions, finely chopped
2 medium carrots, finely chopped
1 can (28 ounces) chopped peeled tomatoes, with liquid
1 can (8 ounces) tomato sauce
2 teaspoons dried oregano, crumbled
2 tablespoons minced fresh parsley
Salt, to taste
Freshly ground black pepper, to taste

❦ In a large heavy skillet, heat olive oil over medium heat and sauté garlic, onions, and carrots, until soft, about 10 minutes. Add tomatoes with the liquid, tomato sauce, oregano, and parsley. Bring to a boil, reduce heat, and simmer, partially covered, until thick, about 20 minutes. Season with salt and pepper to taste. Stir occasionally to avoid sticking. Cool.

Note Refrigerate or freeze leftover sauce and use over meat loaf, baked white fish (it's great with halibut), and even chicken. Will keep in refrigerator for 2 to 3 days and in freezer for at least 2 months.

RICOTTA FILLING

{*Makes about 4 cups*}

2 pounds ricotta cheese
2 tablespoons freshly grated Parmesan cheese
2 eggs, lightly beaten
Salt, to taste
Freshly ground black pepper, to taste

❦ In a large bowl, mix together all ingredients.

ORECCHIETTE MARINARA

{*Serves 8*}

f you're a pasta primavera fan, you'll love this recipe as it utilizes a plethora of fresh vegetables. Orecchiette, which translates as "little ears," hails from Naples and looks like small coins indented with thumbprints. It is sold at most Italian delis. This dish is equally flavorful served cold as a salad.

4 cups Basic Marinara Sauce (page 102)
1 pound dried orecchiette pasta
⅓ cup olive oil
1 carrot
2 small zucchini
2 small yellow crookneck squash
2 stalks celery
Florets from 2 heads broccoli
½ onion
2 tablespoons minced fresh oregano or
    1 tablespoon dried oregano, crumbled
Salt, to taste
Freshly ground black pepper, to taste

❦ Prepare Basic Marinara Sauce and keep warm.

❦ In a large pot of boiling water, cook the orecchiette until al dente, about 10 minutes. Drain, place in a large bowl and toss with 2 tablespoons of olive oil.

❦ Cut carrot, zucchini, squash, celery, broccoli florets, and onion into ½-inch dice. In a nonstick skillet, heat the remaining olive oil over medium heat and saute each vegetable separately until tender. Toss vegetables into the pasta with oregano; add enough sauce to completely coat orecchiette and vegetables, tossing gently. Season with salt and pepper to taste. Reserve remaining sauce for another use.

RIGATONI PUTTANESCA

{*Serves 6 to 8*}

hen enhanced by capers, crushed peppers, olives, and an abundance of herbs, marinara sauce becomes the Roman puttanesca (shady lady–style) sauce. Don't feel locked in by the herbs recommended here; almost any fresh herbs will augment this sauce's fine flavors.

3 cups Basic Marinara Sauce (page 102)
2 tablespoons rinsed capers
Pinch crushed red peppers
2 tablespoons sliced Italian olives
    or cured olives
1 tablespoon *each* fresh oregano, thyme, and
    rosemary or ½ teaspoon *each* dried
    oregano, thyme, and rosemary, crumbled
Salt, to taste
1½ pounds rigatoni pasta
Freshly grated Parmesan cheese, for garnish

❦ Prepare recipe for Basic Marinara Sauce. Measure 3 cups into a large saucepan and reserve remaining sauce for future use. Heat marinara sauce and add capers, crushed red peppers, sliced olives, oregano, thyme, and rosemary.

❦ In a large pot of salted boiling water, cook rigatoni until al dente, about 10 minutes; drain in a colander. Add rigatoni to the sauce and toss until the pasta is evenly coated. Spoon into warm shallow serving bowls and sprinkle with Parmesan cheese.

SPAGHETTI AND MEATBALLS IN MARINARA SAUCE

{*Serves 6 to 8*}

Boil up some spaghetti; drop it into the sauce and toss with the meatballs for a classic Italian specialty.

4 cups Basic Marinara Sauce (page 102)
Italian Meatballs (recipe follows)
1 pound spaghetti
Salt, for water
Freshly grated Parmesan cheese,
　　for garnish, optional

❦ Prepare recipe for marinara sauce. Measure 4 cups of the sauce into a large saucepan or Dutch oven and reserve remaining sauce for future use. Prepare meatballs; add to the sauce, cover, and keep warm.

❦ Just before serving, cook spaghetti in a large pot of salted boiling water until al dente, 8 to 12 minutes; drain well. Using a slotted spoon, transfer meatballs to a large bowl. Toss spaghetti in the sauce, spoon into heated serving plates, and arrange meatballs on top. Pass a bowl of grated Parmesan cheese.

ITALIAN MEATBALLS

{*Makes about 12 meatballs*}

½ pound ground beef
½ pound ground veal
4 slices day-old bread, soaked in water
　　and squeezed dry
1 onion, grated
1 clove garlic, minced
1 small green bell pepper, seeded
　　and finely diced
2 tablespoons minced fresh parsley
1 teaspoon dried oregano, crumbled
1 teaspoon fennel seeds
1½ teaspoons salt
½ teaspoon freshly ground black pepper
3 eggs, lightly beaten
Olive oil, for forming and sautéing meatballs

❦ In a large bowl, mix beef and veal. Tear bread in pieces and add to the meat mixture. Mix in onion, garlic, bell pepper, parsley, oregano, fennel, salt, and pepper. Add eggs and mix well. Oil your hands and shape mixture into 1-inch meatballs. Bake or sauté as follows.

To bake: *Preheat the oven to 385°F. Place meatballs on a baking sheet lined with aluminum foil. Bake until browned and cooked through, 25 to 30 minutes.*

To sauté: *In a large nonstick skillet, heat oil over medium heat and sauté meatballs until brown, about 10 minutes.*

QUICK AND EASY RAVIOLI
IN SAGE BUTTER SAUCE

{Serves 4}

With uncooked fresh or frozen ravioli available at Italian and other delis, as well as some supermarkets, why bother making your own? They're ready to be cooked in a bubbling pot of herb-seasoned butter sauce. This is a substantial pasta dish, which needs only a salad, wine, some breadsticks, and a red-checked tablecloth.

2 dozen uncooked fresh or frozen cheese- or
    meat-filled ravioli
¼ pound unsalted butter
¼ cup loosely packed fresh sage leaves or
    2 tablespoons dried sage, crumbled
½ cup freshly grated Parmesan cheese

❦ When defrosting frozen ravioli, carefully separate them and arrange on a tea towel in a single layer so they don't stick together as they defrost.

❦ In a large skillet, melt butter over medium heat until foamy. Using scissors, snip fresh sage leaves into ⅛-inch strips; add sage to butter and mix well.

❦ In a large pot of salted boiling water cook ravioli covered, over medium-high heat, until al dente, about 5 minutes; drain. Add ravioli to the butter sauce, stirring carefully. Add 2 tablespoons of the Parmesan. Gently coat ravioli with the mixture and simmer over low heat 1 minute. Arrange on heated serving plates and sprinkle with the remaining Parmesan.

CRISPY NOODLE AND FRUIT KUGEL {Serves 8 to 10}

Every Jewish deli or Jewish cook has a favorite kugel recipe. These vary enormously in size, shape, texture, ingredients, and flavor from sweet to savory. This pudding-type kugel is easy; apples, raisins, and apricots add sweetness as well as color to the subtle noodles. Serve as a side dish with roasted chicken or meat, or as dessert with yogurt and brown sugar, or a raspberry sauce.

½ cup raisins

½ cup diced dried apricots

1 cup apple juice

12 ounces flat, wide egg noodles

¼ pound unsalted butter or
    margarine, melted

1 tablespoon sugar, optional

3 eggs, lightly beaten

1 cup peeled, diced apples

1 teaspoon cinnamon mixed with
    2 tablespoons sugar

❦ In a small bowl, plump raisins and apricots in apple juice for 30 minutes; drain well.

❦ Preheat the oven to 375° F.

❦ In a large pot of salted boiling water, cook noodles until al dente, about 10 minutes; drain in a colander.

❦ Brush a 7x11-inch or 9x13-inch baking dish with 1 tablespoon of the butter.

❦ In a large mixing bowl, combine drained noodles, the remaining butter, and sugar, if using, and mix well. Mix in eggs. Fold in drained raisins, apricots, and apples. Spoon into prepared baking dish. Sprinkle generously with cinnamon-sugar mixture. Bake until golden brown and crisp on top, about 30 minutes.

SEAFOOD

The repertoire of fish delicacies served in old-time Jewish delis always includes herring—smoked, pickled, chopped, or smothered in sour cream. Smoked whitefish is also a staple. And the starring fish of Jewish delicatessens is always smoked salmon—"lox" in deli language. Lox is generally served in a sandwich with a small mountain of cream cheese, or presented in rosy slices on a huge platter surrounded by sliced onions, tomatoes, bagels, and cream cheese. Scandinavian delis often feature more variety in their seafood dishes; shrimp, smoked salmon, and sardines are just some of the fish and shellfish used in their open-faced sandwiches and salads. Pickled herring also shows up in Scandinavian delis, but, as in Jewish delis, fresh fish is a rarity. In contrast to the preceding traditional dishes, fresh fish frequently pops up on menus in the more modern delis, because these eateries tend to reflect current culinary trends. More Americans are incorporating fish into their daily diets and expect to enjoy this option in most restaurants, even delis. My own recipe files overflow with fresh fish dishes. Whether broiled, steamed, grilled, sautéed, or baked, all are prepared in the simplest manner to protect their intrinsic good taste. Whichever cooking method you choose, remember that fish cooks quickly so take care not to overcook it and destroy its delicate flavor. Fresh is always preferable to frozen, but be prepared to cook fresh fish ➡

within hours of purchase. If it must wait, cover the fish tightly with plastic wrap and place on a pan of ice in the refrigerator. ¶ When purchasing fish fillets and steaks, try to buy them from a fishmonger who cuts them from a whole fish upon your order. It's impossible to smell precut, prepackaged fish for freshness. ¶ This section offers a melange of fish recipes, both traditional and innovative. One of my all-time favorites is a plate of steaming kippers smothered with fried onions. When I was growing up, it made for many a mouthwatering memory. Today, this dish still makes a terrific Sunday brunch.

DRAGO'S COLD-SMOKED SALMON {Serves 24}

Making lox, cold-smoked salmon, is often a challenge for the home cook. Celestino Drago, chef of Santa Monica's highly acclaimed Drago restaurant, guarantees his method will work if you have the right equipment. A cold-smoker infuses the salmon with flavor without cooking the fish. Try preparing this recipe at home and you will be rewarded with a smoked salmon vastly superior to any commercial deli product. Celestino also suggests, after smoking, preserving the lox with olive oil, sliced onions, juniper berries, and peppercorns. However you prepare it, serve it deli-style with bagels and cream cheese, tomatoes, onions, and cucumbers.

5 to 6 pounds fresh salmon,
    filleted with skin on
4 to 5 cups rock salt

❦ Wash salmon and pat dry with paper towels. Spread half of the salt in a large glass baking dish. Place salmon on top and cover with the remaining salt. The salmon should be completely sealed with the salt. Cover and refrigerate 12 hours.

❦ Remove salmon, place in a large colander, and wash under cold running water for 30 minutes. Dry completely with paper towels; wrap loosely in a kitchen towel, and refrigerate for 24 hours. The fish should be completely dry before smoking.

❦ Follow the manufacturer's directions for cold-smoking. Start the smoker and let it reach full temperature. Place salmon on the rack and let smoke season the salmon through the pipe of the smoker for 45 minutes to 1 hour, but no longer.

❦ Smoked fish may be kept refrigerated for 1 week and in the freezer for up to 1 month, but it's best when fresh.

TO PRESERVE SMOKED SALMON *Place 6 pounds cold-smoked salmon in a glass dish. Scatter over and around fish thin slices of 1 small onion, 1 teaspoon juniper berries, and 1 teaspoon black peppercorns. Pour in enough olive oil to cover. Cover with plastic wrap. This will keep for 2 weeks in the refrigerator.*

COLD POACHED FISH IN RED PEPPER SAUCE

{Serves 8}

The inspiration for this dish came from a chicken and roasted pepper salad developed by one of the first Italian delis in Los Angeles. Serve with cold green beans and crusty bread or focaccia topped with onions and rosemary.

3 Roasted Red Bell Peppers (page 81)

1½ cups fish stock or vegetable stock
(preferably homemade, page 26)

4 pounds fresh fish fillets,
such as sea bass or halibut

2 tablespoons capers, drained and rinsed

½ cup olive oil

3 anchovy fillets in oil

1½ tablespoons all-purpose flour

2 cloves garlic, minced

Freshly ground black pepper, to taste

3 tablespoons red wine vinegar

❦ Prepare Roasted Red Bell Peppers without garlic and oil. Finely chop 1 pepper for the sauce and slice 2 peppers into thin strips for garnish. Set aside.

❦ In a large pot or steamer, bring fish stock to a boil. Add fish, reduce heat, cover, and simmer until fish flakes easily when tested with a fork, 10 to 15 minutes. Remove from heat and allow fish to cool in stock. Drain fish (reserving stock) and then cut into chunks and place on a serving platter. Sprinkle fish with capers, cover with plastic wrap, and chill.

❦ In a small saucepan, bring reserved fish stock to a boil. In a heavy saucepan, heat oil over medium heat and add anchovies, mashing into a paste with a wooden spoon. Add flour and stir until golden. Continue stirring, adding boiling fish stock all at once; stir 2 or 3 minutes. Add the 1 chopped red pepper and garlic. Simmer 10 minutes, remove from heat, and blend well. Season with pepper to taste. Return saucepan to heat and simmer, partially covered, another 10 to 15 minutes. Remove from heat, add wine vinegar, and blend well. Pour the sauce over fish, and garnish with the sliced red peppers. Cool, cover with plastic wrap, and refrigerate at least 4 hours.

PICKLED SALMON WITH
MUSTARD-DILL SAUCE
{*Serves 8*}

This moist salmon is pickled in a savory blend of spices, chilled, and served with Mustard-Dill Sauce. It's cool and refreshing on a hot summer day. Serve with a salad and preceded by a cup of cold borscht. A perfect lunch!

Mustard-Dill Sauce (page 75)
4 cups water
Juice of 3 lemons
½ cup white wine vinegar
3 large onions, thinly sliced
½ cup golden raisins
½ cup firmly packed brown sugar
1 teaspoon ground ginger
2 tablespoons whole pickling spices
Salt, to taste
Freshly ground black pepper, to taste
3 pounds salmon fillets,
    skinned and cut into 2-inch-thick chunks
Fresh dill, for garnish

❦ Prepare Mustard-Dill Sauce, cover with plastic wrap, and chill.

❦ In a large nonreactive saucepan or Dutch oven, combine the water, lemon juice, vinegar, onions, raisins, brown sugar, ginger, and pickling spices; season with salt and pepper to taste. Bring to a boil, add salmon, cover, reduce heat, and simmer 40 minutes. Remove from heat and let salmon cool in the pot for 15 minutes.

❦ Transfer salmon to a glass bowl, cover with plastic wrap and aluminum foil, and chill. Serve on a large platter with Mustard-Dill Sauce and garnish with fresh dill.

SMOKED KIPPERS WITH ONIONS
{*Serves 2 to 4*}

Kippers are smoked herrings that have crossed the ocean from Scotland and found their way into Jewish delis. Quickly sauteing them with onions is an easy way to appreciate their good taste. Present them deli-fashion with bagels, cream cheese, sweet butter, and sliced tomatoes. I also find the smoky, salty flavor of kippers a welcome accompaniment to scrambled eggs. Serve bottles of seltzer to round out an authentic Jewish deli menu. Note that there is no need to add salt and pepper to this dish.

4 tablespoons unsalted butter
2 onions, thinly sliced
2 smoked kippers (about ½ pound each)

❦ In a large nonstick skillet, heat butter over medium heat and sauté onions until golden brown, about 10 minutes. Transfer with a slotted spoon to a warm platter. Arrange kippers, skin side down, in the skillet and brown on each side, about 3 minutes. Return onions to the skillet during the last few minutes.

GEFILTE FISH

{ *Makes about 30 balls* }

An eastern European deli staple, these cold fish balls get their name from the word gefüllt, which means "stuffed" in German. The method of making gefilte fish is similar to that of the French quenelles. The fish is ground with eggs and vegetables and poached in rounds or shaped into an elegant loaf. Serve the gefilte fish chilled on a bed of baby greens with sliced cucumbers and homemade horseradish sauce. Or for a main dish serve with celery root or chayote salad (page 32) and sliced baby pickled beets (page 79).

Creamed Horseradish Sauce (page 74)
3 cups fish stock
  (preferably homemade, page 26)
4 medium onions, sliced and skins reserved
1 cup sliced celery tops
5 medium carrots, peeled and thinly sliced
2 stalks celery, sliced
1 pound filleted cod, cut into chunks
1 pound filleted pike, cut into chunks
2 pounds filleted Chilean sea bass, cut into
  chunks
1½ pounds filleted whitefish, cut into chunks
2 eggs, lightly beaten
About ½ cup matzo meal or cracker meal
½ cup water
Coarse kosher salt, to taste
Freshly ground black pepper, to taste

❦ Prepare Creamed Horseradish Sauce, cover, and chill. Prepare fish stock and cool.

❦ In a large pot or Dutch oven (at least 14 inches in diameter), place 2 of the onions, onion skins (added for color), celery tops, and 2 of the carrots. Pour the cool fish stock over the vegetables and set aside.

❦ In a grinder or food processor, coarsely grind the remaining 2 onions and 3 carrots, celery stalks, and fish chunks. Place ground mixture in a large bowl and blend with eggs and enough matzo meal to bind. Transfer mixture to a large wooden chopping bowl and chop, adding water gradually with 1 tablespoon kosher salt and 2 teaspoons pepper as you chop. Mixture should be soft and light to the touch. Season with additional kosher salt and pepper to taste.

❦ Wet hands with cold water and shape the fish mixture into balls, 2 inches in diameter. Place fish balls in the fish stock on top of the vegetables. Cover, bring to a boil, reduce heat and simmer until tender and cooked through, about 1½ hours. Cool, cover with plastic wrap and aluminum foil, and chill. Serve with horseradish sauce.

GEFILTE FISH LOAF VARIATION *Preheat oven to 350°F. Line 3 or 4 loaf pans with enough plastic wrap to overlap the sides. Spoon in the ground fish mixture and cover with the overlapping plastic wrap. Place loaf pans in a large baking or roasting pan filled with 2 inches of water. Cover with aluminum foil and bake until firm and cooked through, about 1½ hours. Remove from oven and place a heavy weight on top while the loaf is cooling. Makes 3 to 4 loaves; about 30 slices.*

BROILED SALMON WITH
TOMATOES AND BASIL
{ Serves 6 }

These deli-style thick salmon fillets get their flavor from a marinade of olive oil, mustard, and lemon juice. Then they are broiled just until they're pink and flaky. Serve with creamed spinach for the ultimately satisfying meal.

3 large tomatoes, finely diced

2 cloves garlic, minced

¼ cup minced fresh basil

Salt, to taste

Freshly ground black pepper, to taste

6 thick salmon fillets (about 6 ounces each)

3 tablespoons fresh lemon juice

1 teaspoon Dijon mustard

2 tablespoons olive oil

❧ In a medium bowl, combine tomatoes, garlic, and basil. Season with salt and pepper to taste and set aside.

❧ Place fillets, skin side down, in a shallow glass baking dish. In a small bowl, blend lemon juice and mustard. Whisk in olive oil and season with salt and pepper to taste. Pour the mixture over salmon. Cover with plastic wrap and refrigerate at least 2 hours, turning several times.

❧ Preheat the broiler, and line broiler pan with aluminum foil.

❧ Transfer salmon, skin side down, to broiler pan; fish should be about 3 inches from heat. Broil until the flesh is opaque and tender when pierced with a fork, 6 to 8 minutes. Spoon tomato and basil mixture onto 6 serving plates and arrange salmon fillets on top.

SALMON AND HALIBUT KEBABS
{ Serves 6 }

This festive, colorful main course can be prepared in advance and then popped under the broiler at serving time. It goes from oven to table in a matter of minutes and wins compliments every time. For eye and taste appeal, choose the firmest, freshest fish and vegetables. Serve kebabs with garlic mashed potatoes and creamed spinach.

1½ pounds halibut, cut into 1½-inch cubes

1½ pounds salmon, cut into 1½-inch cubes

¼ cup olive oil

3 shallots, chopped

Salt, to taste

Freshly ground black pepper, to taste

6 stainless-steel skewers or wooden skewers,
    soaked in water

2 red bell peppers, seeded and
    cut into 1½-inch slices

2 onions, cut into chunks

❧ In a large shallow glass baking dish, combine fish with olive oil, shallots, and salt and pepper to taste. Cover with plastic wrap and marinate in refrigerator for 2 hours, rotating 3 or 4 times.

❧ On each of 6 skewers, thread a slice of red bell pepper, then alternate with salmon, halibut, and onion; end with another red bell pepper slice.

❧ Preheat the boiler and line broiler pan with aluminum foil. Place kebabs on broiler pan and broil until slightly brown. Turn and broil until done, about 5 minutes on each side, taking care not to overcook. Remove from broiler and arrange each kebab on heated serving plate.

FLORINE'S SEARED TUNA WITH TOMATO SALSA

{Serves 4}

Florine Sikking, a close friend who helped me test recipes for this cookbook, developed this dish when she left the original recipe in her shopping cart at the supermarket. Florine's improvisation is as good, if not better than the lost one.

Tomato Salsa (recipe follows)
1½ pounds fresh albacore or ahi tuna,
    cut into 4 slices (about ¾ inch thick)
1 teaspoon garlic powder
1 teaspoon onion powder
½ teaspoon dried thyme, crumbled
1 tablespoon olive oil
Salt, to taste
Freshly ground black pepper, to taste
Lemon wedges, for garnish

❦ Prepare Tomato Salsa and chill.

❦ Dust tuna slices on each side with garlic and onion powders and thyme.

❦ In a large nonstick skillet, heat oil over high heat and sear tuna slices on one side, about 2 minutes. Turn slices, place about ¼ cup salsa on each slice, and cook no longer than 2 minutes. Do not overcook! Season with salt and pepper to taste. Serve with lemon wedges.

TOMATO SALSA

{Makes about 1 cup}

½ red bell pepper, seeded and finely diced
½ yellow bell pepper, seeded and finely diced
½ medium onion, finely diced
1 medium tomato, finely diced
¼ cup minced fresh parsley or cilantro
1 tablespoon fresh lemon or lime juice
Salt, to taste
Freshly ground black pepper, to taste

❦ In a medium bowl, combine all ingredients. Season with salt and pepper to taste. Cover with plastic wrap and refrigerate.

BAKED TUNA WITH TOMATOES, CAPERS, AND OLIVES

{Serves 4}

A *simple baked fish becomes more delicious when accented with tomatoes, basil, capers, and olives. This works well with firm flesh white fish like cod, halibut, and sea bass. Serve with steamed new potatoes and a seasonal green vegetable. And don't forget a loaf of hot, crusty bread.*

4 fresh tuna steaks, ½ inch thick
    (about 6 ounces each)
Salt, to taste
Freshly ground black pepper, to taste
¼ cup olive oil
2 tablespoons white wine vinegar or
    fresh lemon juice
4 bay leaves
4 medium tomatoes, peeled (page 23),
    seeded, and chopped
2 tablespoons fine bread crumbs
3 tablespoons capers, rinsed and dried
12 black olives, pitted and sliced
1 fresh jalapeño or serrano chili or 2 dried chili
    peppers, seeded and minced
12 fresh basil leaves, coarsely sliced

❦ Remove tough skin from tuna and rub both sides with salt and pepper. Place in a glass baking dish and pour 2 tablespoons of the olive oil and vinegar evenly over the fish. Place a bay leaf on each steak, cover, and refrigerate 1 hour, turning once.

❦ Preheat the oven to 375° F.

❦ Spread tomatoes on top of tuna and sprinkle with bread crumbs, capers, olives, and chilies. Drizzle with the remaining 2 tablespoons olive oil. Cover with aluminum foil and bake until the tuna is cooked through, about 20 minutes.

❦ Transfer to heated serving plates. Discard bay leaves and chilies. Spoon sauce over tuna and sprinkle with basil.

SEAFOOD FRICASSEE

{Serves 6}

A *t Ristorante Il Salotto del Chianti in Tuscany, I was introduced to this seafood stew, which is the Italian version of chicken fricassee. To extract the rich, full flavor of the sea, buy the firmest, freshest fish available. Serve this stew Italian style with toasted crusty bread brushed with fruity olive oil.*

½ pound cold unsalted butter
4 shallots, minced
6 carrots, thinly sliced
2 large leeks (white and green parts),
    thinly sliced
1 cup dry white wine
6 cups fish stock (preferably homemade) or
    vegetable stock (page 26)
Grated zest of 1 lemon
Salt, to taste
Freshly ground black pepper, to taste
1 pound *each* salmon, sea bass, halibut, and
    sole fillets, cut into 1-inch chunks

❦ In a large skillet, melt ¼ pound of the butter over medium heat and sauté shallots, carrots, and leeks until soft, about 5 minutes. Add wine and 2 cups of the stock. Bring to a boil, reduce heat, and simmer until thick. Dice remaining ¼ pound of the butter and add a tablespoon at a time, blending well after each addition. Add lemon zest and season with salt and pepper to taste.

❦ In another large skillet or a Dutch oven, heat remaining 4 cups of stock to a simmer and poach fish until translucent, about 2 minutes. With a slotted spoon, transfer fish to the sauce. Gently spoon sauce over fish to moisten. To serve, spoon fricassee onto serving plates.

MEDITERRANEAN FISH AND POTATO STEW

{ *Serves 8* }

Call it soup or stew, but whatever its title, this dish is a savory treat from the sea! Almost any firm-fleshed, white-meat fish will do, such as halibut, sea bass, or snapper. The accompanying California Aïoli is spread on toast or simply stirred into the soup for a rich, garlicky taste. Since the bones are simmered in the soup, the broth becomes intensely flavorful without the bother of making a fish stock. You probably can buy or beg the bones from your fish market.

California Aïoli (page 76)
3 tablespoons olive oil
4 cloves garlic, minced
2 medium onions, thinly sliced
1 leek (white and greens parts),
    thinly sliced
2 stalks celery, sliced
2 medium carrots, thinly sliced
6 medium tomatoes, roughly chopped
8 sprigs fresh parsley
2 teaspoons fennel seeds
1 teaspoon dried thyme, crumbled
Pinch ground saffron
1 pound fish bones
3 quarts water
2 large potatoes, peeled and diced
Salt, to taste
Freshly ground black pepper, to taste
2 pounds white fish fillets,
    cut into 1-inch chunks

❦ Prepare California Aïoli, cover with plastic wrap, and chill.

❦ In a large heavy pot or Dutch oven, heat oil over medium heat and sauté garlic, onions, leek, celery, and carrots until tender but not brown, about 5 minutes. Add tomatoes, parsley, fennel seeds, thyme, and saffron and simmer another 5 minutes.

❦ Place fish bones in a cheesecloth bag and arrange on top of the onion mixture. Add the water and potatoes, bring to a boil, reduce heat, and simmer 45 minutes, partially covered. Season with salt and pepper to taste. Continue cooking until the soup is thick and flavorful. Remove cheesecloth bag and discard.

❦ Just before serving, add fish fillets and simmer until fish is cooked through, about 10 minutes. Do not overcook. Ladle into hot soup bowls and pass the California Aïoli.

POULTRY

or many people, a deli serves as a home away from home any time of the day, any day of the year, even on holidays like Thanksgiving or Christmas. I believe that people flock to delis on these holidays because delis are renowned for preparing succulent roasted turkeys, tasty enough to rival even those made by Mom. ❦ At a deli, turkey is dished up in a number of ways. You can order juicy slices of white or dark meat, roasted turkey, sliced turkey sandwiches, or even turkey chili. You might find the equivalent of a Thanksgiving feast on your plate, with stuffing, gravy, cranberry sauce, and mashed potatoes no matter that it's July. In a real deli, it's Turkey Day with Trimmings year-round. ❦ Chicken is another popular mainstay of deli cuisine. In old-fashioned delis, chicken in the pot, chicken pot pie, and barbecued chicken are menu perennials. But in more contemporary deli restaurants, chicken takes on all sorts of creative twists. Take traditional roasted whole chickens; they're updated when cooked on the rotisserie with aromatic herbs and served with Garlic Mashed Potatoes or French Fries. ❦ This chapter offers a wealth of deli chicken recipes, both traditional and innovative. One of my favorites, Fifteen-Minute Chicken Mattone, was inspired by roasted butterflied chicken I've enjoyed on numerous visits to the local *rosticcerie* in Italy. I also confess to great fondness for Super-Crispy Fried Chicken, which I developed for purely selfish reasons. Who doesn't love perfectly fried chicken? ❦ A bonus when preparing chicken or turkey is that leftovers contribute to wonderful salads and sandwiches, also included in this book.

DELI CHOPPED CHICKEN LIVERS {*Makes 3 cups*}

This is my time-tested version of chopped liver, the beloved Jewish-style deli sandwich filling and star appetizer. I prefer chicken livers, although veal or beef liver is often used. The more onions you add, the sweeter the chopped liver. Serve on a bed of lettuce for an appetizer or as a deli sandwich. (See page 65 for Chopped Liver Sandwich)

½ cup olive oil

2 onions, thinly sliced

2 pounds chicken livers

2 tablespoons brandy or Cognac

3 hard-cooked eggs, cut up

Salt, to taste

Freshly ground black pepper, to taste

❦ In a large heavy skillet, heat oil over medium-high heat and sauté onions until lightly browned, about 5 minutes. Add livers and sauté, turning them on both sides, until lightly browned, about 5 minutes. Do not overcook. Add brandy, simmer for 2 minutes, and cool slightly.

❦ Spoon liver mixture and eggs into a meat grinder and grind into a large bowl, making sure to add the juices from the skillet. Season with salt and pepper to taste and mix well. Cover with plastic wrap and chill.

OVEN-ROASTED HERB CHICKEN
{*Serves 8*}

Spit-roasted chickens, wrapped or stuffed with fresh herb branches, are found in markets and delis throughout Italy. In this recipe, I re-create the flavor of spit-roasted chicken without using a rotisserie. Best of all, it only takes about 45 minutes to cook. This entrée tastes especially delicious served with French fries.

Fresh Herb Stuffing (recipe follows)
1 onion, sliced and diced
2 cloves garlic, minced
4 carrots, thinly sliced
1 parsnip, thinly sliced
2 tablespoons minced fresh parsley
2 to 2½ cups dry white wine
2 small frying chickens (2½ pounds each)
6 sprigs fresh thyme

❦ Preheat the oven to 450° F.

❦ Prepare Fresh Herb Stuffing.

❦ Arrange onion, garlic, carrots, parsnip, and parsley in a large roasting pan lined with aluminum foil. Pour in 2 cups of the wine.

❦ Beginning at the neck and using your fingertips, separate the skin from the meat of 1 chicken, working down to the thigh. Be careful not to tear the skin. Place half of the herb stuffing under the skin, all the way to the thigh. Smooth skin to disperse the mixture evenly. Repeat the process with the remaining chicken and stuffing.

❦ Place chickens on top of the vegetables and arrange thyme sprigs on top. Bake 30 minutes. (If the chickens are browning too quickly, cover loosely with aluminum foil.) If the liquid has evaporated at this point, add the remaining ½ cup of wine and continue baking until chickens are tender, about 15 minutes.

❦ To serve, cut chickens into quarters, spoon vegetables onto serving plates, and place chicken quarters on top.

FRESH HERB STUFFING
{*Makes about ⅔ cup*}

2 tablespoons minced garlic
2 tablespoons minced fresh rosemary
2 tablespoons minced fresh thyme
2 tablespoons minced fresh basil
2 tablespoons minced fresh chives
2 tablespoons minced fresh parsley
Olive oil, to moisten stuffing
Salt, to taste
Freshly ground black pepper, to taste

❦ In a small bowl, combine garlic, rosemary, thyme, basil, chives, and parsley. Pour in enough olive oil to cover. Season with salt and pepper to taste. Cover with plastic wrap until needed.

ITALIAN BARBECUED CHICKEN SANTINI
WITH SALSA VERDE {*Serves 4 to 6*}

2 cups olive oil

Juice of 2 lemons

½ cup white wine vinegar

4 cloves garlic, crushed and thinly sliced

½ cup minced fresh parsley

Pinch sugar

Salt, to taste

Freshly ground black pepper, to taste

2 small frying chickens (2½ to 3 pounds each),
    cut into pieces

Salsa Verde (recipe follows)

*T*he Santinis, owners of Ristorante dal Pescatore, are our adopted family when we visit Italy. Their restaurant is located in a very small village, Canneto Sull' Oglio, between Cremona and Montava. We love sharing their customs, and one of them is a big Sunday lunch with their entire family. The menu never varies—grilled home-raised chicken with a salsa verde, (green sauce), scented with garlic. This cherished recipe has been in their family for generations. Note that chicken must marinate twenty-four hours.

❡ In a large, shallow glass bowl or pan, combine olive oil, lemon juice, vinegar, garlic, parsley, and sugar. Season with salt and pepper to taste. Arrange chicken pieces in the pan and turn to coat evenly with olive oil mixture. Cover pan with aluminum foil and marinate chicken for 24 hours in the refrigerator, turning pieces occasionally.

❡ Prepare Salsa Verde and chill.

❡ Prepare coals for grilling or preheat the broiler. To barbecue, arrange chicken on a 2-sided grilling basket and enclose the chicken pieces securely. Grill until the chickens are cooked through, about 20 minutes. To broil, place chicken pieces under a hot broiler, skin side down. Turn and broil until brown and crisp on both sides. Pass a bowl of cold Salsa Verde.

SALSA VERDE {*Makes about 3 cups*}

½ cup tightly packed fresh parsley sprigs,
    stems removed

3 cloves garlic, crushed and thinly sliced

Juice of 1 lemon

2 tablespoons white wine vinegar

2 cups olive oil

Salt, to taste

Freshly ground black pepper, to taste

❡ In a large bowl, using a wire whisk, beat parsley, garlic, lemon juice, and vinegar. Continue beating, adding olive oil in a thin stream. Season with salt and pepper to taste. Pour into a smaller bowl, cover with plastic wrap, and chill.

CHICKEN IN THE POT {Serves 8}

Internationally acclaimed chef Jonathan Waxman created this recipe when we cooked together on "Judy's Kitchen," my television program in Los Angeles. I had never had chicken in the pot like this before: it practically bursts with flavor. This recipe is a spin-off of a grilled chicken and vegetable dish that's a signature item in the inspired repertoire that has brought Jonathan fame from Los Angeles to New York and London.

1 jalapeño chili

1 Anaheim chili

1 medium red bell pepper

1 roasting chicken (4 to 5 pounds),
   trussed with string

2 medium onions

3 shallots

1 head garlic, cloves separated

1 teaspoon whole black peppercorns

2 bay leaves, crumbled

6 small red or white new potatoes, unpeeled

4 fresh shiitake mushrooms

4 small turnips, peeled

2 parsnips, peeled

4 small carrots, peeled

2 stalks fennel or celery,
   cut into chunks

8 radishes, stems removed

1 large leek (white and green parts),
   cut in half and soaked in warm water

1 small bunch fresh parsley,
   tied with a string

1 small bunch fresh tarragon

1 teaspoon salt

½ cup whole-grain mustard

1 French baguette, thinly sliced and toasted

❦ Preheat the oven to 350° F.

❦ Roast and seed chilies and bell pepper, according to recipe for Roasted Red or Yellow Bell Peppers on page 81 (omit olive oil and garlic).

❦ Peel onions, place them in a baking pan lined with aluminum foil, and roast until golden brown, about 30 minutes.

❦ In a large pot or Dutch oven, place chicken, roasted onions, shallots, garlic cloves, peppercorns, bay leaves, and roasted chilies. Add enough water to cover, bring to a boil, reduce heat and simmer 30 minutes, partially covered. Add potatoes and continue cooking 15 minutes. Add mushrooms, turnips, parsnips, carrots, fennel, radishes, leek, parsley, tarragon, and ½ teaspoon of the salt. Continue cooking, until chicken is tender when pierced with fork, about 30 minutes.

❦ Remove cooked chicken to a platter and keep hot. Transfer vegetables to a large bowl and keep warm in 2 cups of the broth. Strain the remaining broth into a saucepan, reserving garlic cloves. Bring both to a boil, reduce heat, and simmer 15 minutes, partially covered.

❦ In a blender or food processor, blend roasted red pepper, mustard, 8 of the garlic cloves from the soup, ½ cup of the broth, and the remaining ½ teaspoon salt. Pour mustard sauce into a bowl.

❦ Cut chicken into serving pieces; arrange in large individual heated soup bowls, surrounded by broth and vegetables. Serve with the toasted baguette slices and the mustard sauce.

CHICKEN POT PIE {Serves 6}

The rich flavor and fragrant aroma of this savory pie will remind you of real farmhouse cooking. But the whole recipe can be prepared in a half hour. Another ten minutes will produce a crunchy salad to serve with it. If you prefer turkey, buy breast halves or fillets. They are available fresh or frozen; if frozen, thaw in the refrigerator.

6 Puff Pastry Rounds (recipe follows)
4 cups strong chicken or turkey stock
½ cup sliced carrots (¼-inch thick)
½ cup sliced celery
1 cup fresh button mushrooms,
    stems removed
1 cup fresh or frozen pearl onions
2 pounds uncooked boned chicken,
    skinned and cut into large chunks
2 tablespoons minced fresh parsley
3 tablespoons unsalted margarine
¼ cup unbleached all-purpose flour
2 teaspoons minced fresh tarragon or
    1 teaspoon dried tarragon, crumbled

❦ Prepare Puff Pastry Rounds, bake, and set aside.

❦ In a large pot or Dutch oven, combine chicken stock, carrots, celery, mushrooms, onions, and chicken chunks. Bring to a boil, reduce heat and simmer, partially covered, until tender, about 25 minutes.

❦ In a small heavy saucepan, melt margarine over medium heat and add flour all at once. Cook, stirring constantly, until the mixture turns golden brown. Do not allow to burn.

❦ Remove 2 cups of the broth from the stewed chicken and stir into the margarine-flour paste, mixing until thick. Return to the chicken mixture; add parsley and tarragon and simmer until thick.

❦ Just before serving, reheat pastry rounds. To serve, ladle into 6 heated soup bowls and top with warmed pastry rounds. Serve immediately.

PUFF PASTRY ROUNDS {Makes 6 individual pastry rounds}

1 package (8 ounces) frozen puff pastry sheets
Flour, for rolling

Defrost frozen puff pastry for 20 minutes at room temperature. Line a large baking sheet with aluminum foil or parchment paper. Roll out each sheet of puff pastry on a floured surface into a 11x14-inch rectangle. Cut out six 6-inch circles using a floured sharp cutter or the point of a sharp knife. Transfer to prepared baking sheet. Cover with plastic wrap and refrigerate at least 1 hour.

❦ Preheat the oven to 400° F.

❦ Discard plastic wrap. Prick pastry rounds with a fork and bake until lightly browned, about 30 minutes. Cool on wire racks.

FIFTEEN-MINUTE CHICKEN MATTONE

{ *Serves 4* }

In Italian mattone *means "brick." In this recipe it means that the chicken is weighted down with a brick. This cooking method is impressive; the chicken is done in minutes, resulting in golden-brown, crispy skin and juicy, succulent meat. But you will need a clean brick. Serve with a Caesar salad, French fries, and a seasonal vegetable.*

1 small frying chicken (2½ to 3 pounds)
½ cup fresh lemon juice
¼ cup olive oil
1 clove garlic, minced
Leaves from 1 sprig fresh rosemary
1 teaspoon minced fresh parsley
Salt, to taste
Crushed black peppercorns, to taste

❦ Soak a heavy brick in hot water.

❦ Remove backbone from the chicken and butterfly by cutting chicken in half, removing wing tips, and pressing each half to lay flat.

❦ In a large shallow glass bowl, combine chicken with remaining ingredients and cover with plastic wrap. Marinate chicken in the refrigerator for 2 to 3 hours, turning several times.

❦ Preheat a large cast-iron skillet (preferably with ridges). Place chicken on the hot skillet and place the soaked brick on top. Brown over high heat until crisp, 5 to 10 minutes. Lift the brick, turn chicken, repeat browning, and serve immediately.

SUPER-CRISPY FRIED CHICKEN

{ *Serves 4 to 6* }

Perfect fried chicken can be made with a minimum of oil using a heavy, shallow, nonstick skillet. Placing the seasoned bread crumbs and one or two pieces of chicken at a time in a paper bag makes it easy to coat the chicken evenly—it's neater, too. Draining the fried chicken on paper towels ensures crispness. With these hints, how can you go wrong? Serve with fresh corn on the cob, potato or rice salad, and baked beans.

3 eggs
2 cups fine bread crumbs
½ cup unbleached all-purpose flour
Garlic salt or powder, to taste
Salt, to taste
Freshly ground black pepper, to taste
2 small frying chickens (about 2½ pounds each), cut into serving pieces
Safflower oil, for frying

❦ Place eggs in a shallow dish and beat well. In a brown paper bag, combine bread crumbs, flour, garlic powder, and salt and pepper to taste and shake well. Dip each chicken piece in the beaten egg to coat well and then place in the bread crumb mixture. Shake vigorously to coat chicken, shake off excess crumbs, and place on a baking sheet lined with paper towels.

❦ In a large, heavy skillet (3 inches deep), pour in enough oil to reach about 1 inch deep. Heat oil to about 370°F. Arrange chicken pieces, skin side down (do not crowd); fry on one side until brown, about 10 minutes. Turn and fry on the other side until crisp and brown, about 10 minutes. Transfer to paper towels and drain well.

DELI BARBECUED CHICKEN {Serves 8}

Who has a barbecue spit? Very few home cooks. But you don't need one to make mouthwatering barbecued chicken. Just use your broiler and baste the chicken often with the pungent barbecue sauce. If you still want to use a charcoal grill, the chicken will cook quickly since it's marinated overnight in the barbecue sauce.

2½ cups Deli Barbecue Sauce (page 139)
2 frying chickens (about 3 pounds each),
    cut into serving pieces

❦ Prepare barbecue sauce. Brush both sides of chicken pieces with sauce; place in a large baking dish and cover with plastic wrap. Marinate overnight in the refrigerator.

❦ Preheat the broiler and line a large broiler pan with heavy-duty aluminum foil. Place chicken pieces, skin-side down, in a single layer on broiler pan, 8 inches from the heat. Broil, basting with sauce and turning chicken often (to avoid the sauce from burning) ending with the skin-side up, until the chicken is nicely browned and tender when pierced with a fork, about 30 minutes.

NO-FRILLS ROAST TURKEY {Serves 16}

At last—a juicy, tender bird every time if you follow this recipe. The secret is to coat the turkey lavishly with a delicious barbecue sauce, wrap it in foil, and roast. This recipe makes lots of irresistible deli-style turkey sandwiches. The turkey is roasted wrapped in heavy-duty aluminum foil, ensuring that it's moist, that its flavor penetrates to the bone, and that clean-up is a breeze. Serve with Cranberry-Onion Relish (page 76), along with the vegetable stuffing, if using.

1 double recipe (about 6 cups) Vegetable
   Stuffing (page 133), optional
2 cups Deli Barbecue Sauce (page 139)
1 turkey (15 to 20 pounds)
¼ cup olive oil
¼ cup dry red wine
2 cloves garlic, minced
Salt, to taste
Freshly ground black pepper, to taste

❦ Prepare Vegetable Stuffing, if using, and Deli Barbecue Sauce.

❦ Preheat oven to 325°F.

❦ Rinse turkey and pat it dry with paper towels. Stuff loosely with vegetable stuffing, if desired, and secure opening with skewers or a needle and thread. In a small bowl, mix oil, wine, garlic, and barbecue sauce and rub the outside of turkey. Season with salt and pepper to taste.

❦ Place turkey, breast down, in the center of a large sheet of heavy-duty aluminum foil, long enough to enclose the turkey loosely (or use 2 sheets with a seam in the center). Seal foil securely to make an airtight package. Bake 20 minutes per pound (5 to 7½ hours).

❦ About 30 minutes before turkey is done, open the foil, ladle pan juices into a small saucepan, and chill until the fat rises and hardens. Continue browning turkey with foil open, for the remaining cooking time. Meanwhile, remove saucepan from the refrigerator, skim off fat, bring pan juices to a boil, and keep warm.

❦ To serve, carve turkey and arrange slices with legs and wings on a large platter. Ladle the hot juices over the sliced turkey.

ROAST TURKEY BREAST

{*Serves 10*}

If you're pressed for time, a deli is the best place to buy cooked turkey breasts. You can serve them whole for dinner, or sliced for a buffet or sandwiches. But if you have the time, you'll love turkey prepared this way: it's low in fat, moist, and succulent. Onion Raisin Relish (page 77) is the perfect accompaniment to the sweet, juicy meat.

1 onion, thinly sliced

2 carrots, thinly sliced

1 boned turkey breast (about 6 pounds)

2 cloves garlic, thinly sliced

2 tablespoons peanut oil

Salt, to taste

Freshly ground black pepper, to taste

6 sprigs fresh rosemary

❦ Preheat the oven to 325° F.

❦ Line a shallow baking pan with aluminum foil and arrange onion and carrots on the bottom. Place turkey breast on top, skin side up. Carefully lift skin from meat and insert garlic slices underneath. Rub skin of turkey breast with oil and season with salt and pepper to taste. Arrange rosemary sprigs on top of turkey.

❦ Cover and bake 20 minutes per pound, about 1½ to 2 hours. Transfer turkey to a cutting board; let stand 5 minutes before slicing.

TURKEY CHILI FOR A CROWD {*Serves 8 to 10*}

Turkey is a terrific substitute for beef when making chili. This dish is a huge hit at the Broadway Deli. I like to serve it with Cornmeal Muffins (page 167). If you grind your own turkey, be sure to remove all the skin and fat. It will be leaner than the supermarket variety and fresher, too.

¼ cup olive oil

2 pounds ground turkey breast

½ cup diced onions

8 cloves garlic, minced

½ cup diced celery

½ cup diced carrots

½ cup seeded and diced
   green bell pepper

½ teaspoon cayenne pepper

1 teaspoon chili powder

1 teaspoon dried thyme, crumbled

1 teaspoon ground coriander

1 teaspoon ground cumin

1 can (16 ounces) kidney beans,
   with liquid

1 can (16 ounces) chopped tomatoes,
   with liquid

2 cups canned tomato juice

2 cups chicken stock (page 27)

2 teaspoons freshly ground black pepper

1 teaspoon salt, or to taste

1 cup roughly chopped cilantro

1 cup shredded Cheddar cheese,
   for garnish (optional)

Minced onions, for garnish

❧ In a large, heavy nonreactive pot or Dutch oven, heat oil over medium heat and saute turkey until cooked through and browned, mashing with a fork to break up large chunks. Transfer to a medium bowl.

❧ In the same pot, saute onions, garlic, celery, carrots, and green pepper until soft, about 5 minutes. Add cayenne, chili powder, thyme, coriander, and cumin and cook 2 minutes, stirring occasionally. Add browned turkey and stir to absorb seasonings. Then add kidney beans, tomatoes, tomato juice, and chicken stock and simmer over low heat, partially covered, 45 minutes to an hour, stirring occasionally.

❧ Season chili with salt and pepper to taste and ½ cup of the cilantro. Spoon into heated bowls and garnish with remaining cilantro. Serve with bowls of shredded cheese and onions to sprinkle over tops.

TURKEY SCHNITZEL {Serves 4}

Endless variations of schnitzel are served in German delis worldwide. This version of schnitzel, which means "cutlet," is prepared with economical turkey instead of pricey veal. Turkey fillets are now sold in most supermarkets. Buy an extra package and store it in the freezer for a spontaneous main course that can be ready in minutes. Serve with Garlic Mashed Potatoes (page 85) and Cranberry-Onion Relish (page 76).

8 thinly sliced turkey-breast cutlets
    (about 1 pound total)
2 egg whites
1 teaspoon water
2 tablespoons Dijon mustard
1¼ teaspoons salt
1 cup fine bread crumbs
½ teaspoon freshly ground black pepper
6 tablespoons olive oil

❦ Pound turkey cutlets lightly with a mallet between 2 pieces of waxed paper, for even slices.

❦ In a medium bowl, beat egg whites with the water. Mix in mustard and ½ teaspoon of the salt. In a shallow dish, mix bread crumbs with remaining ¾ teaspoon salt and pepper. Set aside.

❦ Dip each cutlet in the egg white mixture, then coat both sides with bread crumbs. Place on a large platter, cover with plastic wrap, and refrigerate 30 minutes.

❦ In a large nonstick skillet, heat 3 tablespoons of the olive oil over medium heat. Add half of the cutlets and cook, turning once, until golden brown and cooked through, 2 to 3 minutes per side. Transfer to paper towels and drain. Wipe out the skillet and cook the remaining cutlets in the remaining 3 tablespoons oil.

MEATS ou expect to find the predictable sandwich meats—corned beef, pastrami, brisket, tongue—in a deli cookbook. I do promise you all the classics—and much, much more. And I'm also able to share many secrets of famous deli chefs to guarantee both the success and ease of preparation. ❦ Some of my personal favorites appear in this section: meat loaf, stuffed cabbage, short ribs, lamb shanks—all prepared in the style of contemporary delis. These homey dishes offer more than fine flavor. They're easy on the budget, often using cheaper cuts of meat. And they warm the spirit as well as the body, especially on frosty winter nights. ❦ It takes a little extra time to prepare some of these recipes, such as corned beef, but if you have some spare time you'll save an incredible amount of money. And you'll savor the accomplishment of producing in your own kitchen something that you thought only a professional deli chef could turn out. ❦ Browse through this book and look for just the right mouthwatering side dishes to accompany your deli meats. You'll find everything from relishes to super-crisp French fries—even a remarkable creamed spinach.

BAKED MARROW BONES

{*Serves 12*}

I first tasted baked marrow bones as an unusual first course during an elegant food-and-wine gala. Served with tiny spoons for scooping out the velvety marrow, this dish was the topic of conversation throughout the multicourse dinner. Although I haven't seen marrow bones featured this way in a deli, I always think of them as deli food as they're used so often in soups and stews. Marrow is obviously not low fat, but it is delicious. Everything in moderation! Ask your butcher to split the marrow bones for you.

6 marrow bones (4 to 6 inches long),
    split lengthwise
¼ pound unsalted margarine,
    at room temperature
4 cloves garlic
Salt, to taste
Freshly ground black pepper, to taste
1 cup fine bread crumbs
2 teaspoons paprika

▌ Place marrow bones on a baking sheet lined with aluminum foil.

▌ In a blender or a food processor fitted with a knife blade, blend margarine until creamy and continue blending while dropping in the garlic cloves, one at a time. Season with salt and pepper to taste.

▌ Spread margarine mixture generously over the cut sides of the bones. Sprinkle bread crumbs, salt, pepper, and paprika over each bone. At this point, you may cover tightly with aluminum foil and refrigerate until needed.

▌ Preheat the oven to 375° F.

▌ Bake bones until marrow is tender, 20 to 30 minutes. Test for doneness by inserting a fork into the marrow; if prongs go in easily, the marrow is done; the bread crumbs should be golden brown.

▌ Wrap each marrow bone in a napkin and serve at once with small teaspoons (or marrow spoons). Allow each guest to scoop out the delicious garlic-flavored marrow.

SAVORY LAMB SHANKS
WITH ROASTED GARLIC {Serves 6}

Some Americans—unlike our Mediterranean cousins—have yet to indulge in a love affair with lamb. But perhaps this aromatic recipe can help do the trick. The herb-infused, intensely flavored meat slow-cooks until it nearly falls off the bone. Serve the roasted unpeeled garlic with the lamb to enjoy the purée captured inside. You might want to double this recipe, so you'll have lamb left over for a delicious Twenty-Minute Lamb Stew (page oo). Ask your butcher to saw the shanks partially in half across the bone.

6 lamb shanks (about 1 pound each), trimmed of fat and partially cut across the bone

¼ cup olive oil

2 onions, thinly sliced

3 cloves garlic, minced

4 carrots, thinly sliced

2 stalks celery, thinly sliced

1 bay leaf, crushed

3 sprigs fresh oregano, minced, or 1 teaspoon dried oregano, crumbled

½ cup minced fresh parsley

1½ cups dry red wine

1 can (12 ounces) tomato sauce or whole tomatoes, with liquid

Salt, to taste

Freshly ground black pepper, to taste

2 heads garlic, separated into unpeeled cloves

4 sprigs fresh rosemary or 2 teaspoons dried rosemary, crumbled

12 fresh mushrooms, sliced in half

❦ Preheat the oven to 375°F.

❦ Tie string around the meaty portion of each shank to hold its shape.

❦ In a large heavy ovenproof skillet, heat olive oil over high heat and brown shanks on all sides to seal in the juices. Transfer them to a platter. Reduce heat to medium, add onions and minced garlic to the skillet and sauté until soft, about 5 minutes. Add carrots, celery, bay leaf, oregano, parsley, wine, and tomato sauce. Season with salt and pepper to taste. Bring to a boil, reduce heat to low, and simmer until sauce thickens, 5 to 10 minutes.

❦ Add browned lamb shanks and unpeeled garlic cloves to skillet and baste with sauce. Arrange rosemary on top. Cover and bake 1½ to 2 hours, basting and turning lamb shanks every 20 minutes. Uncover, add mushrooms, and bake until shanks are tender, about 30 minutes. If serving immediately, while shanks are baking, skim fat that forms on top. If time permits, cool and refrigerate the entire dish (the fat can be easily removed after it rises to top and hardens). Remove strings and reheat shanks before serving.

❦ Place a lamb shank on each heated serving plate with mushrooms, an unpeeled garlic clove, and spoon sauce on top.

TWENTY-MINUTE LEFTOVER LAMB STEW

{ *Serves 8* }

Recycling is the way of the nineties, so why not use leftover lamb shanks as the base for a hearty lamb stew? When preparing lamb shanks for a special family dinner, I prepare extra shanks, bone them, and combine the meat with steamed carrots, parsnips, and potatoes to make this twenty-minute lamb stew. The lamb and vegetables are enhanced with the rich tomato-wine sauce that is left in the roaster. A perfect main course for another dinner.

Savory Lamb Shanks with
    Roasted Garlic (page 131)
2 medium potatoes, peeled and cubed
6 medium carrots, peeled and
    cut into chunks
2 medium parsnips, peeled and
    cut into chunks
Salt, to taste
Freshly ground black pepper, to taste

❦ Prepare and bake Savory Lamb Shanks with Roasted Garlic. Remove meat from shank bones and place in a large pot or Dutch oven along with the sauce.

❦ In another large pot, place a vegetable steamer; add 2 inches of water, just to reach the bottom of the steamer. Steam potatoes, carrots, and parsnips until tender, about 10 minutes. Add to meat and sauce and toss gently. Season with salt and pepper to taste. Bring to a boil, reduce heat, and simmer until heated through, about 15 minutes.

VEGETABLE-STUFFED
VEAL BREAST

{Serves 6}

What respectable Jewish-style deli would dare to present a menu without stuffed veal breast? An ever-popular entrée, stuffed veal breast is quite easy to prepare at home, if you have your butcher cut the pocket. This cooking method seals in all the juices, so there's no need to baste. If time is short, make the stuffing the day before, cover, and refrigerate.

Vegetable Stuffing (recipe follows)
1 veal breast (about 6 pounds),
    with pocket cut and some fat trimmed
¼ cup olive oil
2 small onions, thinly sliced
3 cloves garlic, minced
4 medium carrots, sliced
2 stalks celery, sliced
1 bay leaf, crushed
1 sprig fresh rosemary, minced
1 cup dry red wine
Salt, to taste
Freshly ground black pepper, to taste

❦ Prepare Vegetable Stuffing.

❦ Preheat the oven to 350°F.

❦ In a large shallow roasting pan, place a large sheet of heavy-duty aluminum foil, long enough to enclose the veal breast loosely. Spoon stuffing into the pocket of the veal breast and close with skewers or a needle and thread. Place stuffed veal breast on the foil.

❦ In a large skillet, heat olive oil over medium heat and sauté onions and garlic until translucent, about 5 minutes. Add carrots, celery, bay leaf, rosemary, and wine and bring to a simmer, about 2 minutes. Pour onion mixture over veal and sprinkle with salt and pepper to taste. Seal foil securely to make an airtight package. Bake until tender, about 2½ hours. Open foil, increase the temperature to 375°F, and bake until browned, about 30 minutes. Slice veal, arrange on heated serving plates, and ladle sauce over top.

VEGETABLE STUFFING

{Makes about 3 cups}

¼ cup olive oil
2 medium onions, finely chopped
3 cloves garlic, minced
2 stalks celery, finely chopped
5 large carrots, peeled and shredded
1 medium parsnip, peeled and grated
1 medium zucchini, shredded
¼ cup minced fresh parsley
2 tablespoons oatmeal
2 tablespoons unbleached all-purpose flour
2 tablespoons fine bread crumbs
¼ cup apple juice
Salt, to taste
Freshly ground black pepper, to taste

❦ In a large skillet, heat olive oil over medium heat and sauté onions and garlic until translucent, about 5 minutes. Add celery, carrots, parsnip, zucchini, and parsley; toss well. Sauté until vegetables begin to soften, about 5 minutes. Blend in 1 tablespoon *each* of the oatmeal, flour, and bread crumbs. Add apple juice and mix well. Add remaining dry ingredients, a little at a time, until the stuffing is moist yet still firm in texture. Season with salt and pepper to taste.

ROASTED VEAL SHANKS {Serves 4}

A favorite of both delis and bistros, this hearty dish perfumes the house as it slowly cooks. Served in big soup bowls, the tender shanks are surrounded by flavorful vegetables in a rich broth to be soaked up with chunks of French bread. A complete meal.

4 meaty veal shanks, about 2 inches thick
Salt, to taste
Freshly ground black pepper, to taste
⅓ cup olive oil
2 medium onions, cut into chunks
6 cloves garlic, finely chopped
2 medium carrots, peeled and cut into chunks
3 bay leaves
2 tablespoons fresh thyme leaves
1 teaspoon dried rosemary, crumbled
1 can (16 ounces) Italian plum tomatoes, chopped with liquid
1 cup dry red wine
3 cups chicken stock (page 27)

❦ Preheat the oven to 350°F.

❦ Season veal shanks with salt and pepper to taste. In a Dutch oven heat 3 tablespoons of the olive oil over high heat and brown shanks on all sides until crusty. (This seals in the juices.) Remove from heat and transfer shanks to a platter.

❦ Return Dutch oven to medium heat, add remaining oil if needed and sauté onions, garlic, carrots, bay leaves, thyme, and rosemary until just tender, about 5 minutes. Add tomatoes and wine, bring to a boil, and simmer 5 minutes. Add shanks and chicken stock to cover veal completely. Cover and bake until tender, about 2½ hours. Serve in large soup bowls with vegetables and broth.

CALF'S LIVER WITH ONIONS AND PEPPERS {Serves 6 to 8}

An all-time deli favorite. I always buy veal liver rather than beef liver. It is more tender and the flavor is so subtle. Sliced very thin and served in small portions in its own juices with onions and peppers, sautéed liver can be both an eye-appealing and taste-appealing dish for company. The addition of crumbled crisp bacon, sliced apples, or raisins complements this simple dish. Serve with Garlic Mashed Potatoes (page 85).

6 tablespoons olive oil
3 medium onions, thinly sliced
3 cloves garlic, thinly sliced
1 large red bell pepper, seeded and thinly sliced
1½ pounds calf's liver, cut into ½-inch strips
Salt, to taste
Freshly ground black pepper, to taste

❦ In a nonstick skillet, heat 3 tablespoons of the olive oil over medium heat and sauté onions, garlic, and red pepper until soft and lightly browned, about 10 minutes. Season with salt and pepper to taste. Transfer to a plate.

❦ In the same skillet, heat the remaining 3 tablespoons of olive oil and cook the liver over high heat until light brown on bottom, about 1 minute; turn and cook 1 minute. Stir in onion mixture, season with salt and pepper to taste, and sauté until liver is cooked to your taste.

ROASTED MEAT LOAF IN TOMATO-WINE SAUCE

{*Serves 12*}

Just when you thought this all-time favorite couldn't get any better, along comes this recipe for meat loaf filled with sautéed vegetables and roasted like pot roast with a garlicky red wine and tomato sauce. It even contains a surprise—hard-cooked eggs hidden in the center. This meat loaf also tastes good cold in sandwiches, served with ketchup and a heap of French fries. Whip up a batch of Alain's Homemade Ketchup (page 73) and use some to make the meat loaf.

Tomato-Wine Sauce (recipe follows)
3 tablespoons olive oil
¾ cup finely chopped yellow onions
¾ cup finely chopped green onions
¼ cup finely chopped celery
¼ cup seeded and diced red bell peppers
¼ cup seeded and diced yellow bell peppers
4 cloves garlic, minced
3 eggs
¼ teaspoon cayenne pepper
1 teaspoon ground cumin
½ teaspoon freshly grated nutmeg
Salt, to taste
Freshly ground black pepper, to taste
¼ cup tomato ketchup
2 pounds ground lean beef
1 pound ground lean veal or turkey
½ cup fine bread crumbs
6 hard-cooked eggs, peeled

❦ Prepare Tomato-Wine Sauce.

❦ In a large heavy skillet, heat olive oil over medium heat and add yellow onions, green onions, celery, red and yellow peppers, and garlic. Sauté, stirring often, until the moisture from vegetables is evaporated, about 5 minutes. Cool.

❦ In a medium bowl, lightly beat raw eggs with cayenne, cumin, nutmeg, and salt and pepper to taste. Add ketchup and blend thoroughly.

❦ Preheat the oven to 375° F.

❦ In a large bowl, combine ground beef and veal with the cooled vegetable mixture and the egg mixture. Using your hands, knead thoroughly. Add bread crumbs and knead 1 to 2 minutes.

❦ Dampen hands and shape half of the meat into a flat loaf 17 inches long. Place on top of the Tomato-Wine sauce in the roasting pan. Place hard-cooked eggs lengthwise along the center of the molded meat loaf. Place the remaining meat mixture on top of the eggs, pressing to make a firm loaf. Bake until the meat is completely cooked through, about 45 minutes.

TOMATO-WINE SAUCE

{*Makes about 3 cups*}

2 tablespoons olive oil
1 onion, thinly sliced
1 can (16 ounces) peeled
    chopped tomatoes, with liquid
1 cup dry red wine
1 head garlic, separated into unpeeled cloves

❦ In a roasting pan long enough to hold a 17-inch meat loaf, heat olive oil over medium heat and sauté onions until soft, about 5 minutes. Add tomatoes with liquid and wine and simmer 5 minutes. Add unpeeled garlic cloves, cover, and set aside.

KERSTIN'S SWEDISH MEATBALLS

{Makes about 6 dozen meatballs; serves about 12}

Kerstin Marsh, a good friend, has served these Swedish meatballs as part of her Christmas Eve smorgasbords for more than thirty years. Her mother's original recipe was made with ground lean fillets of pork, but after a little persuasion, Kerstin agreed to make them for us with ground beef. Kerstin says they are good but not quite the same. You decide. Serve as part of a buffet with the traditional lingonberry sauce or Cranberry-Onion Relish (page 77).

2 eggs

4 slices zwieback, finely ground

2 pounds plus 2 ounces ground beef or pork

2 tablespoons nonfat milk or water

1½ teaspoons salt

¼ teaspoon white pepper

¼ teaspoon paprika

½ pound plus 4 tablespoons unsalted butter or margarine

2¼ cups water

Fresh dill, for garnish

❦ In a large bowl, beat eggs, add zwieback, and soak for 30 minutes.

❦ In a large bowl, combine beef, egg mixture, nonfat milk, salt, pepper, and paprika and mix well. Taste for seasoning (see Note) and shape into 1-inch balls.

❦ In a nonstick skillet, large enough to hold 25 meatballs, heat 6 tablespoons of the butter over high heat until it begins to sizzle. Add ⅓ of the meatballs; shake the pan as you sauté, rolling it back and forth, until meatballs are brown and cooked through, about 10 minutes. Using a slotted spoon transfer meatballs to a large bowl. Over high heat scrape skillet with a spatula adding ¼ cup of the water; stir as water bubbles to mix in pan scrapings for a sauce; add to meatballs.

❦ Repeat procedure in 2 more batches with the remaining butter, meatballs, and water. Serve in a chafing dish or on a platter garnished with fresh dill.

NOTE *To test for seasoning, fry a dab of meat mixture and season with additional salt and pepper to taste.*

SWEET-AND-SOUR STUFFED CABBAGE

{*Makes about 24 cabbage rolls; serves 12*}

S tuffed cabbage is the quintessential comfort food, and it's ideal to serve for any occasion. After all, who doesn't need comfort on a regular basis? This robust recipe is great for buffet parties. Much of it can be prepared in stages and combined just before baking.

Sweet-and-Sour Tomato Sauce
   (recipe follows)
2 medium heads cabbage
   (about 1½ pounds each),
   cores removed
2 pounds ground lean beef
1 small onion, finely chopped
4 cloves garlic, minced
1 small potato, peeled and grated
½ cup quick-cooking white rice
2 eggs, lightly beaten
Salt, to taste
Freshly ground black pepper, to taste

❦ Prepare Sweet-and-Sour Tomato Sauce and keep warm.

❦ In a large saucepan, place cabbage on a rack over simmering water and steam until soft enough to separate the leaves and fold them without tearing or breaking, 12 to 15 minutes.

❦ In a large bowl, combine beef, onion, garlic, potato, rice, and eggs and blend well. Season with salt and pepper to taste. Set aside.

❦ Preheat the oven to 375° F.

❦ Place a cabbage leaf on a flat surface. Shape a portion of the meat mixture into a ball; place it on the core end of the cabbage leaf and roll it up to enclose the filling, envelope style. Place rolls of cabbage, seam-side down, close together and submerged in the pot of tomato sauce; spoon sauce over rolls. Cover pot and bake until meat mixture is cooked through and cabbage is tender, 1 to 1½ hours.

SWEET-AND-SOUR TOMATO SAUCE

{*Makes about 6 cups*}

¼ cup olive oil
2 small onions, chopped
4 cloves garlic, minced
1 stalk celery, chopped
1 medium-size green bell pepper,
   seeded and diced
¼ cup minced fresh parsley
1 can (28 ounces) chopped tomatoes,
   with liquid
1 can (8 ounces) tomato sauce
1 cup dry red wine
¾ cup firmly packed brown sugar
Juice of 3 lemons
Salt, to taste
Freshly ground black pepper, to taste

❦ In a large nonreactive Dutch oven or roasting pan (about 10 quarts), heat oil over medium heat and sauté onions, garlic, celery, bell pepper, and parsley until tender, about 5 minutes. Add tomatoes, tomato sauce, red wine, brown sugar, and lemon juice. Season with salt, pepper, and additional brown sugar or lemon juice to taste. Bring to a boil, reduce heat, and simmer 5 minutes.

ROASTED SHORT RIBS

{Serves 6 to 8}

What do most chefs eat on their days off? Not surprisingly, the meal of choice is often a simple, down-home comfort food. The source of inspiration for this recipe came from a close friend, a deli chef who loves reminiscing about his grandmother's short ribs. She knew how to bring out the full flavor of this budget-priced meat and always served it with mashed potatoes swimming in the pan juices.

¼ cup olive oil
5 pounds beef short ribs
2 medium onions, thinly sliced
2 stalks celery, thinly sliced
2 medium carrots, thinly sliced
1 medium parsnip, thinly sliced
2 bay leaves, crumbled
Salt, to taste
Freshly ground black pepper, to taste
1 cup dry red wine
2 cups beef or chicken stock (page 27)

❦ Preheat the oven to 450° F.

❦ In a large skillet, heat 2 tablespoons of the oil over high heat and brown short ribs on each side, about 2 minutes. Transfer to a large roasting pan and set aside.

❦ Add the remaining 2 tablespoons of oil to the skillet. Over medium-high heat, sauté onions, celery, carrots, parsnip, and bay leaves until brown, about 10 minutes. Add to short ribs and season with salt and pepper to taste.

❦ Bake ribs uncovered for 15 minutes, then add wine and stock. Reduce heat to 350° F, cover, and bake until the meat falls away from the bone, about 2 hours.

ELYSE'S TANGY SHORT RIBS
AND SAUERKRAUT

{Serves 8 to 10}

One day my friend Elyse Grinstein arrived at our home with cans of sauerkraut and stewed tomatoes. Surprisingly, she was ready for some serious cooking. I supplied the meaty short ribs as planned. We simmered this savory dish for several hours and Elyse assured me that it tasted exactly the way her mother used to make it. Hearty and deeply satisfying, these fork-tender short ribs can be showcased at a buffet. And they're great at a party for watching sports on TV. Ask your butcher to cut up the ribs for you.

¼ cup safflower oil
4 pounds meaty short ribs, trimmed of all fat
    and cut into 1½-inch chunks
2 cans (24 ounces each) sauerkraut
4 cans (14½ ounces each)
    stewed tomatoes
½ to 1 cup sugar
Freshly ground black pepper, to taste

❦ In a large Dutch oven, heat oil over high heat and brown short ribs until crusty, turning with a wooden spoon as they brown. Remove from heat and transfer ribs to a large bowl.

❦ Scrape off the browned pieces that formed on the bottom of the Dutch oven, but don't discard. Add sauerkraut and mix well, tossing with the browned pieces. Stir in tomatoes; add browned short ribs and mix well. Add sugar and pepper to taste. (We like it sweet.) Bring mixture to a boil, cover, reduce heat, and simmer for 1½ hours, stirring every 20 minutes. Spoon onto serving plates.

BROADWAY DELI BRISKET

{ *Serves 8* }

he Broadway Deli's recipe for brisket is a popular request from its customers. This dish is simple to make, yet supremely satisfying. The tender, juicy meat is equally inviting in a sandwich or served as a one-pot meal with French bread and salad.

¼ cup olive oil
1 boneless beef brisket (6 to 8 pounds),
    with most of fat trimmed
2 large onions, thinly sliced
6 cloves garlic, thinly sliced
6 large carrots, sliced
4 stalks celery, sliced
2 bay leaves, crumbled
3 sprigs fresh thyme
1½ cups dry red wine
1½ cups beef or chicken stock
Salt, to taste
Freshly ground black pepper

❦ Preheat the oven to 350° F.

❦ In a Dutch oven, heat olive oil over high heat and brown brisket fat side down; turn and brown on other side. Transfer meat to a platter and keep warm.

❦ Reduce heat to medium and add to skillet onions, garlic, carrots, celery, bay leaves, and thyme. Sauté until onions are slightly brown, about 10 minutes. Add wine, raise heat, and boil a few minutes until wine is reduced. Place brisket on top of vegetables and add stock. Season with salt and pepper to taste. Bring to a boil, cover, and bake until meat is tender when pierced with a fork, 2½ to 3 hours. Serve sliced on a platter surrounded by vegetables. Serve sauce on the side.

BAKED KOSHER-STYLE BOLOGNA

{ *Serves 10 to 12, as part of a buffet* }

his deli dish is often the star attraction when my friend Marlene Lochheim, noted Los Angeles hostess and artist, gives informal buffet receptions for the many art groups with which she's involved. She serves it piping hot, with an assortment of grainy breads and a myriad of mustards. Marlene always buys kosher Hebrew National Bologna from Nate & Al's, Beverly Hills' most famous deli, but most other delis sell it too. The secret to this recipe is long, slow cooking.

1 half or 1 whole large bologna
    (about 5 pounds)

❦ Preheat the oven to 225° F.

❦ Wrap bologna loosely in heavy-duty aluminum foil so it has room to expand. Place on a heavy baking sheet and bake 8 hours. Serve hot on a large platter.

BARBECUED RIBS

{Serves 6}

A hearty, spicy all-American favorite, ribs are one of the most popular takeout items at delis. But see how easy it is to duplicate them at home. After much experimenting, I've come up with the perfect barbecue sauce to go with the ribs. It's terrific with chicken, too.

4 pounds beef or pork ribs
Deli Barbecue Sauce (recipe follows)

❦ Prepare barbecue sauce, cover, and keep simmering while basting ribs.

❦ Preheat the oven to 350° F.

❦ Place ribs on a large baking pan lined with aluminum foil and bake until golden brown, about 10 minutes. Pour off the fat and pour half of the barbecue sauce over ribs. Bake for 1 hour, basting every 15 minutes with the simmering sauce. Turn ribs and bake another 30 minutes, basting with the remaining sauce.

DELI BARBECUE SAUCE

{Makes about 2½ cups}

2 tablespoons olive oil
1 small onion, chopped
4 cloves garlic, minced
1 teaspoon dried rosemary, crumbled
1 bay leaf, crumbled
1 can (8 ounces) tomato sauce
1 can (8 ounces) whole peeled tomatoes, with liquid
1 tablespoon dark brown sugar
2 tablespoons red wine vinegar
½ cup dry red wine
½ teaspoon ground cumin
1 tablespoon coarse-grained mustard
Dash Tabasco sauce
Salt, to taste
Freshly ground black pepper, to taste

❦ In a large, nonreactive skillet, heat olive oil over medium heat and sauté onion, garlic, rosemary, and bay leaf until soft, about 5 minutes.

❦ In a blender, blend remaining ingredients and add to onions with rosemary and bay leaf. Bring to a boil, reduce heat and simmer uncovered, stirring often, until sauce is reduced and thickened, about 15 minutes. Use to baste ribs or other meats.

CHEF'S SPECIAL CORNED BEEF

{*Makes about 24 sandwiches*}

The best way to enjoy tender, garlicky corned beef is to make it yourself. It's easy to do and you can vary the seasonings to suit your taste. Serve it hot in sandwiches or turn it into an Irish dish, served with boiled cabbage. Note that you'll need a clean brick to weigh down the beef.

1 first-cut beef brisket
(about 6 pounds)
12 cloves garlic
1 onion, thinly sliced
3 quarts water
1 cup kosher salt
2 cups dark brown sugar
2½ teaspoons bicarbonate of soda
2 teaspoons saltpeter (see Note)
2 teaspoons whole black peppercorns
2 tablespoons pickling spices
4 bay leaves, crumbled

❦ Wipe the meat well with a damp cloth and make several deep punctures with a fork so the pickling brine will be absorbed.

❦ Place meat in a glass or earthenware crock, large enough to hold the meat and pickling solution. Add 8 of the garlic cloves and onion slices.

❦ In a large pot, combine the water, salt, brown sugar, baking soda, saltpeter, 1 teaspoon of the peppercorns, pickling spice, and half of the bay leaves. Bring to a boil and stir until sugar dissolves. Remove from the heat and cool.

❦ Pour brine over beef, making sure meat is completely submerged. Place a heavy brick in a plastic bag, seal, and place on top of the meat. Cover with plastic wrap and aluminum foil and let it soak in a cool place for 8 to 10 days. (Refrigeration is not necessary.) After several days add additional water, if needed, to keep beef completely covered with water. (The longer the meat is left the more mature and corned it will be.)

❦ Preheat the oven to 350° F.

❦ Remove meat from the brine and rinse well in cold water. Place in a deep roasting pan with enough water to come almost to the top of the meat. Add the remaining 1 teaspoon peppercorns, bay leaves, and 4 garlic cloves. Cover loosely with aluminum foil and bake until tender when pierced with a fork, about 3 hours. Transfer to a platter and cool.

❦ Using a very sharp knife, slice the corned beef across the grain, making thin slices for sandwiches and thick slices for corned beef and cabbage.

NOTE *Saltpeter (potassium nitrate) gives the characteristic red color to many cured meats and also acts as a preservative. It is sold in most drugstores. If you are concerned about consuming nitrates, bicarbonate of soda may be substituted, but it is not as effective.*

CORNED BEEF AND CABBAGE {Serves 6 to 8}

Some chefs cook the cabbage with the corned beef, but this contemporary technique produces a tastier version. Cabbage prepared this way is also a fine accompaniment to many other entrées in this chapter. Serve the corned beef and cabbage with a variety of sweet, hot, and horseradish mustards.

4 pounds corned beef
    (preferably homemade, page 141)
2 cups chicken stock
2 medium heads cabbage
    (1½ pounds each), cored, quartered,
    and coarsely shredded
Salt, to taste
Freshly ground black pepper, to taste

❦ Place corned beef in a large pot and cover with water. Bring to a boil, cover, reduce heat, and simmer until completely heated through, about 20 minutes.

❦ In another large pot, bring chicken stock to a boil. Add cabbage and season with salt and pepper to taste; mix well. Cover and steam until tender, about 10 minutes.

❦ Slice corned beef and arrange on heated serving plates. Spoon cabbage alongside.

AUTHENTIC DELI PASTRAMI {Serves 12}

In New York–style delis, pastrami runs a close second to corned beef as the most requested sandwich filling. Leaner and more peppery than its competition, pastrami is made from beef brisket. It's time-consuming, yet simple, to prepare at home if you have a smoker. Here is the authentic way delis make pastrami: the brisket is cured, smoked, and then boiled with most appealing results.

1 cup coarse kosher salt
¼ cup sugar
2 teaspoons saltpeter (see Note)
¼ cup ground ginger
¼ cup crushed black peppercorns
2 to 3 cloves garlic, crushed
1 beef brisket (about 5 pounds),
    trimmed of fat

❦ In a bowl, combine salt, sugar, saltpeter, ginger, peppercorns, and garlic. Rub brisket well with the salt mixture and place it in a glass dish or an enameled pan. Cover with plastic wrap and aluminum foil and weight it down with a board covered with bricks or heavy cans of food. Store in the refrigerator for 3 weeks.

❦ At the end of that time, dry beef with paper towels. Then smoke for 3 hours at 150° F to 170° F, according to the directions on your smoker.

❦ In a large heavy pot, place smoked brisket, cover with water, bring to a boil, cover, reduce heat, and simmer until tender when pierced with a fork, 3 to 4 hours. Cool in the pot; cover with plastic wrap and aluminum foil and chill. This will keep for a week stored in the refrigerator. Slice as needed for sandwiches.

NOTE *Saltpeter (potassium nitrate) gives the characteristic red color to many cured meats and also acts as a preservative. It is sold in most drugstores. If you are concerned about consuming nitrates, bicarbonate of soda may be substituted, but it is not as effective.*

ROASTED TONGUE IN RAISIN SAUCE {*Serves 8 to 10*}

In addition to serving pickled tongue in sandwiches, many delis serve roasted tongue as a main course. When properly prepared, beef, veal, and lamb tongues are tender and tasty. This recipe, which features a full-bodied, tomato-based raisin sauce, is my favorite way of serving tongue. The raisins add a hint of sweetness, providing the ideal counterpoint to the mild taste of the meat.

Raisin Sauce (recipe follows)
1 beef tongue (3 to 4 pounds),
    4 to 6 veal tongues,
    or 16 lamb tongues
Boiling water, for simmering
1 medium onion, diced
2 stalks celery with tops, sliced
1 teaspoon whole black peppercorns
½ teaspoon salt
1 teaspoon whole cloves
2 cloves garlic, minced
1 bay leaf, crumbled
½ cup chopped fresh parsley
8 fresh mushrooms, quartered

❦ Prepare Raisin Sauce and keep warm.

❦ Scrub tongue and place in a large heavy pot with enough boiling water to cover. Add onion, celery, peppercorns, salt, cloves, garlic, bay leaf, and parsley. Bring to a boil, reduce heat to low, and simmer, partially covered, until tongue is tender and the outer skin peels off easily, about 1½ hours. Cool. Remove skin and all the dry hard portions and the root. Preheat the oven to 350° F.

❦ Place tongue in the pot of raisin sauce and baste. Arrange mushrooms around tongue. Cover and bake until tongue is tender, about 30 minutes. Slice tongue and serve with sauce.

RAISIN SAUCE {*Makes about 4 cups*}

¼ cup safflower oil
2 medium onions, diced
3 cloves garlic, minced
1 small green bell pepper,
    seeded and diced
1 can (28 ounces) peeled tomatoes,
    drained
1 cup golden raisins
1 teaspoon minced fresh basil leaves
1 bay leaf, crumbled
½ cup minced fresh parsley
1 teaspoon paprika
2 tablespoons brown sugar
2 tablespoons tomato paste
1 cup dry red wine
Salt, to taste
Freshly ground black pepper, to taste

❦ In a large Dutch oven or heavy nonreactive ovenproof pot, heat oil over medium heat and sauté onions, garlic, and green pepper until soft, about 5 minutes. When onion mixture is soft, add remaining ingredients. Bring to a boil, reduce heat, and simmer, partially covered, until sauce thickens, 5 to 10 minutes. Season with salt and pepper to taste.

HOME-CURED PICKLED TONGUE

{ *Serves 6 to 8* }

This spicy, tender pickled tongue tastes exactly like the sort sold in high-quality delis. Utilizing a professional chef's technique, the tongue is cured for eight to ten days in brine in a heavy duty four-gallon plastic trash bag. Yes, the curing takes time, but it's worth it. Serve as an appetizer or part of a buffet with melon, figs, or cold asparagus; as a main dish with a rice or potato salad; or in a sandwich.

1 tablespoon dry mustard

2 cups plus 3 tablespoons water

¼ cup brown sugar

8 whole cloves

¼ cup pickling spices

1 teaspoon ground ginger

1 tablespoon coriander seeds

1 teaspoon whole allspice

10 cloves garlic, unpeeled and crushed

3 bay leaves

1 tablespoon whole black peppercorns

½ teaspoon red pepper flakes

½ cup coarse kosher salt

1 teaspoon saltpeter (see Note)

Juice and grated zest of 1 lemon

1 large beef tongue (about 3 pounds)

❦ In a small bowl, mix mustard with 3 table-spoons of the water and set aside for 1 hour.

❦ In a medium saucepan, mix the remaining 2 cups water with all the remaining ingredients, except tongue. Add mustard mixture. Bring to a boil, remove from heat, and cool.

❦ Test a heavy-duty 4-gallon plastic bag for leaks by filling it with water. If there are no leaks, pour out water, place tongue in bag, and pour cooled brine mixture over it. Seal securely with the bag wrapper. Place in a shallow bowl and refrigerate, turning the package over every 24 hours.

❦ After 8 to 10 days, remove tongue from the bag, drain, and place in a large pot with enough water to cover. Bring to a boil, reduce heat, cover, and simmer until tender when pierced with a fork, about 3 hours. Allow tongue to cool in its cooked juices. Remove tongue and drain. Pull off the skin and allow to cool further. Wrap with a piece of cheesecloth, then plastic wrap, then foil. Store in refrigerate for up to 2 weeks. Slice before serving.

NOTE *Saltpeter (potassium nitrate) gives the characteristic red color to many cured meats and also acts as a preservative. It is sold in most drug-stores. If you are concerned about consuming nitrates, bicarbonate of soda may be substituted, but it is not as effective.*

PICKLED TONGUE WITH PARSLEY-ANCHOVY DRESSING {*Serves 6*}

I believe no meat is as versatile, economical, and delicious as pickled tongue. At my house, we call it "emergency meat" and always try to keep some in the refrigerator in case unexpected guests drop by. Pickled tongue can be roasted for a main course or made into quick and easy sandwiches and salads. When my children were young, they loved finding tongue sandwiches in their school lunch boxes. Although tongue isn't always thought of as a treat for kids, this tender meat is as appealing and certainly more wholesome than fast-food specialties and packaged "mystery meats." Pickled tongue is available at most ethnic delis and kosher butchers. Or try my Home-Cured Pickled Tongue (page 145).

1 pickled beef tongue (3 to 4 pounds)
Boiling water, for simmering
1 recipe Parsley-Anchovy Dressing (page 50)
Fresh parsley sprigs, for garnish

❦ If the tongue is very salty, soak it in a bowl of cold water to cover for 4 to 5 hours and drain.

❦ Place tongue in a large pot or Dutch oven, pour boiling water over it to cover, and simmer, covered, until tender, 2 to 4 hours. Leave it in the water until it is cool enough to handle. Then skin tongue and remove all the dry hard portions and the root.

❦ Meanwhile, prepare Parsley-Anchovy Dressing. To serve, slice tongue and place it on a large platter in a slightly overlapping pattern. Spoon some dressing on each slice and garnish with parsley. Pass extra dressing on the side.

KNOCKWURST AND BAKED BEANS {*Serves 4*}

This is absolutely my favorite deli food. It was the first dish I ordered at the opening of the Broadway Deli. The knockwurst sausages are served in a shallow soup bowl on top of a mound of bubbling baked beans. Serve with assorted mustards, sauerkraut, and toasted hamburger buns or kaiser rolls.

4 cups baked beans
(preferably homemade, page 85)
8 knockwurst (4 ounces each)

❦ Prepare baked beans and keep warm.

❦ In a large pot of boiling water, place knockwurst, reduce heat, and poach until tender and cooked through, about 20 minutes. Ladle beans into heated, shallow bowls and place knockwurst on top.

FRESH FROM THE DELI BAKERY

CHAPTER 7

Aword about breads: Whether you're in Europe, the Middle East, or the USA, breads are an integral component of deli staples. Breads come in all shapes and sizes and are made with a myriad of different flours and grains. Pumpernickel, focaccia, sourdough—it seems like there's a bread to suit everyone. ❧ The French prefer baguettes, those long skinny loaves, and, of course, their beloved croissants. In Middle Eastern delis, it's pita bread all the way, while in many Scandinavian delis, limpa bread and dark rye hold court. ❧ Jewish-style delis are home to bagels, which now come in a cornucopia of flavors—everything from blueberry to bran. Kaiser and onion rolls and rye bread maintain their stature here, too. ❧ In Europe, I love to watch the different ways that breads are transported from bakery to home. You'll usually spot the loaves unwrapped, resting in baskets, tucked under arms, or tied perilously to bicycle racks. And if you've ever been lucky enough to taste fresh-baked bread in Europe, you'll know why you often see these loaves in transit with a large bite taken out of one end. This chapter is filled with all sorts of classic deli breads and rolls, plus many new varieties that are currently the rage at contemporary delis. Quick Olive-Basil Bread, Deli Onion-Rye Bread, French Country Bread—the recipes are here for your munching pleasure. Recipe testers who worked with me on this book flipped for the Soft Pretzels; they couldn't believe how easy they are to make. ❧ Unless bread is fresh from the oven, it should be heated in the oven or toasted on a griddle over an open fire until the crust is ➜

RECIPES

crunchy. I use a wire camp toaster that I brought back from Italy and toast my bread on top of the gas burner. ❧ I know that it can be difficult to become inspired to bake bread when you can now buy so many great varieties, so I decided to compile a list of motivational reasons:

❧ *You can develop your own variations and limit fats, sugar, and salt as desired.*

❧ *Baking bread is a creative art, and the process can feel extremely rewarding.*

❧ *Making bread is a wonderful project to do with children.*

❧ *Homemade bread freezes well: When defrosted and reheated, it's impossible to taste the difference from bread just out of the oven.*

❧ *Most important of all, your favorite deli, the one with the great breads, isn't always open when you are seized with a craving for fresh-baked bread.*

BAKING WITH YEAST

❧ *Always check the package for expiration date.*

❧ *Active dry yeast and fresh cake yeast are interchangeable; 1 fresh cake (0.6 ounce) of yeast equals 1 package (¼ ounce or 7 grams) of active dry yeast.*

❧ *Active dry yeast is usually dissolved in lukewarm water to proof it.*

❧ *Proofing active dry yeast with warm water and sugar is a test for freshness. It should begin foaming in about a minute.*

❧ *Yeast dough should be thoroughly worked to develop the gluten. Nonyeast dough, as for a pie crust, should always be worked as little as possible to retain the tenderness.*

❧ *While yeast dough is rising, brush the surface with oil and keep covered with a towel to avoid drying out.*

❧ *In my kitchen, a warm place is the cabinet above the ovens. I leave the cabinet door ajar and place the bowl of yeast dough in the cabinet to rise.*

WHOLE-WHEAT BREAD

{*Makes 2 medium loaves*}

L ow-fat, firm, and chewy, this healthful bread makes wonderful toast and great sandwiches. The stone-ground whole-wheat flour is the ingredient that makes this bread so remarkable.

2 packages active dry yeast
2 cups lukewarm water
Pinch sugar
2 tablespoons safflower or vegetable oil,
    plus more as needed
2 tablespoons dark molasses
1 tablespoon coarse kosher salt
2 cups stone-ground whole-wheat flour
3½ cups bread flour, plus more as needed
1 egg, lightly beaten with 1 tablespoon sugar
¼ cup yellow cornmeal

In a glass measuring cup, sprinkle yeast over ½ cup of the lukewarm water. Add sugar, stir to dissolve, and set aside until foamy, about 2 minutes.

In the bowl of a heavy-duty electric mixer, at low speed blend the remaining 1½ cups lukewarm water with oil, molasses, and kosher salt. Add yeast mixture and blend well. In another large bowl combine whole-wheat and bread flours and add to the yeast mixture, 1 cup at a time, blending well after each addition, until dough comes together. Scrape the loose flour from sides of the bowl and continue beating until dough comes together.

Turn out dough onto a floured board and knead 5 minutes, adding additional flour as needed, until dough is smooth and elastic. Place dough in a lightly oiled bowl and brush the top with oil. Cover with a towel and let rise in a warm place until doubled in size, 1½ to 2 hours.

Generously oil two 5½ x 9½-inch loaf pans and sprinkle with cornmeal. Divide dough in half and shape each half into a loaf to fit the prepared pans, kneading out any air bubbles. Place dough in loaf pans, cover loaves with towels, and let them rise in a warm place until doubled in size, about 1½ hours.

Preheat the oven to 375° F.

Brush loaves with beaten egg mixture and bake until they are golden brown and begin to shrink away from the sides of the pan, 35 to 40 minutes. Remove from pans immediately and cool on wire racks.

SQUAW BREAD

{*Makes 2 large round loaves*}

To make squaw bread, the Broadway Deli uses Combi Corn, a mixture of grits, grains, seeds, and flours, used by commercial bakers. I've included it in the recipe, in case you're lucky enough to find it. A local bakery might sell you some. Don't worry if you can't locate it; this dense, slightly sweet, crusty brown bread is delicious without it.

½ cup Combi Corn, optional
½ cup hot water, optional
2½ cups whole-wheat flour
2¾ cups bread flour, plus more as needed
½ tablespoon salt
2 packages active dry yeast
½ cup dark molasses
¼ cup safflower oil or vegetable oil,
    plus more as needed
1¼ cups lukewarm water

❦ If using Combi Corn, combine it in a small bowl with the hot water and set aside for 1 hour.

❦ In the bowl of a heavy-duty electric mixer, on low speed blend whole-wheat and bread flours, salt, and yeast. Add Combi Corn, if using, molasses, oil, and the 1¼ cups lukewarm water and blend until dough is soft and thick enough to work by hand.

❦ Use a bread hook attachment and beat dough for 8 to 10 minutes. Or transfer dough to a floured board and knead it 3 minutes, adding additional flour as needed, until dough is smooth and elastic. Place in an oiled bowl and brush oil on top of dough. Cover with a towel and let rise in a warm place until doubled in size, 1½ to 2 hours.

❦ Generously oil 2 baking sheets. Divide the dough in half and shape each half into a round loaf, kneading out any air bubbles. Place loaves on baking sheets, cover with towels, and let rise in a warm place until doubled in size, about 1½ hours.

❦ Preheat the oven to 375° F.

❦ Bake until the loaves are golden brown, 35 to 40 minutes. Transfer to wire racks and cool.

UNSALTED BUTTER AND MARGARINE

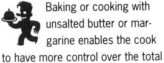
Baking or cooking with unsalted butter or margarine enables the cook to have more control over the total amount of salt in the recipe.

❦ *Unsalted butter has a shorter refrigerator life than salted butter; the salt acts as a preservative. You can tell by the smell when butter is fresh. Butter that is over the hill has a slightly sour smell.*

❦ *Buy extra unsalted butter and store in the freezer. A perfect guarantee for fresh unsalted butter on the spot.*

❦ *You may substitute salted butter or margarine in these recipes, but use less salt.*

❦ *Non-dairy margarine may be substituted for butter or margarine in any of the recipes.*

DELI ONION-RYE BREAD

{*Makes 2 medium loaves*}

ere's how to make a true deli rye bread with a pungent onion flavor. Slice it thin and serve it toasted to accompany a cheese platter, chopped chicken livers, or other appetizers. It's also terrific as a sandwich bread for any of the deli meats in this book.

2 packages active dry yeast
1 cup lukewarm water
1 tablespoon sugar
1 tablespoon vegetable shortening, melted
1 tablespoon coarse kosher salt
1 tablespoon caraway seeds
1 tablespoon minced dried onions
1½ cups rye flour
1½ cups bread flour or high-gluten flour, plus
    more as needed
Safflower oil or vegetable oil, as needed
Yellow cornmeal, for baking sheets
1 egg, lightly beaten

In a glass measuring cup, sprinkle yeast over ½ cup of the lukewarm water. Add a pinch of the sugar, stir to dissolve, and set aside until foamy, about 2 minutes.

❦ In the bowl of a heavy-duty electric mixer, on low speed, add the remaining sugar and ½ cup lukewarm water, vegetable shortening, and salt; blend well. Blend in caraway seeds, onions, and 1 tablespoon at a time of rye flour and bread flour, blending until the dough comes together.

❦ Turn out dough onto a floured board and knead about 5 minutes, adding additional flour as needed, until dough is smooth and elastic. Place dough in an oiled bowl and brush oil on the top. Cover with a towel and let rise in a warm place until doubled in size, 1½ to 2 hours.

❦ Line a baking sheet with aluminum foil, brush with oil, and sprinkle with cornmeal. Divide dough in half and shape each half into a round or oval loaf, kneading out any air bubbles. Place on the prepared baking sheet, cover with towels, and let rise in a warm place until doubled, about 1½ hours.

❦ Preheat the oven to 375°F.

❦ Brush loaves with the beaten egg and bake until golden brown, 35 to 40 minutes. Transfer loaves to wire racks and cool.

WHITE SANDWICH LOAF

{ *Makes 2 loaves* }

H ow can spongy packaged white bread possibly compete with homemade? This light, firm, and flavorful bread tastes delicious plain or toasted.

2 packages active dry yeast

1½ cups lukewarm water

1 teaspoon sugar

1½ teaspoons salt

1 tablespoon vegetable shortening, melted

1 tablespoon egg white

3½ cups bread flour,
    plus more as needed

Safflower oil or vegetable oil,
    as needed

1 egg, lightly beaten with 1 tablespoon sugar

❦ In a glass measuring cup, sprinkle yeast over ½ cup of the lukewarm water. Add sugar, stir to dissolve, and set aside until foamy, about 2 minutes.

❦ In the bowl of a heavy-duty electric mixer, on low speed, blend the yeast mixture, salt, the remaining 1 cup lukewarm water, shortening, and egg white. Blend in flour, 1 cup at a time, until dough is soft and thick enough to work by hand.

❦ Turn out dough onto a floured board and knead 5 minutes, adding additional flour as needed, until dough is smooth and elastic. Place dough in an oiled bowl and brush oil on the top. Cover with a towel and let rise in a warm place until doubled in size, 1½ to 2 hours.

❦ Generously oil two 5½ x 9½-inch loaf pans or 1 large baking sheet. Divide dough in half and shape each into a loaf to fit the prepared pans, kneading out any air bubbles. Place loaves on pans, cover with towels, and let rise in a warm place until doubled in size, about 1½ hours.

❦ Preheat the oven to 375° F.

❦ Brush loaves with the beaten egg mixture and bake until golden brown and loaves begin to shrink away from the sides of the pan, 35 to 40 minutes. Remove from pans immediately and cool on wire racks.

NOTE *If you have a dough-hook attachment, use it to knead the dough for a lighter texture.*

FRENCH COUNTRY BREAD

{*Makes 2 large loaves*}

This is a robust loaf that picks up a warm beige color and firm, grainy texture from the rye flour. Containing no fat, it's a perfect base for hearty sandwiches—toasted it's even better.

1 package active dry yeast
2½ cups lukewarm water
Pinch sugar
5 cups unbleached all-purpose flour,
    plus more as needed
1 cup rye flour
2 teaspoons salt
Safflower oil or vegetable oil,
    as needed

❦ In a glass measuring cup, sprinkle yeast over ½ cup of the lukewarm water. Add sugar, stir to dissolve, and set aside until foamy, about 2 minutes.

❦ In the bowl of a heavy-duty electric mixer, blend the remaining 2 cups lukewarm water and yeast mixture. In another large bowl, combine unbleached flour, rye flour, and salt. Add 4 cups of the flour mixture to the yeast mixture, 1 cup at a time, blending after each addition until dough comes together. It may be wet and sticky.

❦ Turn out dough onto a floured board and knead, adding enough of the remaining flour mixture, until dough is no longer sticky, about 3 minutes. Cover with a towel and let rise in a warm place until doubled, in size, about 1 hour.

❦ Divide dough in half and knead each half into round loaves by rolling dough into a ball and pulling the edges into the center, pinching to seal. Place loaves on lightly oiled baking sheets, seam-side down. Brush with oil, cover with towels, and let rise in a warm place until almost doubled about 1 hour.

❦ Preheat the oven to 400° F.

❦ Using the tip of a sharp knife, cut a 2-inch-square design on the top surface of each loaf. Bake until golden brown and the loaves sound hollow when tapped, about 45 minutes. Cool on a wire rack.

DELI RAISIN-WALNUT BREAD

{Makes 2 large loaves or 2 dozen rolls}

A Broadway Deli signature treat, this popular walnut bread is sweetened by two varieties of raisins and is made without eggs or shortening. An excellent breakfast bread, it tastes especially good toasted and topped with jam. Bake several loaves and freeze; when bread is reheated, no one will have a clue it's not freshly baked. You can also use this recipe to make rolls (see variation).

2 packages active dry yeast

2½ cups lukewarm water

Pinch sugar

4 cups bread flour, plus more as needed

1 cup rye flour

1 tablespoon salt

4 cups toasted chopped walnuts (page 182)

1 cup dark raisins

3 cups golden raisins

Safflower oil or vegetable oil, as needed

❧ In a glass measuring cup, sprinkle yeast over ½ cup of the lukewarm water. Add sugar, stir to dissolve, and set aside until foamy, about 2 minutes.

❧ In the bowl of a heavy-duty electric mixer, combine remaining 2 cups water and yeast mixture. Add both flours, 1 cup at a time, blending each time on medium speed for 2 minutes. Add salt and blend 2 more minutes. Add walnuts and both raisins and blend 2 more minutes.

❧ Turn out dough onto a floured board and knead into a ball. Place dough in a lightly oiled bowl and brush the top with oil. Cover with a towel and let rise in a warm place for 30 minutes.

❧ Line a baking sheet with aluminum foil and oil lightly. Divide dough into 2 halves. Shape each half into an oval loaf and place on baking sheet. Cover with a towel and let rise again in a warm place for 30 minutes.

❧ Preheat the oven to 350° F. Bake loaves until dark brown on the bottom and sides, about 45 minutes. Cool on wire racks.

RAISIN-WALNUT ROLLS *Divide dough into 24 equal pieces (instead of loaves) and shape each piece into round rolls. Place on baking sheets, 2 inches apart, and let rise as directed in bread recipe, but bake about 25 minutes. Cool on wire racks. Makes 2 dozen rolls*

SWEDISH LIMPA BREAD

{ *Makes 2 large or 4 small loaves* }

This aromatic loaf, flavored with fennel and molasses, should be sliced super thin, toasted, and spread lightly with unsalted butter. Serve it with a salad or hearty soup; good for sandwiches, too.

2 packages active dry yeast
½ cup lukewarm water
Pinch sugar
½ cup cracked wheat
2 teaspoons fennel seeds
Grated zest of 1 orange
2 teaspoons coarse kosher salt
⅓ cup dark molasses
3 tablespoons vegetable shortening
1 cup boiling water
¾ cup nonfat milk, heated to lukewarm
2 cups rye flour
4½ cups unbleached all-purpose flour,
    plus more as needed
Safflower oil or vegetable oil, as needed
¼ cup yellow cornmeal
2 tablespoons unsalted butter, melted

In a glass measuring cup, sprinkle yeast over the lukewarm water. Add sugar, stir to dissolve, and set aside until foamy, about 2 minutes.

❦ In the bowl of a heavy-duty electric mixer, at low speed, combine cracked wheat, fennel seeds, orange zest, salt, molasses, and shortening. Pour the boiling water over mixture and mix well. Cool to lukewarm.

❦ Blend in the yeast mixture, milk, and rye flour. Then blend in all-purpose flour, 1 cup at a time, until dough is firm enough to work by hand. Turn out dough onto a floured board and knead until smooth and elastic, about 5 minutes. Brush dough with oil and place in a large oiled bowl. Cover with a towel and let rise in a warm place until doubled in size, about 1 hour.

❦ Punch down and shape into 2 large loaves or 4 small round loaves. Line baking sheets with aluminum foil, brush with oil, and sprinkle with cornmeal. Place the loaves on sheets, cover with a towel, and let rise in a warm place until doubled in size, about 1 hour.

❦ Place an ovenproof pan filled with water on the bottom shelf of the oven. Preheat the oven to 350° F.

❦ Bake bread until crusty, about 1 hour and 15 minutes. While hot, brush with melted butter; cool on a wire rack.

CHALLAH

A deli staple, this European egg bread flaunts a glossy brown crust and a moist, golden interior. Challah upgrades any sandwich and is the undisputed prime choice for making French toast.

1 package active dry yeast
1½ cups lukewarm water
Pinch sugar
3 eggs
⅓ cup honey
4 tablespoons unsalted butter or margarine, melted
1 tablespoon salt
5 to 6 cups unbleached all-purpose flour
Safflower oil or vegetable oil, as needed
Yellow cornmeal, for baking sheet
1 egg white, lightly beaten
Sesame seeds or poppy seeds, for garnish

❦ In a glass measuring cup, sprinkle yeast over ½ cup of the lukewarm water. Add sugar, stir to dissolve, and set aside until foamy, about 2 minutes.

❦ In the bowl of a heavy-duty electric mixer, on low speed, beat together the 3 whole eggs, honey, and butter. Add remaining 1 cup lukewarm water and blend well. Blend in the yeast mixture. Add salt and 5 cups of the flour to the batter, 1 cup at a time, beating after each addition, until the dough is thick enough to work by hand, about 2 minutes.

❦ Turn out dough onto a floured board and knead 5 minutes, adding enough additional flour to make a smooth and elastic dough. Place dough in an oiled bowl; brush oil on top of the dough, cover with a towel, and let rise in a warm place until doubled in size, about 1 hour.

❦ Divide dough into 3 portions. Form each portion into a rope, about 8 inches long. Pinch together 1 end of each of the 3 ropes and braid the ropes, pinching the bottom ends together when you complete the braiding.

❦ Lightly oil a baking sheet and generously sprinkle with cornmeal. Place braided loaf on sheet, cover with a towel, and let rise in a warm place until doubled in size, about 40 minutes.

❦ Preheat the oven to 350° F.

❦ Brush loaf with egg white and sprinkle with sesame or poppy seeds. Bake until golden brown, 30 to 40 minutes. Cool on a wire rack.

FOCACCIA WITH ONIONS AND ROSEMARY

{*Makes 2 focaccia; serves 12*}

In many Italian delis, flat slabs of focaccia bread arrive piping hot the moment you are seated. It's usually topped with anything from Parmesan cheese to sun-dried tomatoes. Sliced onions and fresh rosemary give this version an authentic flavor. The crispy crunch of coarse salt adds a delicious touch. There are very thick focaccia and very thin; I prefer it on the thinner side. The choice is yours. To make this recipe you will need two jelly-roll pans or heavy metal baking pans with sides at least one inch high. The dough for focaccia can also be used to make Italian Bread Sticks (page 161).

2 packages active dry yeast

2 cups lukewarm water

Pinch sugar

½ cup olive oil, plus more as needed

2 tablespoons coarse kosher salt

6½ cups unbleached all-purpose flour,
    plus more as needed

2 small onions, thinly sliced

¼ cup snipped fresh rosemary or
    2 tablespoons dried rosemary, crumbled

❦ In a glass measuring cup, sprinkle yeast over ½ cup of the lukewarm water. Add sugar, stir to dissolve, and set aside until foamy, about 2 minutes.

❦ In the bowl of a heavy-duty mixer, at low speed, blend the remaining 1½ cups lukewarm water, 2 tablespoons of the olive oil, and 1 tablespoon of the salt. Blend in the yeast mixture. Add 5½ cups of the flour, 1 cup at a time, blending after each addition to form a soft dough.

❦ Dust a board with ½ cup flour, turn out dough onto it, and knead 3 minutes, adding additional flour if dough is sticky. When smooth and elastic, shape into a ball, brush with olive oil, and place in an oiled bowl. Cover with a towel and let rise in a warm place until doubled in size, about 30 minutes. Punch down, cover, and let rise for 15 minutes.

❦ In a small bowl, blend 2 tablespoons of the olive oil with onion, rosemary, and remaining 1 tablespoon salt. Cover with plastic wrap and set aside.

❦ Transfer dough to a lightly floured board, divide into halves and knead each half into a rectangle (or oval) measuring about 6x8 inches. Using a sharp knife cut three 1½-inch slashes at both ends. Lift flat dough in the air and stretch gently until cut portions open. Brush each of two 10½x15-inch jelly-roll pans with 2 tablespoons of the olive oil. Place each loaf on prepared baking pan. Using your knuckles, press the surface of the dough all over, making a pattern of indentations. Spread half of the onion mixture over the top, up to 1 inch from the edge. Sprinkle with half of the remaining olive oil. Repeat with the other half. Cover with towels and let rise in a warm place for 20 minutes. Press the surface again making additional indentations.

❦ Preheat the oven to 375°F.

❦ Bake until golden brown, about 20 minutes. Serve hot or cool on wire racks.

VARIATIONS *Instead of the onion-rosemary mixture, sprinkle tops with minced garlic and freshly grated Parmesan cheese or with sun-dried tomatoes and sliced olives.*

QUICK OLIVE-BASIL BREAD

{ *Makes 2 loaves* }

This is truly a quick bread—no kneading or waiting to rise. It's wonderful with pasta dinners or other Italian-inspired foods.

1 cup brine-cured black olives

2½ cups unbleached all-purpose flour,
plus more as needed

1 tablespoon baking powder

2 tablespoons sugar

1 teaspoon salt

½ cup fresh basil leaves, minced

2 eggs

⅓ cup olive oil, plus more as needed

½ cup finely chopped onion

⅔ cup buttermilk

Preheat the oven to 350°F.

On a cutting board, crush olives lightly with the flat side of a large knife and discard the pits. Drain olives on paper towels and chop them.

In a large mixing bowl, stir together flour, baking powder, sugar, salt, and basil. Add olives and toss the mixture well. In a small bowl, whisk together eggs, olive oil, onion, and buttermilk. Add to the flour mixture, stirring until the batter comes together.

Brush two 8x4x2½-inch loaf pans with olive oil. Divide dough in half and transfer to a lightly floured board. Shape each half into a smooth loaf and place in the prepared loaf pan. Bake until a toothpick inserted in the center comes out clean, about 1 hour and 15 minutes. Turn out onto wire racks and cool.

DELI HAMBURGER BUNS

{ *Makes 1 dozen buns* }

Home-baked hamburger buns taste far superior to any store-bought version. You can always double the recipe and store the extra fluffy buns in plastic bags in the freezer for last-minute picnics or barbecues. If you shape the dough into 6-inch ovals, you'll create hot dog buns.

1 recipe White Sandwich Loaf dough (page 153)
Additional flour, as needed
Safflower oil or vegetable oil, for baking sheet

Prepare White Sandwich Loaf dough; knead and let rise as directed in recipe.

Line a large baking sheet with aluminum foil and brush with oil. On a lightly floured board, knead dough into a long rope, pressing out any air bubbles. Cut into 12 equal pieces and shape into buns. Place on the prepared baking sheets, 2 inches apart. Cover buns with a towel and let them rise in a warm place until doubled in size, about 1 hour.

Place another baking sheet on top of buns and gently press down to flatten them slightly. Sprinkle buns with flour and, using a sharp knife or scissors, cut an "X" across the top. Cover and let rise in a warm place for 30 minutes.

Preheat the oven to 375°F.

Bake buns until lightly browned, about 20 minutes. Cool on wire racks.

IZZY'S AUTHENTIC BAGELS {*Makes about 15 bagels*}

I never knew how to make perfect bagels until I met Izzy Cohen, an elderly retired baker, who still makes bagels for his friends. He recently came to my house to demonstrate his technique, bringing his own high-gluten flour. Once you learn the basic process, you'll love making bagels in many varieties—plain, onion, poppy seed, cinnamon, or your own special creations. You might have to go to a health food store to find the malt for this recipe.

2 cups cold water

2 tablespoons sugar

¾ teaspoon salt

1 tablespoon malt

1 tablespoon safflower oil

8 cups high-gluten flour
(12 to 13 percent gluten),
or 8 cups unbleached all-purpose flour
mixed with ¼ cup powdered gluten,
plus more as needed

5 teaspoons active dry yeast

1 tablespoon yellow cornmeal

❧ In the bowl of a heavy-duty electric mixer, blend the water, sugar, salt, malt, and oil on medium speed. In another large bowl, mix 6 cups of the flour with yeast; gradually add flour mixture to water mixture and blend until the dough comes together. Add the remaining 2 cups flour, beating until smooth. (If any dry flour mixture remains in the bottom of the bowl, add several drops of water to moisten it and continue beating 5 minutes.)

❧ Transfer dough to a lightly floured board, cover with a towel and let rest 5 minutes. Divide dough into 15 pieces and cover with a towel while you knead and shape each piece. Knead by folding each piece in half and pushing out any air pockets, then fold in half again and repeat. Shape into a rope about 5 inches long. Form into a doughnut shape, overlap ends by about 1 inch, and knead into a smooth perfect circle. Repeat the process with remaining pieces of dough.

❧ Sprinkle cornmeal on the board and place bagels on top. Cover with a towel and let rest 5 minutes.

❧ Preheat the oven to 425° F.

❧ Fill a large heavy pot with water and bring to a rolling boil. Working in batches, drop 4 to 6 bagels (do not crowd) into boiling water and boil 10 seconds only. At this time, bagels should rise to the top of the water. Transfer with a slotted spoon to a wire rack and drain.

❧ Transfer bagels to a parchment-lined baking sheet 2 inches apart. Bake until golden brown, about 10 minutes. Cool on a wire racks.

VARIATION *Mix together chopped onion and poppy seeds or caraway seeds with a little coarse kosher salt. After boiling and draining bagels, press the top of each bagel into seed mixture and bake as directed.*

ITALIAN BREAD STICKS *{Makes about 6 dozen bread sticks}*

Prepare focaccia dough and make bread sticks with the help of a pasta machine, or use half of the dough for focaccia and the other half for bread sticks. Thin crispy bread sticks, stored in plastic bags and reheated, taste as fresh as the day they were made.

1 recipe focaccia dough (page 00)
Additional flour, as needed
Olive oil, for baking sheets
    and top of bread sticks
Egg white, for brushing bread sticks
Coarse kosher salt, for bread sticks

❦ Prepare focaccia dough (omitting onion and rosemary). Knead and let rise 2 times as directed in recipe.

PASTA MACHINE METHOD
❦ Pinch off a ball of dough 2 inches in diameter and flatten it with the palm of your hand to a ½-inch thickness. Lightly dust with flour. Set the pasta machine rollers as far apart as possible. Guide the dough between the rollers and roll it through. Coat with flour and feed the sheet through the wide noodle-cutting blades, cutting it into strips about ¼ inch wide and 10 to 15 inches long. Carefully place the sheet of cut strips on floured board and quickly separate each strip.

HAND-ROLLED METHOD
❦ Divide the dough into 4 portions and roll out each portion on a floured board into rectangles ⅓ inch thick. Cut each rectangle into 2-inch squares; roll each square up tightly and then roll back and forth with the palm of your hand into a long, narrow stick, as thin as a pencil and 10 to 12 inches long.

SHAPING AND BAKING BREAD STICKS
❦ Line baking sheets with aluminum foil and brush with olive oil. Shape strips into straight bread sticks or twist them into other shapes, such as canes. Place bread sticks on prepared sheets. Cover and let rise in a warm place for 15 minutes.
❦ Preheat the oven to 350° F. Brush with egg white, sprinkle with salt, and bake until lightly browned, about 10 to 15 minutes.

WHOLE-WHEAT BRAIDED ROLLS {Makes 1 dozen rolls}

*O*ne morning I watched and worked with Machelle Toman, the Broadway Deli's baker and pastry chef, as she baked these marvelous twisted rolls. Once you learn the braiding technique, you will be as thrilled as I was by the professional-looking results.

1 recipe Whole-Wheat Bread dough (page 150)
Safflower or vegetable oil, for baking sheet
¼ cup yellow cornmeal
1 egg, lightly beaten
Sesame seeds, for garnish

❦ Prepare Whole-Wheat Bread dough; knead and let rise as directed in recipe.

❦ Line a baking sheet with aluminum foil, brush lightly with oil, and sprinkle with cornmeal.

❦ Knead dough into a long rope about 18-inches long and 2 inches thick; cut into 12 equal pieces. Knead each piece into a smooth rope, about ¼ inch thick and 14 inches long. With right end of rope form a loose loop by crossing the end over the rope and then back up through the center of the loop, leaving a little knob within the circle. Take left end of rope and bring it over and down through the center of the circle two times and tuck end under. It will resemble a round braid effect.

❦ Place braided rolls on the prepared baking sheet 2 inches apart. Cover with a towel and let rise in a warm place 1 hour.

❦ Preheat the oven to 375° F.

❦ Brush rolls with beaten egg, sprinkle with sesame seeds, and bake until golden brown, about 20 minutes. Cool on wire racks.

VARIATION *For pretzel shape or knot: Pull off golf-ball-size pieces of dough. Roll each piece into a 10-inch strip. Knead each piece into a smooth rope, then tie into a knot. Makes about 18.*

KAISER ROLLS

{*Makes about 1 dozen rolls*}

The crusty kaiser roll is compatible with almost every sandwich filling. The classic shape sports five petals and is completely covered with poppy seeds. The secret to achieving crusty rolls is to brush them with water and bake them in an oven that is moistened with a pan of water.

4½ cups unbleached all-purpose flour
1 package active dry yeast
1 tablespoon sugar
1 teaspoon salt
1½ cups hot water
1 teaspoon malt extract, optional
1 egg
1 egg white
1 tablespoon vegetable shortening
Safflower oil or vegetable oil, for bowl
½ cup rye flour, for dusting
1 cup poppy seeds

❦ In the bowl of a heavy-duty electric mixer, blend 3½ cups of the flour with yeast, sugar, and salt. Pour in the hot water and malt extract, if using. Blend until smooth, about 1 minute. Add egg, egg white, and shortening and beat until mixture is smooth. Add the remaining 1 cup flour, ¼ cup at a time, until dough comes away from the sides of the bowl. Transfer dough to a floured board. Knead 5 minutes, adding flour if dough is wet.

❦ Place dough in an oiled bowl, cover with a towel, and let rise in a warm place until doubled in size, about 1 hour. Uncover bowl and punch down dough. Cover and let rise again in a warm place until doubled, about 45 minutes.

❦ Roll out dough into an 18-inch-long rope and cut into 12 pieces, each about 1½ inches long. Shape each piece into smooth rounds. Cover and let rest 5 minutes.

❦ Flatten each round to about ¼ inch thick. Dust lightly with rye flour. Place your thumb in the center of a round. With the forefinger of your other hand pick up a section equal to about ⅕ of the dough and fold the portion slightly over your thumb. Pick up the second section and repeat the procedure, overlapping slightly. Repeat this 3 more times and press the last piece into the gap made by removing your thumb.

❦ Sprinkle baking sheets liberally with poppy seeds. Place each roll face down on the sheet, 2 inches apart. Cover with a towel and let rise in a warm place until doubled in size, about 45 minutes.

❦ Carefully place a pan of water on the bottom shelf of the oven. Preheat the oven to 450° F.

❦ Uncover rolls and turn them right side up. Bake until crispy and brown all over, about 25 minutes. Cool on wire racks.

SOFT PRETZELS

{Makes 12 to 14 pretzels}

H omemade soft pretzels are addictive. These are chewy on the outside and soft and moist inside. Form your own shapes.

1 package active dry yeast
1½ cups lukewarm water
1 tablespoon sugar
4 cups unbleached all-purpose flour,
    plus more as needed
1 teaspoon salt
⅛ teaspoon ground ginger
Safflower oil or vegetable oil,
    for baking sheets
Coarse kosher salt, as needed
1 egg, lightly beaten

❧ In a glass measuring cup, sprinkle yeast over ½ cup of the lukewarm water. Add 1 teaspoon of the sugar, stir to dissolve, and set aside until foamy, about 2 minutes.

❧ In the bowl of a heavy-duty electric mixer, on medium speed, blend flour, the remaining 2 teaspoons sugar, the 1 teaspoon salt, and ginger. Add yeast mixture, rinse out cup with the remaining 1 cup lukewarm water and add to dough. Beat on medium speed until dough comes together.

❧ Turn out dough onto a lightly floured board and knead until smooth, 3 to 5 minutes. Divide dough into 12 to 14 small pieces. With the palms of your hands roll each piece into a rope about 1 foot long. Twist into pretzel shapes of your own design.

❧ Preheat the oven to 425°F.

❧ Brush baking sheets lightly with oil and sprinkle with kosher salt. Arrange pretzels 2 inches apart on baking sheets. Let rise in a warm place 20 minutes. Brush with beaten egg and sprinkle lightly with kosher salt. Bake until brown, about 15 minutes. Cool on wire racks.

VARIATION *Sauté minced onions or minced garlic, lightly season with salt, and sprinkle on unbaked pretzels. Or, instead of twisting the dough into pretzels, make bread sticks out of the ropes.*

MUFFINS AND DANISH

The muffin is fast catching up with the bagel in deli bakeries. I have included several best-sellers, including some mouthwatering bran muffins. But wait until you see the real star of this section—the Broadway Deli's recipe for a Danish pastry dough that is pure magic. This one recipe provides professional-looking (and tasting) bear claws, cinnamon snails, sticky buns, and croissants. You will be inspired to add your own fillings and flavorings. Sure, it takes a little time, but the spectacular results are worth it. For good measure, you will find scones too. Muffins freeze well. Just cool and place in plastic freezer bags. They will keep up to 3 months. Defrost and heat before serving for a just-baked flavor.

BANANA-BRAN MUFFINS   {Makes 16 muffins}

There's much more to these muffins than just bananas and bran. Raisins, apricots, and dates go a long way toward creating a breakfast treat that's a healthful and flavorful way to begin the day.

2 cups unsweetened low-sodium
  All-Bran cereal
1 cup milk
¼ pound unsalted butter or margarine,
  at room temperature
¾ cup sugar
2 tablespoons honey
3 eggs
½ cup mashed bananas
2 cups unbleached all-purpose flour
1 tablespoon baking powder
½ teaspoon salt
½ cup golden raisins
½ cup diced dried apricots
½ cup diced pitted dates
16 paper liners or vegetable oil,
  for muffin cups

❦ Preheat the oven to 400° F.

❦ In a medium bowl, stir together bran and milk. Cover and let stand, mixing occasionally to keep bran moistened, about 10 minutes.

❦ In a large bowl, using an electric mixer, cream butter, sugar, and honey. Blend in eggs, 1 at a time, until mixed well. Blend in bananas and bran mixture. In another bowl, combine flour, baking powder, and salt, and blend into butter mixture. Fold in raisins, apricots, and dates.

❦ Line 16 muffin cups with paper liners or brush with oil. Spoon batter into the cups ⅔ full. Bake until golden brown and a toothpick inserted in the center comes out clean, about 30 minutes.

JOAN'S BEST BRAN MUFFINS   {Makes 1 dozen muffins}

Joan Bram, a great friend and enthusiastic recipe tester, shared this bran muffin recipe after experimenting with many others. It's her favorite. For freshly baked bran muffins, store the batter, well covered, in the refrigerator and bake as needed.

½ cup golden raisins
½ cup apple juice
12 paper liners or vegetable oil,
  for muffin cups
¼ cup vegetable shortening
½ cup brown sugar
¼ cup molasses
2 eggs
1 cup milk
1½ cups 100 percent natural
  unprocessed bran
1 cup unbleached all-purpose flour
1½ teaspoons baking soda
¾ teaspoon salt

❦ In a small bowl, plump raisins in apple juice until soft, about 30 minutes, and drain.

❦ Preheat the oven to 400° F.

❦ Line 1 dozen muffin cups with paper liners or brush with oil.

❦ In a large bowl, using an electric mixer, cream shortening and sugar. Add molasses and eggs and beat well. Mix in milk and bran.

❦ In another bowl, sift together flour, baking soda, and salt. Stir into the batter just until thoroughly blended. Fold in the drained raisins.

❦ Spoon batter into prepared muffin cups ⅔ full. Bake until a toothpick inserted in the center comes out clean, 15 to 20 minutes.

CORNMEAL MUFFINS

{*Makes 18 muffins or about 6 dozen miniature muffins*}

Large or small, these moist muffins are a welcome addition to any breakfast or brunch. They are particularly enticing when hollowed out in the center and filled with Turkey Chili for a Crowd (page 127) for an attention-getting appetizer at a buffet party.

3 eggs
3 cups buttermilk
2 tablespoons sugar
1 teaspoon salt
4 tablespoons vegetable shortening or
    unsalted butter, melted,
    plus more for muffin cups
2 cups yellow cornmeal
2 cups unbleached all-purpose flour
2 tablespoons baking powder
1 teaspoon baking soda
½ cup fresh or frozen corn kernels

❦ Preheat the oven to 450°F.

❦ In a large bowl beat eggs. Add buttermilk, sugar, salt, and shortening and blend well.

❦ In a medium bowl, combine cornmeal, flour, baking powder, and baking soda. Stir into egg mixture; add corn kernels, and mix lightly; do not beat.

❦ Line 18 large (2½-inch) muffin cups with paper liners or brush with butter. Or brush 5 to 6 dozen (1¼-inch) miniature muffin cups with butter. Spoon batter into the cups ⅔ full. Bake until a toothpick inserted in the center comes out clean, 15 to 18 minutes (or 10 to 12 minutes for minature muffins). Serve hot.

ZESTY ORANGE MUFFINS

{*Makes 1 dozen muffins*}

The flavor of fresh oranges really comes through in these muffins. Coating the orange zest and sections with flour before adding to the batter keeps them from becoming soggy. This technique preserves their zesty citrus taste throughout the baking process.

Grated zest of 2 oranges
1 cup seeded and chopped orange sections
    (membrane removed)
1¾ cups sifted cake flour
¼ pound unsalted butter,
    at room temperature
1 cup sugar
2 eggs
2 teaspoons baking powder
½ cup milk
¼ cup fresh orange juice
12 paper liners or vegetable oil,
    for muffin cups

❦ Preheat the oven to 400°F.

❦ Using a strainer, toss orange zest and sections with ¼ cup of the flour, shaking excess flour off. (Keeps zest from settling to bottom.) Set aside.

❦ In a large bowl, using an electric mixer, cream butter and sugar. Add 1 egg at a time, blending well after each addition.

❦ Combine the remaining 1½ cups flour and baking powder and blend into butter mixture alternately with milk and orange juice. Mix in the floured orange zest and orange sections.

❦ Line 1 dozen muffin cups with paper liners or brush with oil. Spoon batter into prepared muffin cups ¾ full. Bake until golden brown and a toothpick inserted in the center comes out clean, 25 to 30 minutes.

BROADWAY DELI SCONES {*Makes about 1 dozen scones*}

The Broadway Deli makes the best scones I've ever eaten—even surpassing those I've enjoyed in London's elegant tearooms. To make whole-wheat scones, substitute whole-wheat flour for half of the cake flour.

3 cups cake or pastry flour,
    plus more for board
1 tablespoon baking powder
3 tablespoons sugar
6 tablespoons unsalted butter,
    cut into pieces
½ cup currants
½ cup yellow raisins
1 cup sour cream
Vegetable oil, for baking sheet

❦ Preheat the oven to 350°F.
❦ In the bowl of a heavy-duty electric mixer, combine flour, baking powder, sugar, and butter until fine crumbs form. Add currants and raisins, and beat 30 seconds. Mix in the sour cream (do not overmix).
❦ Transfer dough to a floured board and knead into a smooth ball. Pat out dough about 1½ inches thick. Using a 2-inch-round cookie cutter, cut dough into rounds. Knead scraps into a ball, roll and cut into rounds.

❦ Line a baking sheet with aluminum foil and brush with oil. Place dough rounds on sheet, 2 inches apart, and bake until golden brown, about 20 minutes.

DELI DANISH PASTRY DOUGH

{ *Makes about 2¾ pounds dough* }

This is a versatile pastry dough that is well worth the time and effort. The noted chef Michel Richard, one of the Broadway Deli partners, began his career as a pastry chef in France. I watched him preparing pastry dough, step by step, and was inspired to use it in several varieties of Danish pastries. Cinnamon Danish Snails, Bear Claws, and Pecan Sticky Buns are just a few of the goodies you can make with this recipe. This dough recipe and each of the pastry recipes yield a large quantity. But the pastries freeze very well after baking.

¾ pound unsalted butter

4 cups bread flour,
  plus more for board

½ cup sugar

1 teaspoon salt

2 packages active dry yeast

3 tablespoons grated lemon zest, optional

4 eggs

⅓ to ½ cup milk, heated until lukewarm

❦ Cut ¼ pound of the butter into small pieces. In the bowl of a heavy-duty electric mixer, at medium speed, blend flour, sugar, salt, yeast, lemon zest, if using, and butter pieces until the dough is fine crumbs. Blend in eggs. Then blend in enough of the milk to make a soft dough. Use a dough hook attachment and knead for 5 minutes on medium-high speed, or transfer dough to a floured board and knead 10 minutes. Transfer to a floured board and work into a soft ball, then flatten slightly with the palm of your hand. Wrap in plastic wrap and refrigerate while preparing the butter.

❦ Place the remaining ½ pound butter between 2 sheets of plastic wrap. Using a rolling pin, tap butter to flatten until it forms a 6-inch square; wrap with plastic wrap and refrigerate.

❦ Lightly flour a pastry board. Roll out dough into a 14x16-inch rectangle. Place pounded butter in the center, fold the 4 sides of the dough inward over the butter, so it is completely enclosed by the dough, like an envelope.

❦ Sprinkle a work area with flour. Roll out dough, not pressing down too hard, into a 10x20-inch rectangle. Fold in thirds and turn seam-side down; roll out again into a 10x12-inch rectangle and fold in thirds. Wrap in plastic wrap and place in a plastic bag. Refrigerate overnight.

❦ Repeat rolling and folding 2 more times; refrigerate 2 hours each time.

CINNAMON DANISH SNAILS {Makes about 4 dozen pastries}

Once you've mastered the technique of working with pastry dough, you can create endless varieties of delicious pastries like these flaky, spice-scented snails. An irresistible, delightful breakfast treat with a cappuccino.

1 recipe Deli Danish Pastry Dough (page 169)
Flour, for dusting board
½ pound unsalted butter, melted
¼ cup ground cinnamon mixed with
      ¾ cup sugar
Apricot Glaze (recipe follows)

❦ Prepare pastry dough. Divide into 4 portions. Work with 1 portion at a time, keeping the remaining dough covered and refrigerated. Roll out dough on a lightly floured board into a rectangle, about 14 inches long and ¼ inch thick. Brush one half, lengthwise, with melted butter and sprinkle the other half generously with cinnamon-sugar mixture. Fold in half and run rolling pin over the top surface to seal.

❦ Cut dough into ½-inch strips and twist each strip into a rope, about 14 inches long. Starting with one end of the rope, coil it into a snail shape, working from the center to the outside, tuck the other end under the snail. Line baking sheets with aluminum foil and brush with melted butter. Arrange pastries 2 inches apart on the prepared baking sheets. Cover with a towel and let rise in a warm place until doubled, about 1 hour.

❦ Preheat the oven to 375° F and prepare Apricot Glaze.

❦ Bake snails until golden brown, about 15 minutes; brush with Apricot Glaze and cool on wire racks.

APRICOT GLAZE {Makes about 1½ cups}

2 cups apricot preserves
2 tablespoons brandy or apple juice

❦ In a small heavy saucepan warm preserves over low heat until melted. Stir in brandy. Press through a fine strainer into a small bowl.

BEAR CLAWS

{*Makes about 40 Bear Claws*}

Years ago I spent eight hours in a tiny bakery in Del Mar, California, watching the owner, a Swedish pastry chef, making pastries. The bear claws were outstanding. His method of folding, filling, and coating the pastry dough with almonds until it became a batch of succulent bear claw was fascinating. I could hardly wait to try them in my kitchen.

1 recipe Deli Danish Pastry Dough (page 169)
Flour, for dusting board
½ pound unsalted butter, melted
¼ cup ground cinnamon mixed with
    ¾ cup sugar
2 cups toasted sliced almonds (page 182)
½ cup sugar

❦ Prepare pastry dough. Divide dough into 4 portions. Work with 1 portion at a time, keeping remaining dough covered and refrigerated.

❦ On a lightly floured board, roll out dough ¼ inch thick into a 6x20-inch strip. Brush with melted butter and sprinkle generously with cinnamon-sugar mixture. Fold both long sides to meet in the center and turn over seam-side down. Sprinkle a long sheet of waxed paper with sliced almonds. Brush seamless side of prepared pastry generously with melted butter and turn over onto almonds. Press down so almonds adhere to the butter.

❦ Turn over pastry and sprinkle sugar over almonds. Using a sharp knife, cut dough crosswise into 2-inch pieces. Cut three 1-inch slits at wide end of each piece.

❦ Line baking sheets with aluminum foil and brush with melted butter. Arrange filled pastry on baking sheets, 2 inches apart, fanning out the slits to resemble bear claws. Cover with a towel and let rise in a warm place until doubled, about 30 minutes. Repeat with remaining dough.

❦ Preheat the oven to 375° F.

❦ Bake pastries until golden brown, about 15 minutes. Cool on wire racks. Store leftover pastries in plastic bags in freezer. Reheat before serving.

PECAN STICKY BUNS

{Makes about 4 dozen buns}

This recipe makes enough sticky buns for a big breakfast party. For a smaller group, bake a dozen at a time. Or use one portion of pastry dough for sticky buns and the remaining dough for bear claws or snails.

1 recipe Deli Danish Pastry Dough (page 169)
Pecan Filling (recipe follows)
Sticky Glaze (recipe follows)
Flour, for dusting board
¼ pound unsalted butter, melted
2 tablespoons ground cinnamon
3 cups toasted pecan halves (page 182)

❦ Prepare pastry dough, filling, and glaze.

❦ Divide dough into 4 portions. Work with 1 portion at a time, keeping the remaining dough covered and refrigerated.

❦ Punch down dough on a floured board and roll out to an 8x13-inch rectangle. Brush with melted butter and sprinkle about ¼ cup of the filling evenly over the butter. Roll up as for a jelly roll, starting from the long side. Cut into 12 slices.

❦ Pour ¼ cup of the glaze into an 8-inch square baking pan, sprinkle with ½ tablespoon of the cinnamon, and arrange ¼ cup of the pecan halves evenly on the glaze. Place the dough slices, cut side down, onto the mixture in the baking pan. Cover with a towel and let rise in a warm place until doubled in size, about 30 minutes. Repeat with the remaining pastry dough, filling, and glaze.

❦ Preheat the oven to 375° F.

❦ Bake buns until golden brown, about 35 minutes. Cool in the pan 5 minutes, then carefully invert onto a large platter. Store excess pastries in plastic bags in freezer. Reheat before serving.

PECAN FILLING

{Makes about 3½ cups}

½ cup golden raisins
Apple juice, for plumping
1½ cups finely ground cookie or
    cake crumbs
½ cup granulated sugar
2 tablespoons brown sugar
1 teaspoon ground cinnamon
½ cup chopped toasted pecans (page 182)

❦ In a small bowl, plump raisins in apple juice to cover 30 minutes and drain.

❦ In a medium bowl, combine cookie crumbs, both sugars, and cinnamon. Mix in raisins and pecans.

STICKY GLAZE

{Makes about 3 cups}

¼ pound unsalted butter
1 cup dark corn syrup
1 cup light corn syrup
½ cup honey

❦ In a heavy medium saucepan, combine all ingredients over medium heat. Simmer until butter melts and mix well. Cool.

BROADWAY DELI CROISSANTS

{Makes about 2 dozen croissants}

Making light, fluffy croissants is easy once you master some special techniques, including the method of rolling and shaping the triangles of pastry. The following is a technique I learned from chef Michel Richard, who is noted for his expertise in pastry making along with his many other accomplishments.

1 recipe Deli Danish Pastry Dough
(page 169)
Flour, for dusting board
2 egg yolks, lightly beaten with
1 tablespoon milk

❦ Prepare pastry dough and divide into 4 portions. Work with 1 portion at a time and keep remaining dough covered and refrigerated.

❦ Roll dough into a 10-inch circle, about ¼ inch thick. Cut each circle into 6 triangles. Starting at widest end of each triangle, roll up toward opposite point fairly tight unroll halfway then, using a stretching and rolling motion from the point, roll up again. Press point to seal and shape into a croissant by bringing both ends together in a crescent shape with 1 inch space between the 2 ends. Place on baking sheets lined with aluminum foil, 2 inches apart.

❦ Repeat with remaining pastry dough. Cover with a tea towel and let rise in a warm place until doubled in bulk, about 30 minutes. Brush top of pastries with yolk mixture.

❦ Preheat the oven to 400° F.

❦ Bake the croissants for 5 minutes, reduce the heat to 350° F, and bake until golden brown, about 15 minutes.

DELI DESSERTS

T

he dessert counter is my favorite deli section. No matter which deli I visit in any corner of the world, I have to check out the desserts first. ❦ I've included many Broadway Deli favorites, which are quite different from those of traditional delis. Although it offers classics like cheesecake, the Broadway Deli also features an array of sweets influenced by many countries. For example, its tiramisu is similar to those showcased in Italian delis, except that the Broadway Deli makes a delicate chocolate shell to substitute for the glass bowl that usually holds the filling. ❦ Tiramisu, Apple Strudel, Giant Chocolate Marshmallows, Old-Fashioned Rice Pudding—these are just some of the contemporary and classic recipes that follow. ❦ And there are some real family heirlooms like my Aunt Betty's fabulous Chocolate Spice Cake. Tested and improved over many years, this cake has become almost impossibly light and even more delicious than I remember from my childhood. ❦ Whether collected from the Broadway Deli, from family favorites, or from my travels, these recipes are easier to make at home than you ever imagined.

RECIPES

CHAPTER 8

MACHELLE'S BROWNIE CHEESECAKE

{Makes one 10-inch cake; serves 12}

Machelle Toman, the Broadway Deli's pastry chef, developed this clever double-layer cheesecake. This marriage of a brownie and a cheesecake, two of America's favorite desserts, is ingenious. Allow plenty of time to make this cake; it must be refrigerated overnight.

½ pound unsalted butter,
    at room temperature,
    plus more for cake pan
2 cups sugar
2 teaspoons vanilla extract
4 eggs
1 cup cake flour
½ teaspoon baking powder
Pinch salt
¾ cup cocoa powder
1 cup chopped walnuts
1 cup chocolate chips
Creamy Cheesecake Filling (recipe follows)
4 ounces semisweet chocolate, melted

❦ Preheat the oven to 350°F.

❦ Butter a 10-inch-round, 3-inch-deep cake pan and line the bottom with a round of parchment or waxed paper.

❦ In a large bowl, using an electric mixer, beat butter and sugar on medium speed until light and fluffy, about 2 minutes. Blend in vanilla. Beat in eggs, 1 at a time, until well blended.

❦ In a medium bowl, combine cake flour, baking powder, salt, and cocoa powder. Spoon the flour mixture into the butter mixture and beat until completely blended. Stir in walnuts and chocolate chips.

❦ Pour brownie batter into the prepared cake pan. Bake until semifirm, 15 to 20 minutes. Cool in pan and refrigerate overnight.

❦ Preheat the oven to 350°F.

❦ With a sharp knife loosen the cake from the sides, place a piece of plastic wrap on top, and flip over (do not remove the parchment paper). Wipe the pan clean and return the brownie to the pan.

❦ Prepare Creamy Cheesecake Filling. Carefully pour filling over the brownie, place the cake pan in a larger pan, and pour in hot water to reach halfway up the sides. Spoon melted chocolate into a pastry bag, fitted with the smallest plain metal tip. Pipe 8 lines of chocolate across the cake in one direction. Using a toothpick, working quickly in the opposite direction, crisscross 8 lines across the chocolate, to make a chevron pattern. Bake until lightly browned, 30 to 35 minutes. Cool in the water bath, cover with plastic wrap, and chill.

CREAMY CHEESECAKE FILLING

2 pounds cream cheese,
    at room temperature
2 cups sugar
4 whole eggs
4 egg yolks
1 cup sour cream
Pinch salt
1 teaspoon vanilla extract

❦ In a large bowl, using an electric mixer, blend cream cheese and sugar. Add remaining ingredients and blend well.

THE QUINTESSENTIAL CHEESECAKE

{ *Makes one 9-inch cheesecake; serves 12* }

This cheesecake recipe, the best in my vast collection, comes from a neighborhood Los Angeles deli. Unlike most cheesecakes, it never sinks in the middle and seldom cracks on top because it's baked in a bain-marie (water-bath) and then gently cooled in the oven for two hours.

1 Classic Graham Cracker Crust
   (recipe follows)
2 pounds cream cheese,
   at room temperature
2 cups sour cream
6 eggs, lightly beaten
1 cup sugar
¼ teaspoon salt
1 tablespoon vanilla extract
1 tablespoon fresh lemon juice

❦ Prepare and refrigerate Classic Graham Cracker Crust.

❦ Preheat the oven to 325°F.

❦ In the bowl of a heavy-duty electric mixer, beat cream cheese on medium speed until soft and fluffy. Using a rubber spatula, loosen the cream cheese from the blades. Blend in sour cream. Blend in eggs, 1 at a time, mixing well after each addition. Blend in sugar and salt and continue beating 2 minutes. Blend in vanilla and lemon juice and beat until mixture is light and fluffy.

❦ Place the springform pan with the graham cracker crust in the center of a large sheet of heavy-duty aluminum foil; bring the foil up the sides of the pan and press to seal. Pour the cream cheese filling into the pan. Place inside a larger baking pan and pour boiling water into the larger pan until it rises halfway up the sides of the springform pan.

❦ Bake 2 hours, turn off heat, and leave in oven another 2 hours before removing. Cool to room temperature, then refrigerate until ready to serve.

CLASSIC GRAHAM CRACKER CRUST

{ *Makes one 9-inch crust* }

1¾ cups graham cracker crumbs
1 tablespoon sugar
5 tablespoons unsalted butter or margarine,
   at room temperature

❦ In a medium bowl, thoroughly blend crumbs, sugar, and butter. Spoon the mixture evenly into the bottom of a 9-inch springform pan and press it down firmly. Refrigerate at least 15 minutes.

CHOCOLATE SWIRL CAKE {*Makes 1 loaf cake; serves 12*}

t's taken many years to perfect this marble-patterned chocolate pound cake. I remember making a special trip to a tiny Jewish bakery to buy it when I was a young bride. Make it a chocolate trio with chocolate chip ice cream and chocolate sauce.

½ pound plus 4 tablespoons unsalted butter, at room temperature
3 ounces unsweetened chocolate
¼ cup light corn syrup
2 tablespoons hot water
¼ teaspoon baking soda
1½ cups sugar
4 eggs
2 teaspoons vanilla extract
2½ cups unbleached all-purpose flour, plus more for loaf pan
1 teaspoon baking powder
½ teaspoon salt
⅔ cup nonfat milk

❦ Preheat the oven to 325°F.

❦ In a small saucepan, combine 2 tablespoons of the butter, chocolate, corn syrup, and the hot water. Cook over low heat, stirring until thick and smooth. Add baking soda and mix well. Set aside.

❦ In a large bowl, using an electric mixer, cream the ½ pound butter and add sugar, beating until light and fluffy. Add eggs and blend well. Mix in vanilla.

❦ In a small bowl, combine flour, baking powder, and salt. Add to batter in large bowl alternately with milk and beat until just combined. Transfer ½ cup of the batter to a medium bowl and blend in the chocolate mixture.

❦ Grease a 9x5x3-inch loaf pan with 2 tablespoons of the butter and dust with flour. Spread half of the batter remaining in large bowl into the prepared loaf pan. Spread the chocolate batter on top and then spread the plain vanilla batter over it. Using a knife, swirl through the batter 5 times for a marbled effect. Bake until a toothpick inserted in the center comes out clean and the cake pulls away from the sides of the pan, about 1 hour and 15 minutes. Cool on a wire rack. Using a metal spatula, carefully loosen sides of the cake from the pan.

MELTING CHOCOLATE

❦ Melt chocolate in a double boiler, over hot, not yet simmering, water.
❦ Grated or chopped chocolate melts more quickly and evenly than larger chunks.

❦ Never add cold liquids when melting warm chocolate. Butter, cream, or flavoring should be warm when added to the melted chocolate.

ORANGE-GLAZED BUNDT CAKE

{ Makes one 10-inch cake; serves 12 }

One of my fondest childhood memories is of the orange-glazed bundt cake that was showcased in almost every Jewish bakery in Los Angeles during the forties. I remember this cake, bursting with pure orange flavor, possessing a tender crumb, and flaunting a shiny glaze that runs dramatically down its sides. My version is fancy enough to serve for any special occasion, and it stays fresh for days.

½ pound plus 1 tablespoon unsalted butter, at
    room temperature
3 tablespoons finely ground almonds
2 cups sugar
4 eggs
3 cups unbleached all-purpose flour
2½ teaspoons baking powder
1 teaspoon salt
1 cup whipping cream,
    at room temperature
2 teaspoons vanilla extract
Grated zest of 2 oranges
½ cup strained fresh orange juice
½ cup honey
½ cup strained orange marmalade

❦ Preheat the oven to 350°F.

❦ Grease a 10-inch bundt pan or fluted tube pan with 1 tablespoon of the butter and sprinkle with ground almonds.❦

❦ In the bowl of a heavy-duty electric mixer, cream the remaining ½ pound butter and sugar on medium speed until fluffy. Add eggs, 1 at a time, beating well after each addition. In a medium bowl, combine flour, baking powder, and salt. Add to butter mixture alternately with cream, beating at medium-low speed. Stir in vanilla and orange zest.

❦ Pour the batter into prepared tube pan. Bake until lightly golden and a toothpick inserted in the center comes out clean, about 1 hour.

❦ Meanwhile in a saucepan, combine orange juice and honey. Cook over low heat, stirring once or twice, until honey is completely dissolved, about 3 minutes. Cool.

❦ Cool baked cake in pan set on a wire rack for 5 minutes. Invert onto a cake plate and brush with orange marmalade. Spoon honey-orange juice over cooled cake.

AUNT BETTY'S CHOCOLATE SPICE CAKE

{Makes one 10-inch cake; serves 16}

This is a special recipe from my aunt, who was a fabulous baker. With its rich chocolate and spice flavors, this unfrosted cake deserves to become a staple in your dessert repertoire. It's truly classic, old-fashioned comfort food.

¼ pound plus 6 tablespoons
    unsalted butter or margarine,
    at room temperature
½ cup finely ground walnuts
1 ½ cups sugar
4 eggs, separated
1 ¾ cups sifted cake flour
2 teaspoons baking powder
½ teaspoon ground cloves
½ teaspoon ground cinnamon
½ teaspoon ground allspice
¼ teaspoon salt
1 cup milk
4 ounces unsweetened chocolate, melted
1 cup toasted chopped walnuts (page 00)
1 teaspoon vanilla extract

❦ Preheat the oven to 325°F.

❦ Grease a 10-inch bundt pan or fluted tube pan with 2 tablespoons of the butter. Sprinkle with ground walnuts.

❦ In the bowl of a heavy-duty electric mixer, beat the remaining ¼ pound plus 4 tablespoons butter and the sugar on medium speed until light and fluffy. Beat in egg yolks, 1 at a time, until well blended.

❦ In a medium bowl, sift flour, baking powder, cloves, cinnamon, allspice, and salt. Spoon flour mixture into butter mixture alternately with milk until completely blended. Stir in melted chocolate, toasted walnuts, and vanilla.

❦ In a clean bowl, using clean beaters, beat egg whites on high speed until stiff; fold into the batter.

❦ Pour the batter into the prepared pan. Bake until a toothpick inserted into the center of the cake comes out clean and the cake begins to shrink away from the sides of the pan, about 50 minutes. Cool cake in pan set on a wire rack. Carefully loosen sides and center of the cake from the pan and invert onto a cake plate.

FIG AND NUT LOAF

{Makes 1 loaf; serves 12}

This flavor-packed fruit and nut loaf is found in Jewish as well as Italian delis. Similar to a fruitcake, it's made with chunks of chocolate, dried fruit, candied citrus peels, and nuts and is a delicious finale to almost any meal.

¾ cup toasted chopped hazelnuts
⅔ cup toasted chopped almonds
¾ cup chopped dried figs
⅓ cup diced candied orange peel
⅓ cup diced candied lemon peel
3 ounces semisweet chocolate, finely chopped
3 eggs
½ cup sugar
1¼ cups unbleached all-purpose flour
1¾ teaspoons baking powder
¾ teaspoon salt
Unsalted butter, for loaf pan

❦ Preheat the oven to 300°F.

❦ In a medium bowl, combine hazelnuts, almonds, figs, candied peels, and chocolate; mix well.

❦ In the bowl of a heavy duty electric mixer, beat eggs and sugar until thick and fluffy. Gently fold in the nut mixture.

❦ Sift flour, baking powder, and salt over the egg mixture and fold in. Spoon the batter into a generously buttered 8x4-inch loaf pan and smooth the top. Bake until the top of the loaf is deep golden-brown and a toothpick inserted into the center comes out clean, about 1 hour.

❦ Transfer pan to a wire rack for 5 minutes. Remove loaf from the pan and cool on a wire rack at least 45 minutes before slicing.

TOASTING NUTS

❦ Toast nuts in a single layer on a baking pan lined with aluminum foil. Bake at 350°F until fragrant and golden brown, 3 to 5 minutes. (Hazelnuts take longer, 10 to 15 minutes.) Toss twice to brown evenly.

❦ Always cool toasted nuts before chopping in food processor.

❦ Toast twice as many nuts as needed in a recipe. Fill bowls with toasted nuts, such as pecans, hazelnuts, cashews, and macadamia nuts, and watch them disappear. Better than popcorn.

❦ Shelled nuts should be stored in the refrigerator and will keep up to 6 months in the freezer.

THE BEST CARROT CAKE

{ Makes one 10-inch cake; serves 12 }

I've yet to find anyone who can resist a good carrot cake. The Broadway Deli always keeps a couple of these freshly baked cakes on hand, but orders go quickly. Be sure to use very fresh, sweet carrots: the sweeter the carrots, the tastier the cake.

Unsalted butter or margarine,
    for baking pan
¼ cup ground pecans
4 eggs
¾ cup granulated sugar
1¼ cups brown sugar
1¼ cup safflower oil
2 teaspoons vanilla extract
2½ cups grated carrots (about 1 pound)
2 cups cake or pastry flour
2 teaspoons baking powder
1 teaspoon baking soda
1 teaspoon salt
2 teaspoons ground cinnamon
1 cup chopped toasted pecans (page 182)
⅔ cup plus 1 tablespoon flaked or
    shredded coconut
Cream Cheese Icing (recipe follows)
½ cup diced, canned pineapple, drained

❦ Preheat the oven to 350°F.

❦ Butter a 10x2-inch round cake pan and line with waxed paper. Sprinkle with ground pecans.

❦ In the bowl of a heavy-duty electric mixer, beat eggs and both sugars until smooth. Add oil gradually; beat until smooth. Beat in vanilla.

❦ In a medium bowl, toss carrots with ¼ cup of the flour; set aside. Into another medium bowl, sift the remaining flour, baking powder, baking soda, salt, and cinnamon. Spoon the flour mixture into the egg mixture and blend well. Stir in carrots, toasted pecans, and ⅔ cup of the coconut. Pour batter into the prepared cake pan. Bake until a toothpick inserted into the center comes out clean and the cake begins to shrink away from the sides of the pan, about 50 minutes. Cool for 15 minutes in the pan, then invert on a wire rack to cool to room temperature. Peel off the waxed paper.

❦ Prepare Cream Cheese Icing. Toast the remaining 1 tablespoon coconut. Slice cake across the center into 2 equal layers; ice the bottom layer; top with pineapple; cover with the top cake layer; ice the entire cake; and dust the surface with toasted coconut.

CREAM CHEESE ICING

{ Makes about 3 cups }

1 pound cream cheese
¼ pound unsalted butter,
    at room temperature
2 cups powdered sugar
1 teaspoon vanilla extract

❦ In a large bowl, using an electric mixer, whip cream cheese and butter until light and fluffy. Beat in sugar and vanilla until completely blended.

CHOCOLATE STREUSEL COFFEE CAKE

{Makes one 9- or 10-inch cake; serves 12}

This recipe dates back to the late 1960s, when we lived on a ranch and entertained every Sunday. Although traditionally homey, this recipe differs from many coffee cakes because it has a semisweet-chocolate and walnut mixture baked into the batter and sprinkled over the top. My family includes many chocolate enthusiasts, most notably my husband. So I add chocolate to everything I can.

Chocolate-Nut Topping (recipe follows)
¼ pound unsalted butter or margarine, at room temperature, plus more for pan
1 cup sugar
2 eggs
1 teaspoon vanilla extract
2 cups unbleached all-purpose flour
1 teaspoon baking soda
1 teaspoon baking powder
½ teaspoon salt
2 teaspoons chopped, candied orange peel
1 cup sour cream
½ cup finely ground walnuts

▓ Preheat the oven to 350°F.

▓ Prepare Chocolate-Nut Topping.

▓ In the bowl of a heavy-duty electric mixer, cream butter and sugar until fluffy. Blend in eggs and vanilla. In a medium bowl combine flour, baking soda, baking powder, salt, and orange peel. Add flour mixture to butter mixture alternately with sour cream, ⅓ of each at a time.

▓ Lightly butter a 9- or 10-inch tube pan and sprinkle with ground walnuts. Pour half of the batter into prepared pan, spreading evenly. Sprinkle with half of the topping. Spoon the remaining batter on top and carefully spread over topping. Sprinkle with remaining topping.

▓ Bake until the cake is golden brown, begins to come away from the sides of the pan, and a toothpick inserted in center comes out clean, about 45 minutes.

CHOCOLATE-NUT TOPPING

{Makes about 2 cups}

1 cup toasted chopped walnuts or pecans (page 182)
1 cup chopped semisweet chocolate (about 6 ounces)
2 to 3 tablespoons sugar
½ teaspoon ground cinnamon

▓ In a medium bowl, mix together all ingredients.

FAMILY-STYLE BANANA CAKE

{Makes one 9-inch cake; or 2 dozen cupcakes; serves 14 to 16}

Sometimes I make this cake just for the wonderful aroma that fills my kitchen. It's so easy to whip up, too, using only the simplest ingredients. Chocolate lovers will add the glaze, but the cake is also delicious with just a sprinkle of powdered sugar.

½ cup vegetable shortening

1½ cups granulated sugar

2 eggs

1 teaspoon vanilla extract

1 cup mashed bananas (about 2 large)

2 cups unbleached all-purpose flour

¾ teaspoon baking powder

¾ teaspoon baking soda

½ teaspoon salt

¼ cup milk

½ cup chopped toasted walnuts
     (page 182)

Powdered sugar, for garnish

Chocolate-Strawberry Glaze
     (page 189), optional

❦ Preheat the oven to 350°F.

❦ In a large bowl, using an electric mixer, blend shortening and granulated sugar until light and fluffy. Beat in eggs and vanilla and then bananas.

❦ In a medium bowl, combine flour, baking powder, baking soda, and salt. Beat into the shortening mixture alternately with milk. Fold in walnuts. Pour batter into a well-buttered 9-inch bundt pan or angel food pan. Bake until golden brown and a toothpick inserted in the center comes out clean, about 45 minutes. Cool in pan on a wire rack.

❦ Meanwhile prepare Chocolate-Strawberry Glaze, if using, and spread on top and sides of cake. Or sprinkle with powdered sugar.

BANANA CUPCAKES *Fill 24 buttered muffin pans ⅔ full with batter and bake 25 to 30 minutes.*

BROWNIES À LA MODE

he Broadway Deli serves these brownies topped with a scoop of vanilla ice cream and chocolate sauce. The end result tastes like a one-of-a-kind chocolate sundae.

1 pound plus 2 tablespoons unsalted butter,
    at room temperature
4 cups sugar
4 teaspoons vanilla extract
8 eggs
2 cups pastry flour or
    unbleached all-purpose flour
1 teaspoon baking powder
Pinch salt
1⅓ cups cocoa powder
2 cups toasted chopped walnuts (page 182)
1 package (12 ounces) semisweet
    chocolate chips
Signature Chocolate Chip
    Ice Cream (page 202) and
    chocolate sauce, for topping

❦ Preheat the oven to 375°F.

❦ Melt 2 tablespoons of the butter and brush it over the bottom and sides of a 12x17x2-inch baking pan (jelly-roll pan). Line the bottom with parchment or waxed paper and set aside.

❦ In the bowl of a heavy-duty electric mixer, beat the remaining 1 pound butter with sugar on medium speed until light and fluffy, about 2 minutes. Blend in vanilla. Beat in eggs, 1 at a time, until well blended.

❦ In a medium bowl, combine pastry flour, baking powder, salt, and cocoa powder. Spoon flour mixture into butter mixture and beat until completely blended. Stir in 1½ cups of the walnuts and 1½ cups of the chocolate chips.

❦ Pour batter into the prepared pan and spread evenly with a rubber spatula. Sprinkle with the remaining ½ cup walnuts and ½ cup chocolate chips. Bake 30 minutes, then turn the pan in oven to bake evenly. Continue baking until the top is dry, about 20 minutes longer. (Do not overbake; the brownies will firm up as they cool.)

❦ Cool cake in pan set on a wire rack. Invert onto a wooden board and cut into 2-inch squares. Serve topped with ice cream and chocolate sauce. Wrap unused brownies individually in plastic wrap and store in the refrigerator or freezer.

TUNNEL OF FUDGE CUPCAKES {Makes 1 dozen cupcakes}

The legendary Canter's Deli and Bakery in Los Angeles has always been renowned for its shiny, smooth chocolate-frosted cupcakes. It's impossible to visit this deli and not walk out with a box of them. This is my version of Canter's cupcakes. Instead of the smooth frosting, mine have a creamy chocolate filling and are generously sprinkled with toasted cake crumbs. The technique of using a food processor to combine zest and sugar results in a wonderful orange flavor.

Grated zest of 2 oranges
1 cup sugar
¼ pound unsalted butter,
    at room temperature
2 eggs
1 teaspoon vanilla extract
½ teaspoon almond extract
2 cups unbleached all-purpose flour
1 teaspoon baking powder
½ teaspoon baking soda
¼ teaspoon salt
⅔ cup buttermilk
Chocolate Cream Filling (recipe follows)

❦ Preheat the oven to 375°F.

❦ In a food processor or small bowl, blend orange zest and sugar.

❦ In a large bowl, using an electric mixer, beat butter and sugar mixture until light and fluffy. Add eggs, 1 at a time, beating well after each addition. Blend in vanilla and almond extracts.

❦ Into a medium-bowl, sift together flour, baking powder, baking soda, and salt. Add flour mixture, alternately with buttermilk, to the butter mixture, blending thoroughly, but not overbeating.

❦ Line 1 dozen muffin cups with paper liners or grease with butter. Spoon batter into muffin cups ⅔ full. Bake until a toothpick inserted in the center comes out clean, 20 to 25 minutes. Cool on a wire rack.

❦ Prepare Chocolate Cream Filling. Preheat broiler.

❦ Cut a small cone (about 1 teaspoon) from the center of each cupcake, crumble cones, and toast under the broiler. Spoon Chocolate Cream Filling in the center of each cupcake. Sprinkle toasted crumbs over the filling.

CHOCOLATE CREAM FILLING {Makes about 1½ cups}

¼ cup sugar
1½ tablespoons water
1 ounce unsweetened chocolate
1 egg, separated
½ teaspoon vanilla extract

❦ In the top of a double boiler, over simmering water, combine 2 tablespoons of the sugar, the water, and chocolate. Cook, stirring constantly, until chocolate melts. Remove from the heat and blend in egg yolk with a whisk, beating well. Stir in vanilla.

❦ In a medium bowl, using an electric mixer, beat egg white until soft peaks form. Gradually add the remaining 2 tablespoons sugar and beat until stiff peaks form. Fold chocolate mixture into egg white gently but thoroughly.

DOUBLE CHOCOLATE ECLAIRS {*Makes about 1 dozen eclairs*}

Every ethnic deli has its own variation of eclairs. These are my favorite. Flaky pastry combines with chocolate filling and an elegant chocolate-strawberry glaze for melt-in-your-mouth creamy richness. Try these; they're really quite easy to make. Of course you can always substitute the usual filling of whipped cream or ice cream, if you like.

Chocolate Pastry Cream (recipe follows)
Chocolate-Strawberry Glaze (recipe follows)
1 cup water
¼ pound unsalted butter,
　　at room temperature
1 cup sifted unbleached all-purpose flour
Pinch salt
1 teaspoon sugar
4 eggs

❦ Prepare Chocolate Pastry Cream and Chocolate-Strawberry Glaze; cover and chill.

❦ Preheat the oven to 375°F.

❦ In a heavy saucepan, bring the water and butter to a boil over high heat. Stir until butter is melted. Remove from the heat and add flour, salt, and sugar, all at once, stirring vigorously until the mixture begins to come away from the sides of the pan.

❦ Turn the mixture into the bowl of a heavy-duty electric mixer. Beat in 1 egg at a time, beating well after each addition until completely blended, scraping the bowl occasionally with a rubber spatula.

❦ Line a baking sheet with aluminum foil. Spoon batter into a pastry tube equipped with a No. 6 tip and pipe onto baking sheet strips of batter about 2½ inches long (the shape of a finger), placed 2 inches apart. Bake until golden brown, about 30 minutes; turn off oven and leave eclairs for a few minutes to firm up. Remove from baking sheets and cool on wire racks.

❦ To fill cream puffs, fit pastry bag with plain tube No. 3 and fill with pastry cream. Either cut each puff in half to fill or push the pointed end of the tube into the side of each puff and squirt in cream. (Do not fill puffs until just before serving or they may become soggy.) Glaze tops with Chocolate-Strawberry Glaze.

CHOCOLATE PASTRY CREAM   *{Makes about 3 cups}*

½ cup sugar
¼ cup cocoa powder
2 cups milk
Pinch salt
1 vanilla bean, split lengthwise
4 egg yolks
⅓ cup unbleached all-purpose flour

❦ In a medium saucepan, combine ¼ cup of the sugar and cocoa. Add milk and salt. Bring to a boil over medium heat. Remove from the heat, add vanilla bean, and let steep 10 minutes. Scrape seeds from vanilla bean into the milk mixture and discard the bean.

❦ In a large bowl using an electric mixer, beat egg yolks with the remaining ¼ cup sugar until thick and pale yellow in color. Mix in flour. Reheat milk mixture and gradually beat it into the yolks. Return the batter to the saucepan. Whisk over medium-high heat until the mixture begins to bubble. Whisk until smooth, about 2 minutes. Press a sheet of plastic wrap onto the cream and chill.

CHOCOLATE-STRAWBERRY GLAZE   *{Makes about 2 cups}*

1 cup clear strawberry jelly (no seeds or pulp)
½ cup sifted cocoa powder
1½ ounces semisweet chocolate, chopped

❦ In a heavy saucepan, heat jelly over medium-low heat until melted. Add cocoa powder and stir until dissolved. Add chocolate and stir until melted. Strain into a small bowl and cover with plastic wrap. This will keep for several months stored in the refrigerator.

GIANT CHOCOLATE MARSHMALLOWS

{Makes 1 dozen marshmallows}

This is a creation of the highly acclaimed chef-owner of Citrus restaurant. Michel Richard, who is also a partner in the Broadway Deli. An accomplished pattissier. Michel said that these sweets remind him of the French dessert, Floating Island. But to me, they are more like a giant-size version of the packaged marshmallow cookies my children used to love.

Sugar Cookie Rounds (recipe follows)
Sponge Cake (recipe follows)
6 egg whites
1 cup sugar
½ cup raspberry jam
1 pound semisweet chocolate,
　　melted with 1 tablespoon safflower oil

❦ Preheat the oven to 300°F.

❦ Prepare and bake Sugar Cookie Rounds. Prepare Sponge Cake. Cut cake into twelve 3-inch rounds and set aside.

❦ In a large bowl, using an electric mixer, beat egg whites until soft peaks form. Slowly add sugar, beating until stiff. Line a baking sheet with waxed paper. Fill a pastry bag (with a large tip) with the egg-white mixture and pipe into twelve 3½-inch rounds on prepared baking sheet. Bake until golden, 10 to 15 minutes. Cool in the refrigerator.

❦ To assemble: Place a large rack over a sheet of waxed paper. Spread raspberry jam onto each sugar cookie and place on rack. Place each sponge cake round on top of raspberry jam. Using a spatula, place a cooled egg-white round over each cake round. Pour melted chocolate over the top, allowing excess chocolate to drizzle onto waxed paper. Cool before serving.

SUGAR COOKIE ROUNDS

{Makes 1 dozen cookies}

1½ tablespoons unsalted butter,
    at room temperature
⅓ cup sugar
Pinch salt
¼ cup finely ground almonds or pecans
1 cup unbleached all-purpose flour,
    plus more for board
1 egg

❦ In a large bowl, using an electric mixer, blend butter, sugar, salt, and almonds. Add flour gradually, mixing well. With the machine running add egg and continue mixing until dough comes together. Transfer dough to a floured board and knead into a compact ball. Wrap in plastic wrap and chill for 1 hour.

❦ Preheat the oven to 350°F.

❦ Line 2 baking sheets with waxed paper. On a floured board, roll out dough ¼ inch thick; cut into 3½-inch rounds and place 2 inches apart on baking sheets. Bake until golden brown, about 20 minutes

SPONGE CAKE

{Makes one 12x17-inch sponge cake}

1 tablespoon unsalted butter,
    at room temperature, for baking pan
½ cup plus 2 tablespoons sugar
6 eggs, separated
1 teaspoon vanilla extract
½ cup plus 1 tablespoon unbleached
    all-purpose flour

❦ Preheat the oven to 350°F.

❦ Line the bottom of a buttered 12x17x2-inch baking pan with waxed paper. Grease paper with more butter, sprinkle with 2 tablespoons of the sugar, shaking out excess sugar. Sprinkle with 1 tablespoon of the flour and shake out excess.

❦ In a large bowl, using an electric mixer, beat egg yolks, the remaining ½ cup sugar, and vanilla on high speed until thick and pale, about 2 minutes. Sift the remaining ½ cup flour over the mixture and fold it in.

❦ In another large bowl, beat egg whites on high speed until soft-firm, peaks form. Whisk ¼ of the beaten whites into the egg yolk mixture. Using a rubber spatula, gently fold in the remaining whites.

❦ Pour batter into the prepared pan, smooth the top with a spatula, and bake until golden and the cake pulls away from the sides of the pan, about 10 minutes. Cool in pan set on a wire rack 5 minutes. Run a thin knife around the edges and invert onto a cake rack. Remove the waxed paper and cool.

APPLE STRUDEL

Strudel is popular at most delis, but it's better made at home. Fresh filo dough is sometimes available at Greek or Middle Eastern bakeries, but you'll probably have to settle for frozen filo from the supermarket—thawed overnight in the refrigerator. Strudel (before it's baked) freezes very well. So you might want to make several batches of this (to use up all the filo from a package). You'll then have on hand a fabulous, crispy dessert in no time at all.

1 cup golden raisins
½ cup apple juice
¾ pound unsalted butter
½ cup sugar
1 teaspoon ground cinnamon
2 pounds pippin apples (about 5 medium), peeled, quartered, cored and cut into ¼-inch-thick slices
⅓ cup applesauce
¼ cup cake crumbs
16 sheets filo dough
1 cup finely ground graham cracker crumbs
¼ cup sugar mixed with about 1 teaspoon ground cinnamon

❦ In a small bowl, plump raisins in apple juice until soft, about 30 minutes.

❦ Preheat the oven to 350°F.

❦ In a large, heavy nonstick skillet, melt ¼ pound of the butter. Add the ½ cup sugar and the 1 teaspoon cinnamon and stir until dissolved. Add apples, increase heat, and cook until just tender and caramelized, about 15 minutes. Add applesauce, cake crumbs, and drained raisins and toss. Cover and cool.

❦ In a small saucepan, melt the remaining ½ pound butter. Place a damp towel on a work area and cover with waxed paper. Remove 8 sheets of filo from the package. (Cover the remaining sheets with waxed paper and a damp towel until ready to use.)

❦ Fold filo leaves in half like a closed book and unfold 1 page. Brush with melted butter and sprinkle with graham cracker crumbs. Continue turning the pages of the filo, brushing each with butter and crumbs until you come to the center. Do not brush the center with butter yet. Close the second half of the "book" over the first and work backward: Open the last leaf and continue spreading butter and crumbs until you come back to the center. Gently press down the layered filo. Now brush the center with melted butter and sprinkle with crumbs.

❦ Spread half of the reserved apple filling lengthwise on top of the layered filo, 2 inches from the edge closest to you and 2 inches from the sides. Cover the filling with the closest unspread edge and fold the sides over. Brush the sides with butter and continue rolling up the filo, jelly-roll fashion. Cover a baking sheet with aluminum foil and brush with butter. Place the rolled strudel on the foil, seam-side down, brush with melted butter and sprinkle with cinnamon-sugar mixture.

❦ Repeat entire procedure with another 8 sheets of filo and the remaining half of the apple mixture. (Strudel can be frozen at this point.) Bake until golden brown, about 45 minutes. Slice immediately.

FRESH FRUIT COBBLER WITH STREUSEL TOPPING

{ Serves 6 }

Fresh-baked cobbler is an ideal showcase for luscious summer fruit. Serve with crème fraîche, vanilla sauce, or ice cream; the taste of the rich, cool cream against the warm cobbler is sinfully sensational. If you don't have individual baking dishes, you can make this cobbler in an 8-inch-square baking dish.

Streusel Crumb Topping (recipe follows)
8 pears or peaches, peeled, pitted,
    and sliced, or 1 pint strawberries,
    hulled and sliced (about 2¼ cups)
⅓ cup granulated sugar
Grated zest of 1 lemon
Powdered sugar, for garnish

❦ Preheat the oven to 350°F.
❦ Prepare Streusel Crumb Topping.
❦ In a large bowl, combine fruit, granulated sugar, and lemon zest and toss gently. Spoon equal portions of the fruit mixture into six 6-ounce ovenproof baking dishes. Sprinkle 3 tablespoons of Streusel Crumb Topping evenly over the fruit. Bake until brown and bubbly, 25 to 30 minutes. Then preheat broiler and broil until crumb topping is crisp. Sprinkle with powdered sugar and serve hot.

STREUSEL CRUMB TOPPING

{ Makes about 2 cups }

1½ cups unbleached all-purpose flour
¼ cup granulated sugar
¼ cup brown sugar
¼ cup slivered almonds
½ teaspoon ground cinnamon
¼ pound unsalted butter, cut into small pieces

❦ In a large bowl, using an electric mixer, combine all ingredients and blend until mixture resembles coarse crumbs. Do not overblend.

BEATING EGG WHITES

❦ Use a copper or stainless-steel bowl large enough so egg whites have plenty of room to expand to 6 times their original volume.
❦ In preparing meringues, always add a pinch of cream of tartar to stabilize the egg whites.

❦ Use a wire whisk and beat as much air as possible into egg whites. Never overbeat egg whites or they are impossible to fold into a batter. They become jelly-like in consistency.

LEMON MERINGUE TARTLETS {*Makes 1 dozen tartlets*}

These elegant lemon tartlets are ideal for a party menu as they're prepared in steps. The filling can be made up to two days in advance; it needs to cool for at least five hours. The shells are best baked the day they are served. Only the meringue is made at the last minute. With all the lemon juice in this recipe, you must use a double boiler with a nonreactive surface—glass, enamel, or stainless steel. Or you can improvise by placing a heatproof glass bowl over a pan of simmering water. Tartlet shells freeze well before or after baking.

12 Tartlet Shells (recipe follows)
¾ cup fresh lemon juice
10 egg yolks, at room temperature
1¼ cups sugar
6 tablespoons unsalted butter,
    cut into pieces
Grated zest of 3 lemons
Meringue Topping (recipe follows)

❦ Prepare and bake Tartlet Shells.

❦ In the nonreactive top of a double boiler, over simmering water, whisk lemon juice, egg yolks, and sugar until thick, about 5 minutes. Add butter and lemon zest stirring until the mixture is smooth. Press a piece of plastic wrap onto sauce. Cool, then refrigerate at least 5 hours.

❦ Prepare Meringue Topping. Preheat the broiler.

❦ Spoon about 2 tablespoons of filling into each baked tart shell. Fill a pastry bag (using a No. 8 metal tip) with the meringue. Beginning at the edge of the tartlet, pipe the meringue in circles ending in the center. Place on a baking sheet and broil about 4 inches below heat source until the meringue browns, about 3 minutes, watching carefully. Cool on wire racks and then remove tartlet tins.

TARTLET SHELLS   {*Makes 1 dozen 3½-inch tartlet shells*}

1¼ cups unbleached all-purpose flour,
  plus more for board
¼ cup ground almonds
¼ cup sugar
Pinch salt
¼ pound cold unsalted butter,
  cut into pieces
1 egg

❦ In a large bowl, using an electric mixer, blend flour, almonds, sugar, and salt. Blend in butter until the mixture resembles coarse meal. Add egg and blend until dough begins to come together. Transfer to a floured board and knead into a ball (do not over-mix). Wrap in plastic wrap and chill for at least 30 minutes.

❦ Preheat the oven to 350°F.

❦ Roll out dough on a floured sheet of waxed paper until ⅛ inch thick. Cut into twelve 6-inch rounds. Fit pastry rounds into 3½-inch round tartlet tins (preferably with removable bottoms). Trim and finish edges. Line each tartlet with parchment or waxed paper and fill with pie weights or beans. Bake until crust is firm, about 15 minutes. Remove weights and parchment. Continue baking until well-browned, about 10 minutes. Cool; wrap in plastic wrap and aluminum foil and store in refrigerator or freezer. Bake in oven to crisp up.

MERINGUE TOPPING   {*Makes about 4 cups*}

4 egg whites
Pinch salt
Pinch cream of tartar
6 tablespoons sugar

❦ In a large bowl, using an electric mixer, beat egg whites, salt, and cream of tartar until soft peaks form. Beat in sugar, 1 tablespoon at a time, and continue beating until stiff, but not dry.

THE BEST APPLE PIE

I could hardly believe what I saw, just before Thanksgiving at the Broadway Deli—ninety pounds of caramelized apples rolled out of a huge pot for over two hundred pies. But for this book, the pastry chefs reduced their recipe to just this one pie. Serve with vanilla ice cream or whipped cream.

Sweet Pie Dough (recipe follows)
8 large Granny Smith or pippin apples
    (about 4 pounds)
Juice of 1 lemon
5 tablespoons unsalted butter
½ cup granulated sugar
½ cup dark brown sugar
1 teaspoon ground cinnamon
2 tablespoons cornstarch
¼ cup cold water

❦ Preheat the oven to 375°F.

❦ Prepare Sweet Pie Dough.

❦ Peel, core, and cut apples into thin slices, about ¼ inch thick. In a large bowl, toss apples with lemon juice.

❦ In a large, heavy saucepan, combine butter, both sugars, cinnamon, and sliced apples. Bring to a boil, reduce heat, and simmer until apples are tender and sauce thickens, about 5 minutes.

❦ In a small bowl, combine cornstarch and the water, mixing to dissolve. Add to apple mixture and simmer until syrup is translucent, about 2 minutes. Cool.

❦ Spoon the apple filling into the prepared pie crust forming a pyramid shape. Lightly moisten the edge of the bottom crust with water and cover with the top crust. Press the crusts together to seal; crimp the edges and make a few slits in the center of the top crust to allow steam to escape. Place on a baking sheet and bake until crust is golden brown, 45 minutes to 1 hour.

SWEET PIE DOUGH

{*Makes 2 crusts for a 9-inch pie*}

2 cups unbleached all-purpose flour,
    plus more for board
2 tablespoons sugar
⅛ teaspoon salt
¼ pound plus 2 tablespoons cold
    unsalted butter, cut into pieces
¼ cup cold water
½ cup ground almonds

❦ In a large bowl, using an electric mixer, combine flour, sugar, salt, and butter. Blend until the mixture is crumbly. Blend in the water until the dough begins to come together. Do not overmix. Transfer dough to a floured board and knead into a ball. Divide into 2 flat discs; wrap 1 in plastic wrap and chill.

❦ Roll out the remaining disc on a large sheet of floured waxed paper to a round large enough to cover and overlap a 9-inch pie pan. For easier handling, cover the pastry with another sheet of waxed paper and fold pastry in half. (The waxed paper protects the center of the pastry from sticking together.) Lift the pastry from the bottom waxed paper and place on half of the pie pan. Unfold the pastry and remove the paper that covers it. Sprinkle the bottom pastry with ground almonds. Roll out remaining dough for the top crust.

DELI BAKED APPLES

{*Serves 6*}

elect large red apples for this homey dessert; Rome Beauties work best. Glazed with honey and filled with a sweet and spicy mix, these baked apples are a welcome finale for any brunch. Add whipped cream, vanilla ice cream, or Vanilla Bourbon Sauce (page 200) for extra allure.

6 large Rome Beauty apples
Juice of 2 lemons
3 tablespoons brown sugar
¼ cup golden raisins
1 teaspoon grated lemon zest
2 tablespoons honey
1 teaspoon ground cinnamon
½ teaspoon freshly grated nutmeg
1½ cups unsweetened apple juice

❦ Preheat the oven to 375°F.

❦ Using an apple corer or sharp paring knife, core apples to just 1 inch above the bottom of each apple. Spoon equal amounts of lemon juice into each well.

❦ In a small bowl, mix brown sugar, raisins, and lemon zest and spoon an equal amount into each cavity of the apples. Arrange apples in a baking dish. Drizzle honey over each apple and sprinkle with cinnamon and nutmeg. Pour apple juice around apples. Cover loosely with aluminum foil and bake until apples are tender when pierced with a toothpick, about 1 hour and 15 minutes. Serve hot or at room temperature.

TAPIOCA CRÈME BRÛLÉE {Serves 8}

*P*earl tapioca is the Broadway Deli's secret ingredient in this sin-*fully rich dessert. It adds texture, as does the crunchy brown sugar crust that's caramelized under the broiler. The vanilla beans also play a big role in making this recipe so special; try to use them instead of vanilla extract.*

3 cups water
2 tablespoons pearl tapioca
Ice water, for cooling
¾ cup milk
2¼ cups whipping cream
2 vanilla beans, cut in half lengthwise or
    1 teaspoon vanilla extract
½ cup granulated sugar
Pinch salt
10 egg yolks
½ cup dark brown sugar

❦ Preheat the oven to 300°F.

❦ In a small saucepan, bring the 3 cups water and pearl tapioca to a boil, reduce heat, and simmer until tapioca is translucent, about 20 minutes. Strain and place tapioca in ice water to stop the cooking process. Strain again and rinse with cold water, to remove the starch. Place 1 tablespoon each of tapioca on the bottoms of eight 8-ounce ovenproof custard cups or bowls.

❦ In a large heavy saucepan, heat over medium heat milk, cream, vanilla beans, granulated sugar, and salt and whisk until well blended. Reduce heat to low and simmer until mixture begins to boil. Remove from the heat, remove vanilla bean halves, and scrape seeds into the cream mixture. Cover and let infuse for 30 minutes. Then add egg yolks to cream mixture whisking until well blended.

❦ Strain custard mixture into a large bowl and carefully pour or spoon over the tapioca in each bowl until ¾ full. Place custard cups in a baking dish filled halfway with hot water. Bake until set, and a knife or tooth-pick inserted in center comes out clean, about 1 hour. Remove the cus-tard cups from the hot water and cool on wire racks. If you are making these ahead, you may cover and refrigerate until ready to serve.

❦ Preheat the broiler to very hot. Just before serving, sift 1 tablespoon of the brown sugar on the top of each custard. Place under red-hot broiler until the sugar bubbles and browns. Or you can caramelize the topping with a blowtorch as the professional chefs do.

OLD-FASHIONED RICE PUDDING

{ Serves 12 }

Deli afficionados always light up at the sight of rice pudding! Small wonder that it's always on deli menus; I think there'd be a mutiny if anyone dared to take it off. At the Broadway Deli, rice pudding is a popular takeout order for those who wish to curl up with a bowl at home. Lavishly spiced, noticeably creamy, and scented with fragrant orange zest, this rendition is simple for even the novice home cook to prepare.

1 navel orange

½ cup raisins

4 cups milk

½ cup long-grain rice

½ cup sugar

2-inch piece cinnamon stick

½ teaspoon salt

1 cup half-and-half

3 large egg yolks

1 teaspoon vanilla extract

1½ teaspoons ground cinnamon
mixed with 1½ teaspoons sugar

Whipped cream, for garnish

❦ Using a sharp paring knife, remove the peel from the orange in 1 long spiral. Squeeze orange juice, strain into a small bowl, and add raisins to plump.

❦ In the top of a double boiler combine orange peel, milk, rice, sugar, cinnamon stick, and salt. Cook, covered, over simmering water, stirring occasionally, until rice is almost tender, 45 to 50 minutes. Discard the peel.

❦ In a medium bowl, whisk together half-and-half and egg yolks. Add in a thin stream to the rice mixture in the double boiler, stirring constantly. Cover and cook over simmering water until thick, about 20 minutes. Discard cinnamon stick and stir in vanilla.

❦ Drain raisins and stir them into the pudding. Spoon pudding into twelve 4-ounce custard cups or small ovenproof ramekins. Cover with plastic wrap and chill for at least 1 hour and up to 24 hours. Sprinkle with cinnamon-sugar mixture and serve with whipped cream.

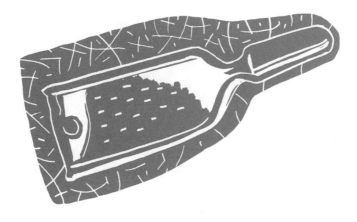

BOURBON BREAD PUDDING {Serves 8 to 10}

Nostalgia lovers flock to delis and bread puddings are often the dessert they most demand. This pudding may be the consummate rendition of this comforting finale. Although it calls for egg bread (challah), you can substitute leftover croissants or brioche and still achieve sweet success.

Vanilla-Bourbon Sauce (recipe follows)
1 tablespoon unsalted butter, melted
1 small egg bread (about 1 pound),
    crust trimmed
¼ cup golden raisins
¼ cup sugar mixed with
    1 tablespoon cinnamon
4 cups milk
1 cup sugar
7 eggs
1 teaspoon vanilla extract

❦ Prepare Vanilla-Bourbon Sauce; cool, cover, and chill.

❦ Preheat the oven to 350°F.

❦ Brush an 8-inch-square baking pan with butter. Slice bread into 1-inch cubes and arrange in the buttered pan. Sprinkle with raisins and half of the cinnamon-sugar mixture.

❦ In a large heavy saucepan, combine milk and sugar, and bring to a boil, stirring until sugar dissolves. Cool.

❦ In a large bowl, beat eggs until light in color. Add 1 cup of the milk mixture slowly to the eggs; then add the remaining milk mixture beating well. Blend in vanilla. Pour half of the custard mixture over bread cubes, gently press with hands; let it absorb; then add the remaining custard mixture. Sprinkle with the remaining cinnamon-sugar mixture.

❦ Place baking pan in a larger pan of hot water. Bake until a knife inserted in the center comes out moist (not wet) and the top springs back when touched, 45 minutes to 1 hour. Cut into squares and serve warm with chilled Vanilla-Bourbon Sauce.

VANILLA-BOURBON SAUCE {Makes about 1¾ cups}

3 egg yolks
⅓ cup sugar
⅓ cup milk
1 cup whipping cream
Pinch salt
¼ cup bourbon
½ teaspoon vanilla extract

❦ In a medium bowl, whisk egg yolks with sugar until well blended. In a medium saucepan, combine milk, cream, and salt, bring to a boil and reduce heat to medium low. Whisk ½ cup of the cream mixture into the egg-yolk mixture. Slowly whisk back into the saucepan. Continue whisking over medium low heat until the sauce begins to thicken. Do not boil. Remove from heat and add bourbon and vanilla. Strain through a fine strainer into a bowl. Cool, cover with plastic wrap, and chill.

TIRAMISU IN SMALL CHOCOLATE BOWLS

{*Serves 4*}

This original Broadway Deli dessert was created by chef Michel Richard. It's his answer to the traditional Italian tiramisu and it's sensational! To make the chocolate bowls, you will need one or two small stainless-steel bowls, about five inches in diameter, to use as molds.

Chocolate Bowls (recipe follows)

½ recipe Sponge Cake (page 191)

3 eggs, separated

6 tablespoons sugar

1 pound mascarpone cheese or
　ricotta blended until smooth

1 teaspoon Frangelica, other almond liqueur,
　or almond extract

1 teaspoon dark rum

1 teaspoon Kahlúa

1 cup whipping cream

2 cups espresso or strong brewed coffee

Cocoa powder, for garnish

❦ Prepare Chocolate Bowls and store in the refrigerator or freezer until needed. Prepare Sponge Cake batter and bake in an 8-inch square baking pan; cover until ready to use.

❦ In a heavy saucepan, over medium heat, beat egg yolks, sugar, and mascarpone until light in color. Cool. Add Frangelica, rum, and Kahlúa.

❦ In a large bowl using an electric mixer, beat egg whites until stiff, but not dry, peaks form. Gently fold egg whites into the cooled marscarpone mixture. In another bowl, whip cream until stiff peaks form and fold into mascarpone mixture. Spoon into a pastry bag fitted with a No. 6 plain tip.

❦ Pour espresso into a shallow bowl. Cut sponge cake in half and cut each half into eight 1x4-inch strips; dip each into the espresso. Place 2 strips of cake in the bottom of each chocolate bowl. Pipe or spoon a layer of custard on top. Cover with 2 more cake strips and top with more custard. Sprinkle a generous amount of cocoa over the entire surface. Place bowls on a baking pan, cover with plastic wrap, and refrigerate until ready to serve.

CHOCOLATE BOWLS

{*Makes 4 bowls*}

2 pounds semisweet coating chocolate or
　tempered chocolate

Safflower oil, as needed

Ice water, for molds

❦ In the top of a double boiler, over hot water, melt chocolate and keep warm, adding a little safflower oil if chocolate begins to harden when dipping.

❦ Fill a 5-inch-round stainless-steel bowl with ice water. Place a short-handled wooden spoon in the center and place in the freezer. When the water begins to freeze straighten the spoon to an upright position and continue to freeze until solid.

❦ Remove the block of ice from the bowl and wipe off any moisture with a terrycloth towel. Holding it by the wooden-spoon handle, dip the block of ice evenly into the warm melted chocolate, 1 time only. Lift quickly and chocolate will set in less than 1 minute; then it will slide off easily. (Do not allow any water to drop into the chocolate.) Place chocolate bowl on a baking pan, cover with plastic wrap, and store in refrigerator or freezer until ready to use.

❦ Rinse off any chocolate from the block of ice and return it to the metal bowl. Add more ice water to fill bowl and return to the freezer to reuse. Repeat 3 more times.

SIGNATURE CHOCOLATE CHIP ICE CREAM

{Makes about 3 pints}

This cookbook would not be complete without my signature chocolate chip ice cream. It is always there in my freezer to be enjoyed—day and night. This recipe is a cross between the famous Wil Wright's Chocolate Chip Ice Cream and the stracciatella gelato (chocolate chip ice cream) we look forward to eating when vacationing in Italy. Serve with apple pie, brownies, or topped with chocolate sauce for serious chocolate lovers.

2 cups milk
1 cup sugar
1 vanilla bean, split lengthwise, or
    2 teaspoons vanilla extract
7 egg yolks
Ice water, for cooling custard
2 cups whipping cream
6 to 8 ounces semisweet chocolate, melted

❦ In a medium heavy saucepan, over medium heat, combine milk with ½ cup of the sugar and bring to a boil, mixing until sugar is dissolved. Turn off heat, add vanilla bean, cover, and let steep 5 minutes. Remove vanilla bean and scrape seeds into milk mixture. Stir until seeds separate; then add vanilla bean pod.

❦ In a large bowl, using a wire whisk or an electric mixer, beat egg yolks and the remaining ½ cup sugar until light and fluffy. In a slow stream, pour ½ cup of the heated milk mixture into the egg mixture and blend well. Pour the egg mixture back into the saucepan with the milk mixture, mixing to blend well. Cook over medium-low heat, stirring constantly, to just below the boiling point (170° to 180°F), about 5 minutes.

❦ Pour custard into a fine strainer suspended over a large bowl set over a larger bowl filled with ice water. Scrape up thickened cream that settles on bottom of pan. Add whipping cream and mix until cooled. Cover with plastic wrap and refrigerate until cold.

❦ Remove vanilla bean pod from custard mixture. Freeze mixture in an ice cream maker according to manufacturer's instructions. When very cold and thick, and machine is still running, pour warm melted chocolate in a thin stream. The chocolate will quickly harden and break up into small pieces. Continue to freeze ice cream. Spoon into plastic containers; cover and freeze until ready to serve.

COOKIES

Delis are known for giving cookies to the kids, and the Broadway Deli has followed that tradition. And what an array the children can choose from—French Lemon Sable Crisps; Italian Biscotti, studded with hazelnuts; that all-American favorite, Double Chocolate Chip cookies; and many more. Grown-ups look longingly as these treats are distributed, but why should they? They can go home and make their own from the delectable variety of cookie recipes in this section. ❦ The old-fashioned, crockery cookie jar has gone the way of the wooden icebox. But if you peek into my freezer, you'll find lots of homemade cookie dough, tightly wrapped in plastic, ready to be baked into fresh hot batches when we need a cookie spree. ❦ Cookie-baking is marvelous family entertainment. It also rewards children with the opportunity to gobble up straight-from-the-oven treats—to say nothing of scraping the dough from the bowls, which they sometimes prefer to the baked product. ❦ Nowadays it's my grandchildren who get the free cookies at the deli and who help me with home baking. Amazingly, even three-year-old Ariella and four-year-old Zane keep busy while sampling the dough and watching the baking. Pretty soon, they will be able to grease the cookie sheets and sprinkle the cookies with powdered sugar.

LEMON SABLE CRISPS

{ *Makes about 5 dozen cookies* }

L ight on sugar, these delicate French cookies possess a sparkling
lemon flavor. I had so many requests for this Broadway Deli
recipe that I asked the chef to supply it for this book.

½ pound plus 4 tablespoons
    unsalted butter or margarine,
    at room temperature
3/4 cup sugar
2 eggs
1 teaspoon vanilla extract
Pinch salt
2¾ cups pastry or cake flour
⅓ cup fresh lemon juice
2 tablespoons grated lemon zest
1 egg white, lightly beaten
½ cup crystallized sugar

❦ In a large bowl, using an electric mixer, cream butter and sugar until light and fluffy, 1 to 2 minutes. Add eggs and blend well. Blend in vanilla. Add salt and flour, ½ cup at a time, alternately with lemon juice and zest. (Dough may be a little sticky.) Cover with plastic wrap and refrigerate 4 hours.

❦ Divide dough into 4 parts and shape each into a rope, about 7 inches long. Wrap with plastic wrap and freeze until firm enough to slice, about 30 minutes.

❦ Preheat the oven to 350°F.

❦ Brush ropes with egg white and roll in crystallized sugar; then cut into ¼-inch-thick slices and place on baking sheets lined with aluminum foil. Bake until the cookies brown around the edges, 20 to 25 minutes. Transfer cookies to wire racks to cool.

HAVE COOKIE DOUGH ON HAND ALL YEAR

❦ *When mixing a batch of cookie dough it is not necessary to bake all the cookies the same day. Store unbaked dough, wrapped in plastic wrap, in the refrigerator and bake as needed. Dough will keep for 3 or 4 days in the refrigerator and at least 2 months in the freezer.*

❦ *Cookie dough freezes better than the baked cookies. Just shape the unused dough into long rolls or flat discs; wrap in plastic wrap, place in a plastic bag and freeze.*

❦ *Label wrapped dough with the name and storage date. Defrost for 2 to 3 hours, or until it can be handled easily and proceed with your recipes.*

❦ *Fresh warm cookies right out of the oven are always a treat and the kitchen always smells so inviting and good.*

DOUBLE CHOCOLATE CHIP COOKIES

{Makes about 5 dozen cookies}

've been baking chocolate chip cookies since I was nine years old, so I know a good recipe when I see one. The Broadway Deli's version is irresistible to chocolate lovers—dense and incredibly chocolatey, with both chocolate chips and chocolate chunks. And no, I didn't forget the baking powder and baking soda; the pastry chef doesn't use any.

¾ pound plus 1 tablespoon
　　unsalted butter or margarine,
　　at room temperature
1 cup granulated sugar
1 cup light brown sugar
2 eggs
1 teaspoon vanilla extract
12 ounces semisweet chocolate, coarsely
　　chopped
3 cups unbleached all-purpose flour
1½ cups toasted chopped pecans (page 182)
12 ounces semisweet chocolate chips

❧ In a large bowl, using an electric mixer, cream ¾ pound of the butter and both sugars. Add eggs, 1 at a time, and beat until light and airy. Blend in vanilla and chopped chocolate. Add flour and beat for 20 seconds. Stir in nuts, chocolate chips, and mix by hand just until well blended. (The chopped chocolate and chocolate chips should not be too soft or the dough will turn brown and not bake properly. Do not overmix after adding chopped chocolate or chocolate chips.)

❧ Line baking sheets with parchment paper or aluminum foil. Melt the remaining 1 tablespoon butter and brush over parchment paper or foil. Use a small ice cream scoop to scoop out dough and transfer to the prepared baking sheets. (Bake in batches, if necessary.) Press dough with the palm of your hand to flatten cookies. Cover with plastic wrap and refrigerate 1 hour.

❧ Preheat the oven to 325°F. Bake cookies 6 minutes, then turn baking sheet for even baking. Bake 6 minutes longer, turn baking sheet again, and bake 3 minutes longer. (Total baking time is 15 minutes.) Transfer cookies to wire racks to cool.

BISCOTTI

Known as cantucci in parts of Italy, these almond cookies are baked twice, resulting in a crisp, flavorful biscuit. This recipe is versatile: try substituting hazelnuts or pistachio nuts for the almonds. Or add chocolate chips, poppy seeds, or even dried fruit. You can also substitute some whole-wheat flour for the white.

2 cups unbleached all-purpose flour,
    plus more for board
½ teaspoon baking powder
½ teaspoon baking soda
¼ teaspoon salt
1 teaspoon ground fennel or anise seeds
¾ cup coarsely ground almonds
½ cup whole almonds
2 extra-large whole eggs
1 teaspoon vanilla extract
¼ teaspoon almond or anise extract
1 cup sugar
Vegetable oil, for baking sheet
1 egg white

❦ Preheat the oven to 350°F.

❦ Place flour, baking powder, baking soda, salt, and fennel seeds in a mound on a floured board. Surround the outside of the mound with coarsely ground and whole almonds. Make a well in the center of the mound and place whole eggs and both extracts in the well. Using a fork, beat the egg mixture; beating constantly, gradually add sugar until it is dissolved. Continue beating with a fork, incorporating the flour mixture and almonds. Knead into a firm, pliable dough.

❦ Divide dough into 3 portions. With lightly oiled hands, shape each portion into a long thick loaf (resembling a rope). Place loaves 2 inches apart on lightly oiled baking sheets. Brush with egg white and bake until golden brown, 15 to 20 minutes.

❦ Remove loaves from the oven and, using a spatula, transfer to a cutting board. (Do not turn off oven.) While still hot, slice loaves into ½-inch-thick slices at a 45 degree angle. Place cut sides down onto the baking sheets and return to the hot oven. Turn off oven and leave the slices until golden brown on top, about 5 minutes; turn and brown on the other side 5 minutes. Transfer slices to wire racks and cool. To recrisp after a day or two, place remaining biscotti on baking sheets and bake at 350°F 5 to 10 minutes.

HAZELNUT VARIATION *Place 2 cups hazelnuts on a baking sheet lined with aluminum foil. In a preheated 350°F oven, bake until the skins begin to crack and loosen, 5 to 10 minutes. Transfer to a clean towel and rub until most of the skins separate from the nuts. Add to recipe in place of almonds.*

CHOCOLATE-HAZELNUT COOKIES

{Makes about 4 dozen cookies}

These melt-in-your-mouth cookies are baked daily at the Broadway Deli. The dough can be prepared in big batches, wrapped in plastic wrap, and refrigerated for as long as one week. Bake as many as you like and you can have them fresh daily—just like a deli!

1 cup toasted hazelnuts (page 206)

1 cup sugar

¼ pound unsalted butter or margarine, at room temperature

1 teaspoon almond or vanilla extract

2 cups unbleached all-purpose flour, plus more for board

1 teaspoon baking powder

¼ teaspoon salt

½ cup unsweetened cocoa powder

2 egg whites

❧ Preheat the oven to 350°F.

❧ In a food processor fitted with a steel blade or using a hand chopper, grind hazelnuts with sugar until very fine and mixture begins to come together.

❧ In a large bowl, using an electric mixer on medium speed, cream butter with hazelnut mixture and almond extract until well blended.

❧ In a medium bowl, blend flour, baking powder, salt, and cocoa. Add to butter mixture alternately with egg whites, beating at medium speed until dough comes together.

❧ Line baking sheets with aluminum foil. Divide dough into quarters and roll each quarter out on a floured board to ¼ inch thick. Using a cutter with scalloped edges, cut into 2-inch rounds. Place 1 inch apart on baking sheets. Bake until firm, about 10 minutes. Cool on baking sheets and transfer with a spatula to wire racks to cool completely.

HONEY-ALMOND COOKIES

{Makes about 2 dozen cookies}

Dipped in honey and rolled in almonds, these porcupine-like cookies often pop up in ethnic bakeries and delis. They're crunchy on the outside and buttery on the inside, with orange juice and zest contributing a citrus sparkle to their remarkable flavor. For holiday gift-giving, these cookies can't be beat.

¼ pound unsalted butter or margarine,
    at room temperature
¼ cup olive oil, plus more for baking sheet
¼ cup sugar
1 egg
½ teaspoon ground cinnamon
½ cup fresh orange juice
Grated zest of 2 oranges
2¼ cups unbleached all-purpose flour,
    plus more for board
1½ teaspoons baking powder
Pinch salt
2 cups lightly toasted, finely ground almonds
1 tablespoon water heated
    with ½ cup honey

❦ Preheat the oven to 375°F.

❦ In a large bowl, using an electric mixer, beat butter until creamy. Add olive oil and sugar and beat until fluffy. Add egg, cinnamon, orange juice, and zest and blend well.

❦ In a separate bowl, mix together flour, baking powder, and salt; then add to the butter mixture a little at a time, beating after each addition. Add ½ cup of the almonds and mix well. Turn out dough onto a floured board and shape into two 12-inch-long rolls. Cover with plastic wrap and refrigerate until firm.

❦ Line a baking sheet with aluminum foil and brush with olive oil. Cut rolls of dough into ¼-inch slices and arrange cookies 2 inches apart on baking sheet. Bake until golden brown, about 15 minutes.

❦ While still warm, dip each cookie in the warm honey mixture and roll in the remaining almonds. Cool on wire racks.

BROADWAY DELI RUGELACH {*Makes about 5 dozen pastries*}

A rolled filled pastry, rugelach is an old-fashioned European bakery and deli specialty, which has now found its way into chic patisseries. In this recipe, the dough is filled with jam, nuts, and cinnamon-sugar. However, you can opt for chocolate, cheese—any filling you like.

¾ pound unsalted butter,
 at room temperature,
 plus more for baking sheets
¾ cup powdered sugar
1 teaspoon vanilla extract
12 ounces cream cheese,
 at room temperature
3⅓ cups pastry flour,
 plus more for board
2 cups apricot jam
2 cups chopped toasted walnuts or
 pecans (page 182)
1¼ cups granulated sugar mixed with
 1 tablespoon ground cinnamon
1 egg, beaten with 1 tablespoon water

❦ In a large bowl, using an electric mixer, cream butter, powdered sugar, and vanilla. Add cream cheese and blend until smooth. Add flour all at once and blend until mixture comes together. Cover bowl with a towel and refrigerate 2 hours.

❦ Preheat the oven to 375°F.

❦ Divide dough into 4 equal portions; work with 1 portion at a time and keep the other portions in the refrigerator, covered with a towel. On a lightly floured board, roll out each portion into a ⅛-inch-thick rectangle (about 13x16 inches). Spread with ½ cup of the apricot jam and sprinkle with ½ cup of the walnuts and ¼ cup of the cinnamon-sugar mixture. Roll dough up along the long edge into a log, cover, and refrigerate.

❦ Line 2 baking sheets with aluminum foil and grease with butter. Brush the top of each log with egg mixture and sprinkle each with 1 tablespoon of the remaining cinnamon-sugar mixture. Cut logs into 1-inch slices and place 1 inch apart on prepared baking sheets. Bake until lightly browned, 20 to 30 minutes. Cool slices on wire racks.

DOUBLE CHOCOLATE HAMANTASCHEN

{ Makes about 4 dozen pastries }

Hamantaschen are triangular pastries served during the Jewish holiday of Purim. They are traditionally filled with poppy seeds, fruit preserves, or prune jam. But this updated recipe is based on a chocolate cookie dough and includes a rich chocolate filling. The cookie dough can be made ahead and refrigerated up to three days or frozen for one month.

1 recipe Chocolate-Hazelnut Cookie dough
    (page 207)
1 egg white, optional
1 cup cocoa powder
1 cup sugar
½ cup milk, whipping cream, or coffee
2 cups chopped toasted hazelnuts (page 206)
Flour, for dusting board
Melted butter, for baking sheets

❦ Prepare cookie dough, adding 1 or 2 teaspoons additional egg white if dough is too crumbly to shape into triangles. Wrap in plastic wrap and chill.

❦ In a large bowl, combine cocoa, sugar, milk, and hazelnuts and blend thoroughly. Cover with plastic wrap and chill.

❦ Preheat the oven to 350°F.

❦ Divide dough into quarters and roll out each quarter on a floured board ¼-inch thick. Using a cutter with scalloped edges, cut into 2-inch rounds. Fill a pastry bag with the chocolate-hazelnut mixture and pipe about a teaspoon in the center of each round. Fold the edges of the dough toward the center to form a triangle, leaving a bit of the filling visible in the center. Pinch the edges to seal them.

❦ Line a baking sheet with aluminum foil and lightly brush with butter.

❦ Place hamantaschen ½ inch apart on baking sheet. Bake until crisp, about 15 minutes. Transfer pastries to wire racks to cool.

CHOCOLATE-COVERED HALVAH

{ Makes about 4 dozen halvah cups }

At most Middle Eastern and Jewish-style delis, you can always find Greek or Turkish halvah at the check-out counter. Its creamy, nutlike flavor comes from sesame seeds. Beware, it's habit-forming. I love to buy a giant hunk of this marbled treasure, coat small pieces with chocolate, and serve them with espresso.

1 pound semisweet chocolate,
    cut into small pieces

4 dozen ruffled paper baking cups

½ pound marble-pistachio or plain halvah,
    cut into 1-inch chunks

❦ In the top of a double boiler, over hot water, melt chocolate. Arrange ruffled paper baking cups on baking sheets lined with waxed paper. Pour a teaspoon of melted chocolate in the bottom of each paper cup. Place a chunk of halvah in center of the chocolate and spoon enough chocolate over the halvah to cover completely. Cover baking sheet with plastic wrap and refrigerate until chocolate is set.

DELI ENTERTAINING
FOR SPECIAL
OCCASIONS

CHAPTER 9

There are countless special occasions year-round when we feel the urge to entertain—a birthday, an anniversary, the Fourth of July, Labor Day, an outdoor concert, a tailgate picnic before a sports event, and, of course, Thanksgiving. Then there's a child's graduation, a reception for an artist or author, a brunch for out-of-town guests, or a spur-of-the-moment get-together. You'll think up a lot more. ❦ Deli foods lend themselves to all of these occasions. An assortment of deli meats and poultry, lots of salads, a variety of ethnic breads and rolls, fresh fruit, and some satisfying sweets from the deli bakery are the basics. ❦ With the help of my book you can prepare all of the salads and meat and poultry selections yourself; many of the bakery items are also easy and fun to make. And if you're energetic, you can try the breads (nothing is better than home-baked bread). ❦ Most of the menus can be served buffet style, especially when the guests list is over twenty-five. Most deli food has an advantage; it requires no last-minute anxiety. What you see is what you get. And everybody loves it! ❦ For several of the menus, the food can be prepared in advance, then arranged on a large buffet table, allowing the guests to do all the work. You just supply the mouthwatering selections, and they can create their own fantasies. For a large crowd, hire someone to keep the platters full and to clean up afterwards. ❦ More elaborate deli food can become the basis of an international buffet. Serve a mix of hot and cold dishes—soups, pastas, salads, and main courses from around the world. ❦ Following are some of my personal favorite and proven deli-style menus to serve as guidelines for various types of entertaining. Most of the recipes can be found in this book. But of course you can also substitute store-bought items from your favorite deli for some of the dishes.

M E N U S

DO-IT-YOURSELF SALAD BAR

This is a perfect way to entertain a large crowd. Much of the preparation may be done in advance, stored in the refrigerator, and finished just before serving time. What makes this buffet fun and exciting is the presentation. Use your most colorful bowls, platters, and accessories. Heavy coated and decorated paper plates will be just fine, and so will large paper napkins—lots of them. Prepare the salad dressings and assemble salads, but combine just before serving—it only takes a few minutes. Wine, beer, soft drinks, tea, and coffee are suggested beverages.

PREPARED SALADS
Santa Fe Chicken and Black Bean Salad (page 45)
Best-Ever Potato Salad (page 38)
Rice and Garden Vegetable Salad (page 37)
The Best Caesar Salad (page 31)

SALAD FIXINGS AND RELISHES
Romaine lettuce
Cucumber slices
Red onion slices
Tomato slices
Olives
Quick Dill Pickles (page 78)

SALAD DRESSINGS
Mustard Vinaigrette (page 49)
Italian Herb Vinaigrette (page 48)
Thousand Island Dressing (page 53)

BREAD AND ROLLS
French Country Bread (page 154)
Whole-Wheat Rolls (page 162)
Soft Pretzels (page 164)

DESSERT BAR
Chocolate-Hazelnut Cookies (page 207)
Biscotti (page 206)
Brownies (page 186)
Signature Chocolate Chip Ice Cream (page 202)

DO-IT-YOURSELF SANDWICH BAR

This is so simple you will wonder why you never thought of it before. Don't make any sandwiches—let your guests make them! The basic components of this crowd-pleasing menu are a variety of unusual breads and rolls; an appealing selection of hearty deli meats and other sandwich fillings; and some flavorful relishes and accompaniments.

BREADS
Squaw Bread (page 151)
French Country Bread (page 154)
Deli Onion-Rye Bread (page 152)
Kaiser Rolls (page 163)
Hamburger Buns (page 159)

DELI MEATS AND CHEESES
Chef's Special Corned Beef (page 141)
Authentic Pastrami (page 142)
Roast Turkey Breast (page 126)
Home-Cured Pickled Tongue (page 144)
Deli Chopped Chicken Livers (page 118)
Swiss cheese
Fontina cheese
Provolone cheese

RELISHES AND SAUCES
Deli Hot Mustard (page 73)
Alain's Homemade Ketchup (page 73)
Pickled Baby Beets (page 79)
Deli Sauerkraut (page 80)
Roasted Red and Yellow Bell Peppers (page 81) with anchovies

ACCOMPANIMENTS
Arugula
Red leaf lettuce
Tomato slices
Fresh fennel
Sliced cucumbers
Minced green onions
Red and green bell pepper slices
Classic Creamy Coleslaw (page 31)

DESSERTS
Lemon Meringue Tartlets (page 194)
Machelle's Brownie Cheesecake (page 177)

YEAR-ROUND BASIC DELI BUFFET

Here is the marvelous mix of hot and cold dishes that delis are famous for. This menu may be easily adapted to the season or occasion, but it's a perfect guideline for easy, informal hospitality. You may serve the buffet in three courses: cold foods first, hot foods next, and finally a dessert buffet, along with hot and cold drinks. If you wish to simplify, choose fewer dishes and bigger plates and serve the hot and cold foods on one long table, arranging the salads at one end and hot dishes at the other. Then, you can just clear the table and arrange the dessert course while guests are eating their meal. This menu is splendid for brunch as well as dinner and may be eaten indoors or out. You'll need lots of bowls and serving platters. So buy, beg, or borrow whatever you need in advance, and decide which food will look best in the appropriate serving piece.

SALADS
French Potato Salad (page 37)
Tabbouleh (page 36)
Dallmeyer's Tomato, Pepper, and Mozzarella Salad (page 33)
Chinese Chicken Salad (page 42)

HOT FOODS
Barbecued Ribs (page 139)
Deli Barbecued Chicken (page 124)
Old-Fashioned Vegetarian Beanpot (page 85)
Deli Sauerkraut (page 80)

BREADS AND ROLLS
Swedish Limpa Bread (page 156)
Quick Olive-Basil Bread (page 159)
Kaiser Rolls (page 163)

DESSERTS
Apple Strudel (page 192)
Broadway Deli Rugelach (page 209)
Aunt Betty's Chocolate Spice Cake (page 181)

SPECIAL-OCCASION SUNDAY BRUNCH

One of my favorite ways to celebrate a red-letter day is with a Sunday brunch. It's especially nice when the weather is warm and we can serve outside in the garden, which gives us room for lots of friends. Fill large platters and bowls with enormous amounts of each food so they don't have to be filled so often. Then have additional bowls and platters covered with plastic wrap in the refrigerator ready to replace when needed. (Nothing looks more unappetizing than nearly empty or even half-empty serving dishes, filled with spills and remnants of food.) For this menu, slightly undercook omelets and keep warm in a very low oven until ready to serve.

Champagne, blinis, and caviar
Izzy's Authentic Bagels (page 160) with cream cheese
Lox and Onion Omelets (page 94)
Sliced tomatoes and red onions
Thin slices of Swiss or jack cheese
Olives

DESSERT TABLE
Chocolate Swirl Cake (page 179)
Fresh Fruit Cobbler with Streusel Topping (page 193)
Rugelach (page 209)
Fresh strawberries with bowls of sour cream and brown sugar

ALL-AMERICAN PICNIC

This menu is not absolutely original or unique, but it is foolproof, delicious, and fast and easy for impromptu celebrations. Be sure to bring along hearty red wine, beer, soft drinks, and a thermos of hot coffee.

Super-Crispy Fried Chicken (page 123)
Best-Ever Potato Salad (page 38)
Classic Creamy Coleslaw (page 31)
Cherry tomatoes
Radishes
Green onions
Quick Dill Pickles (page 78)
Kaiser Rolls (page 163)
Focaccia with Onions and Rosemary (page 158)
Orange-Glaze Bundt Cake (page 180)
Fig and Nut Loaf (page 182)
The Best Apple Pie (page 196)
Chilled melon wedges

TABLE OF EQUIVALENTS

> *The exact equivalents in the following tables have been rounded for convenience.*

US/UK

oz = ounce
lb = pound
in = inch
ft = foot
tbl = tablespoon
fl oz = fluid ounce
qt = quart

LENGTH MEASURES

1/8 in	3 mm
1/4 in	6 mm
1/2 in	12 mm
1 in	2.5 cm
2 in	5 cm
3 in	7.5 cm
4 in	10 cm
5 in	13 cm
6 in	15 cm
7 in	18 cm
8 in	20 cm
9 in	23 cm
10 in	25 cm
11 in	28 cm
12 in/1 ft	30 cm

OVEN TEMPERATURES

Fahrenheit	Celsius	Gas
250	120	1/2
275	140	1
300	150	2
325	160	3
350	180	4
375	190	5
400	200	6
425	220	7
450	230	8
475	240	9
500	260	10

METRIC

g = gram
kg = kilogram
mm = millimeter
cm = centimeter
ml = milliliter
l = liter

WEIGHTS

US/UK	Metric
1 oz	30 g
2 oz	60 g
3 oz	90 g
4 oz (1/4 lb)	125 g
5 oz (1/3 lb)	155 g
6 oz	185 g
7 oz	220 g
8 oz (1/2 lb)	250 g
10 oz	315 g
12 oz (3/4 lb)	375 g
14 oz	440 g
16 oz (1 lb)	500 g
1 1/2 lb	750 g
2 lb	1 kg
3 lb	1.5 kg

LIQUIDS

US	Metric	UK
2 tbl	30 ml	1 fl oz
1/4 cup	60 ml	2 fl oz
1/3 cup	80 ml	3 fl oz
1/2 cup	125 ml	4 fl oz
2/3 cup	160 ml	5 fl oz
3/4 cup	180 ml	6 fl oz
1 cup	250 ml	8 fl oz
1 1/2 cups	375 ml	12 fl oz
2 cups	500 ml	16 fl oz
4 cups/1 qt	1 l	32 fl oz